D1564176

On
Universals

On
Universals
An Essay in
Ontology

NICHOLAS WOLTERSTORFF

THE UNIVERSITY OF
CHICAGO PRESS

Chicago and London

International Standard Book Number: 0–226–90565–9
Library of Congress Catalog Card Number: 73–121819

The University of Chicago Press, Chicago 60637
The University of Chicago Press, Ltd., London

Contents

v

Contents

5 / Predicate Entailment / 105

1. Arguments in favor of the view that there are predicables must now be considered. / 105
2. The first sort of argument considered is The Argument from Resemblance. Arguments of this sort are seen to depend on the acceptability of what are called "predicate entailment principles." / 108
3. A second sort of argument considered is The Argument from Multiple Affirmability. Arguments of this sort are also seen to depend on the acceptability of "predicate entailment principles." / 116
4. It is concluded that predicate entailment principles are acceptable. / 123
5. There seems to be no *argument,* however, for thinking that predicate entailment principles are acceptable. And the situation is that many philosophers would insist that they are unacceptable. / 126

6 / Abstraction / 128

1. The occurrence of "abstractive attention" provides us with another argument for the conclusion that there are predicables. Before it is concluded that this is a satisfactory argument, consideration is given to the view that the object of abstractive attention is never some predicable but always a *case* of such. / 128
2. The view of Aquinas, that though one can abstractively attend to universals, yet there are no universals in the things, is seen to be ingenious but incoherent. / 141

7 / The Nature of Predicable Entities / 150

1. Identity criteria for predicables are proposed. / 150
2. Existence criteria for predicables are proposed. / 158
3. Can predicables act? / 170

8 / Identification / 173

1. Predicable entities cannot be identified with any sort of classes. / 173
2. Ockham's suggestion, that the concept of some predicable is identical with the concept of cases of that predicable, is highly original but not acceptable. / 181

9 / Reduction / 194

1. Predicables are reducible, in the sense that propositions which can be stated by referring to some predicable or by using a term which must be reckoned as true of some predicable, can also be asserted without referring to any predicable and without using any term which must be reckoned as true of some predicable. / 194

Preface

That there are colored things, few will doubt. But are there colors as well?

That there are things that act in various ways, few will doubt. But are there actions in addition?

That there are things of various kinds, this too, few will doubt. But are there kinds as well as things of those kinds?

That performances of symphonies take place, few will doubt this either. But are there symphonies 'over and above' performances of symphonies?

And if there are colors as well as colored things, actions as well as acting things, various kinds of things as well as things of various kinds, symphonies as well as performances of symphonies, what sort of entities are these? What is their 'nature'? What is their 'status' among the other entities to be found in reality?

These are the sorts of questions that I shall raise and try to answer in the following essay.

This, accordingly, is an essay in ontology.

Though it is an essay *in,* not *on,* ontology, yet it may be worthwhile to make a few remarks here *on* ontology. For it is true of ontology, as of any other branch of philosophy—indeed, of any other branch of the theoretical disciplines—that one's conception of what one is doing influences what one is doing.

Ontology, as I understand it and shall try to practice it, is a description of the most general structure of what there is. It is a description of a structure so general that every other discipline will deal with some detail of the structure.

I do not, accordingly, identify ontology with what P.F. Strawson calls "descriptive metaphysics," and which he explains as the attempt to describe the most general features of our human conceptual scheme (compare Kant's conception of "critical metaphysics"). For I hold that we can know not only our conceptual scheme but that to which our conceptual scheme applies. Indeed, one of the main uses of our conceptual scheme is to gain knowledge of that to which the scheme applies. It is with a description of the most general structure of *this,* that ontology, as I wish to practice it, occupies itself. Of course, there is nothing 'wrong' in describing the general structure of our conceptual scheme, nor in asking in what ways it might have been different and yet applicable to reality, nor in asking in what ways reality might have been different and our conceptual scheme yet applicable. But such questions are simply not the questions that I shall here be asking.

I also do not understand the project of ontology as does Gustav Bergmann—namely, as the attempt to construct a system which explains or accounts for what is presented to us. Though the ontologist certainly should, wherever possible, argue for and defend his claims, I doubt that such argumentation, in any reasonable sense of the word "explain," always has or should have the structure of an explanation for what is presented. We are sometimes presented, I suppose, with red things. But does one provide an explanation of that with which one is thereby presented by claiming that in such a situation there is something which exemplifies redness? Further, I find that I cannot draw any clear distinction whatever between what is presented to me and what, though it is the case, yet is not presented to me.

So I understand ontology as descriptive, not explanatory; and descriptive of the most general structure of what there is, not descriptive of the most general structure of that conceptual scheme of ours which we apply to what there is.

When I speak of "description," no Kantianism or positivism

must be heard as lurking behind this phrase. We are not limited in our descriptions to the perceptible; factually meaningful assertions are not confined to the verifiable. The lesson of the collapse of positivism must not be lost on us. Indeed, all those old dualisms which have haunted modern philosophy—appearance/reality, the knowable/the unknowable, the given/the interpreted—have collapsed, and will play no role in our discussion. The infatuation of the modern philosophers with the drawing of epistemological boundaries will not enthrall us.

It is my conviction that all of us, apart from ontology, are aware of the structure of reality—always, of course, dimly, always somewhat askew, always overlooking things, never getting the whole picture. Yet the task of the ontologist is not to postulate new and astonishing entities, not to take us aback with his surmises, not to reveal secrets never suspected. His task is to describe that rich reality in the midst of which we live and act, believe and disbelieve, hope and despair. If he is successful, and if we are at all perceptive, we will not find him describing a terrain which, by his description, is astonishingly different from that in which we thought we lived. We will find him describing that terrain which has all the features of the familiar. The ontologist does not postulate unfamiliar things to account for the familiar. He calls our attention to the familiar. The danger that he courts in his reader is not that of annoyed shock, but of dozing familiarity. He does not take us on long trails through dark woods into sunlit openings beyond. He points out to us the structure of the ground on which we have stood all along.

But let us not be snared by the delusion that the ontologist's description of the structure of reality can be unbiased, unprejudiced. It will invariably be shaped and formed by many factors—cultural, linguistic, religious, and more. The ontologist explores how things seem to him to be. In the course of doing so he finds others claiming that things are different from the way they seem to him to be. He should, then, if he does not conclude that he was mistaken, search for considerations in favor of his own view which his disputants will find decisive. Sometimes he will find such, sometimes not. Sometimes, that is, he will discover that when productive argument has ceased, disagreement remains. What he needs then is just the courage of his convictions.

In the course of our discussion we will have to pay close, sometimes excruciatingly close, attention to ordinary language. The aim of such scrutiny is not to find ontology in language; we shall not assume that some ultimate ontological wisdom is to be discerned in the distinctions found in ordinary language. The aim is solely to make clear, to ourselves and the reader, what it is that we are claiming. For ordinary language is the language familiar to all of us. Though of course we can and shall introduce new words and give old words new meanings, in so doing we shall have to probe in order to find that point in ordinary language on which we can rest our explanations of our novelties. That linguistic novelties cannot merely be hurled at readers, expecting the stoned to understand, this, at least, the last fifty years of philosophy have taught us. The result of our caution will look, to a traditionalist, like the slimy trail of the linguistic serpent spread across our pages. I, for my part, see it only as putting into practice the lesson that every ontologist should learn from the linguistic turn in philosophy.

I said earlier that what follows is an essay in ontology. It is, speaking more precisely, an essay in a part of ontology. Our discussion focusses solely on the cluster of issues directly involved in what has traditionally been known as "the problem of universals." Those issues are as ancient and as contemporary as philosophy itself. They are, in that way, the delightful despair and the despairing delight of philosophers. I have tried, in the discussion, to allow the ancient and the medieval, as well as the contemporary philosophers, to have their say. I do so not at all out of antiquarian interests, but solely because these philosophers did and do have something to say.

My indebtedness to my philosophical colleagues at Calvin College, particularly Alvin Plantinga and Peter deVos, is great. But for the criticisms and suggestions which they offered in the seminar in which we discussed these matters, this book would be much the worse.

Introduction

Our topic in the following discussion is that cluster of issues known as the problem of universals. Of course we shall not and can not simply accept all the received formulations of those issues and proceed to give answers to them. For those formulations incorporate presuppositions, ontological and otherwise, which in many cases we shall not want to accept and which considered all together are inconsistent. Yet these formulations point—whether badly or well—to genuine and important issues. These issues are our concern.

In order to gain an entrance into a discussion of these issues, we begin, in the two chapters which comprise Part One, with a consideration of two different distinctions which have traditionally been drawn between words or expressions. One is a distinction between parts of sentences, namely, between logical subjects and logical predicates. The other is a distinction between terms, namely, between general terms and singular terms. These distinctions are alike in that each is based on a distinction as to the way in which words can be related to what is other than words.

The justification for thus beginning our ontological inquiry with a consideration of certain topics in the philosophy of language is not that the philosophy of language is so intimately associated with ontology that an infection in the former will spread to the latter, for the reverse is true as well. Nor is the justification that questions of ontology are all to be settled by an appeal to the workings of human language, for this is decidedly not the case. Rather, it will prove to be the case that if we are to engage in a full and clear discussion on universals we must have a clear understanding of certain fundamental relations between words and things. And those very relations are of central concern in the distinctions between logical subjects and logical predicates, and between singular terms and general terms. Furthermore, it has almost always been the case that doctrines about these particular relations between words and things have played a pivotal role in discussions concerning universals. Accordingly, for a critical discussion concerning alternative views on universals, as well as for a development of our own positive views, there is no better place to begin than with an explanation of some of the basic concepts underlying the subject-predicate distinction and the general term-singular term distinction.

In addition, in our own discussions concerning universals we shall make considerable use of these distinctions themselves. We shall use them in ways such that it will be important to see clearly what the distinctions amount to; it will not be satisfactory to trust to some rough, prior understanding. It may be added that discussions on universals have almost always been inextricably intertwined with the distinction between subjects and predicates and with the distinction between general and singular terms. There is almost no traditional or contemporary discussion of universals in which one or the other of these distinctions themselves does not play a key role. If we are to attain a critical understanding of what has been said on the topic of universals, we shall have to see clearly what these distinctions amount to.

So the philosophy of language—or better, some parts thereof—is a ladder to be used in building our ontology of universals. It should be added that the ladder we use is not independent of the nature of the building we erect. One's philosophy of language is not ontologically neutral.

Armed with some understanding of those relations between words and things which underlie the subject-predicate and the general term-singular term distinctions, we proceed to our discussion concerning the being and the nature of universals. The question which confronts us first is this. Which entities are they that we mean to discuss? Universals, yes; but the use of the term "universal" is scarcely so uniform that we can proceed without explanation or scruple.

In the course of our discussion of subjects and predicates the verb "to predicate" is given a sense such that it is *words* which are predicated—"is wise," for example, of the person Socrates, by assertively uttering "Socrates is wise." There is in ordinary speech, however, quite a different use of the verb "to predicate." In this alternative use, it is nonlinguistic entities which are predicated. For example, in assertively uttering "Socrates is wise," I predicate *wisdom* of Socrates; and though it may be obscure what sort of entity wisdom is, certainly it is not a word. By using this concept of nonlinguistic predication, we can differentiate entities into those which can be predicated, these appropriately being called *predicables;* and those which cannot be predicated, these, following the tradition, being called *substances.* Further, among predicables are to be found some which can be truly predicated of more than one thing, for example, *being red;* and some which cannot be truly predicated of more than one thing, for example, *being identical with the planet Venus.* The former may be called *predicable universals.* Later in the discussion another sort of universal will be considered, *nonpredicable universals* or *substance universals.* But first, predicable universals call for discussion; it is to this that Part Two is devoted. However, since almost all the interesting philosophical issues that arise concerning predicable universals arise as well concerning predicable nonuniversals, the distinction between these two sorts of predicables will seldom be of any importance in this part of the discussion. Part Two is, in effect, a discussion of predicables generally.

One of the defects in most traditional discussions concerning predicables, or predicable universals, is that philosophers have concentrated all their attention on just one sort of predicable—properties, for example. They have failed to note that there are other sorts as well. One can indeed predicate wisdom of Socrates, and wisdom might naturally be called a property. But equally one can predicate *being wise, walking,* and *that he is wise,* of

Socrates. I call such entities as these, respectively, states, actions, and assertibles. The distinction between properties, states, actions, and assertibles is made by reference to the particular relation which is claimed to hold between the entity predicated and that of which it is predicated. For in predicating some nonlinguistic entity of something—in assertively uttering "Socrates is wise"— one claims some relation to hold between those entities, a relation which does hold if and only if one's original assertion is true. But there is a different relation claimed to hold between properties and that of which they are predicated from that which is claimed to hold between actions and that of which they are predicated. On the basis of the different relation claimed to hold, one can draw a distinction between what might naturally be called properties and what might naturally be called actions.

The delineation of the concept of a predicable, and the drawing out of the main distinctions between various sorts of predicables, is accomplished in chapter 3. In the course of the discussion, an important point concerning the relation of words to things is discovered. Two expressions may name or denote the same thing even though, when interchanged in sentences in which they occur, the result is not new sentences but rather ill-formed sequences of words. For example, "Socrates is in the state of being wise" is a well-formed sentence; "Socrates is in the state of wisdom" is not. We cannot conclude from this however, that "wisdom" and "being wise" name different entities, on the ground, say, that being wise possesses the property of being something that Socrates is in the state of, whereas wisdom does not. For the fact that the sentence "Socrates is in the state of wisdom" is ill-formed does not establish that wisdom lacks the property of being something that Socrates is in the state of. A general maxim appropriate to the principle here espoused is this: Beware of arguing from what it does or does not make good sense to say, to how things are. Ontology cannot be conducted by scrutiny of language.

An important and well-known objection to our line of thought thus far is that there is something incoherent in the concepts of the various predicative relations distinguished, or something incoherent in the supposition that a pair of things can stand in any of these relations. There are no such relations, many have held, for entities to stand in. Plato, already, in the *Parmenides* and the

Philebus, expressed serious doubt as to whether his concept of participation had any sense. And, in the contemporary world, Gilbert Ryle and F.H. Bradley have both argued that to view things as standing in some predicative relation is to commit oneself to a vicious infinite regress. What we need to do, then, is to consider in detail these various objections to predicative relations. This we do in chapter 4. The conclusion reached is that all these arguments fall far short of yielding the desired conclusion. There seems no reason to hold, on account of these arguments, that two things cannot stand in some one or other of the various predicative relations distinguished.

This still leaves us with the question as to whether there are in fact any predicables. To hold that there is nothing incoherent in the notion of one thing standing in some predicative relation to another is not yet to have shown that there are in fact entities which can be predicated. What we need is some reasons for or against the conclusion that there are predicables. In chapters 5 and 6 arguments are advanced in favor of the conclusion that there are predicables. Along the way our ontological inventory is expanded by what I call *cases* of predicables, *Socrates' wisdom* being a case of wisdom, *Bannister's running* being a case of running, and the like.

Having concluded that there are predicables, what we want next is some understanding of their nature. For certainly predicables do not wear their natures on their faces. Even if it be granted that there *are* predicables, we want to know *what* they are. What *is* a property? What *is* an action? What *is* an assertible? What *is* a relation? Some readers, indeed, may feel so strongly that they do not know what predicables are that they will not be willing to admit that there are any until told *what* they are. I think such unwillingness would be misguided. One can very well know that there are cats without being able to answer the philosopher's question as to the 'nature' of a cat. So also, with predicables. One can recognize that there are predicables, and be able to single some of them out from the manifold of entities, without being able to say, in philosophically satisfactory fashion, *what* they are.

It is not wholly clear what sort of answer would satisfy our longing to understand the nature of predicables. But if we knew the conditions under which predicable A is identical with predicable B, if we knew the conditions under which there is such an entity as predicable A, and if we knew whether predicables are actors or not, we would then at least be well on the way to understanding the nature of predicable entities. These, accordingly, are the questions considered in chapter 8. In the course of considering these questions, we arrive at something of a rapprochement between classical realism and classical nominalism.

Another way of domesticating predicables in one's thought, of making them seem less mysterious and puzzling, of coming to the feeling that one understands their 'nature,' is to identify them with one or another sort of entity which, for whatever reason, seems less puzzling and mysterious. The history of philosophy is replete with suggestions along these lines. It has been suggested that predicables are to be identified with certain classes (sets) of nonpredicables, or that they are to be identified with concepts, or, in the subtle suggestion of William of Ockham, that the concept of a predicable is to be identified with the concept of the cases of that predicable. I conclude, after scrutiny, that none of these traditional views is acceptable.

A further question which comes naturally to the mind of anyone lettered in contemporary philosophy is this. Are predicables reducible? That is, can every fact which can be stated by referring to some predicable also be stated without referring to any predicable; and, can every fact which can be stated by using a term which must be true of some predicable if the sentence containing it is to be used to state the fact, also be stated without using such a term? All the facts which we now state by using terms standing for and terms true of predicables—can all those facts be stated without using such terms? I conclude, in chapter 9, that predicables are in fact reducible. But I also conclude that there is nothing of ontological significance in this fact. In particular, it does not follow from this fact that there are no predicables. All that follows is that we can, if we wish, state the facts without referring to predicables and without using terms true of predicables. We can, if we wish, close the eyes of our language to predicables.

This concludes our discussion of predicables. It does not, however, conclude our discussion of universals generally. It is to this topic that we turn in Part Three.

A predicable universal is something which can be truly predicated of many, and which, accordingly, can be exemplified by many. I think we all feel some analogy between this phenomenon, and such facts as the following: that a symphony can have many performances, that a species can have many examples, that a book can have many copies, that a word can have many occurrences, that a disease can have many cases, and so on. On the ground of this analogy, I also call such entities as symphonies, species, books, words, and diseases universals. They are *substance* universals, not predicable universals.

The main question which calls for consideration here is whether we can find some ground for our feeling of analogy between certain substances, on the one hand, and predicable universals, on the other. The tradition suggests to us immediately that what we must look for is some difference between the way universals—predicable or substance—fit into time and space, and the way in which nonuniversals fit into time and space. One doctrine, for example, is that universals are repeatable, whereas nonuniversals are not. After probing, in chapter 10, various suggestions on this point, the conclusion is drawn that no distinction between universals and nonuniversals can be made by reference to some difference in the ways in which they fit into space and time.

Are we then left with nothing but a vague, ungrounded feeling of analogy? I think not; and in chapter 11 a unifying theory is suggested. All universals, I suggest, are *kinds*—not sets or classes, but kinds. A property, for example, is the kind whose examples consist of the cases of the property—wisdom is identical with the kind, case of wisdom. A symphony is identical with the kind whose examples are the performances of that symphony—Beethoven's Ninth is identical with the kind, performance of Beethoven's Ninth. This, then, is our major thesis concerning the nature of universals generally, substance as well as predicable. Universals are, all of them, kinds.

What remains to be done, in Part Four, is to give some consideration to the 'existential' and theological significance which, in the course of Western thought, has been assigned to predicables and to universals. We have said that predicables enter into human life through such activities as predication, perception, thought, and the like. But this is very low-key indeed compared to Plato's conviction that predicables and species ought to be paradigms

for all human and divine thought and action, and compared to
the conviction of the medieval theologians, from Augustine on,
that predicables and species function as exemplars for God's
creative activity.

In Part Four, which comprises our last chapter, these religious
and theological convictions concerning universals are discussed.
I conclude that whatever else may be the role of universals in
human life, Plato cannot be right in saying that they ought to
serve as paradigms to be imitated. For underlying the Platonic
conviction that predicables and natural kinds ought to function
as paradigms is the conviction that predicables are perfect examples of themselves. But this is incoherent. Circularity is not
the perfect circle. Thus circularity is not the sort of thing that
any draftsman, even if he wished, could imitate. Plato's religion
of forms is unacceptable. But equally the medieval theology of
exemplars is unacceptable. For though at least some predicables
are as eternal as God himself, predicables and species cannot
function as exemplars for anyone's creative activity. God no
more than man can make horses in accord with his idea of the
horse, nor circles in accord with his idea of circularity.

Words and Things

PART ONE

1

Subjects and Predicates

1. When philosophers and others have considered various sentences in our language, they have discerned, or thought that they discerned, a distinction between a part of the sentence which can stand for what something is said about, and a part which can stand for or express what is said about something. The former they have called a *logical subject;* the latter they have called a *logical predicate.* For example, in the sentence "Socrates is wise," "Socrates" is thought to be capable of standing for what something is said about, and is on that account called the logical subject of this sentence; whereas "is wise" is thought to be capable of standing for or expressing what is said about something, and is on that account called the logical predicate of this sentence.

In what follows, I shall try to discover what there is of truth to these ideas. I shall do so by exploring definitions of "subject term" and "predicate term," trying to arrive at satisfactory definitions. Satisfactory definitions must, I judge, do at least two things. They must have as their *basis* the distinction between standing for what something is said about, and standing for or expressing what is said about something. Secondly, they must yield certain rather definite *results.* The subject-predicate distinction is designed

to cut up sentences in a certain way; and for a great number of
sentences there is general agreement as to which part of the
sentence is to be the subject and which the predicate. In "Socrates
is wise," for example, it is agreed that "Socrates" is to be the
subject and "is wise" is to be the predicate.

If there were no way of drawing the distinction between that
part of a sentence which can stand for what something is said
about and that part which can stand for what is said about something, except a way which yielded results diverging radically from
the generally agreed on ways of cutting up sentences, then I
think we would have to allow that traditional thought on this
matter was so confused as to make it misleading to speak, any
more, of logical subjects and logical predicates. And contrariwise,
if no differences in function can be correlated with the generally
agreed on ways of cutting up sentences into subjects and predicates, except a difference quite other than the distinction between
that part of a sentence which can stand for what something is
said about and that part which can stand for what is said about
something, then again I think we would have to allow that traditional thought on this matter was so confused as to make it
misleading to speak, any more, of logical subjects and logical
predicates.

It should also be said at the beginning that what we are here
really interested in defining is "subject of a certain sentence" and
"predicate of a certain sentence," not "subject" and "predicate"
tout court. We want to find out what it is to function as the
logical subject of a sentence, and what it is to function as the
logical predicate of a sentence. We want a definition which enables
us to tell, *given an actual sentence,* which expression(s) can be
regarded as subject(s) of that sentence, and which as predicate.
Sometimes, though not very frequently, a different approach has
been taken to the matter. Sometimes "subject" has been defined
as that which *can* play a certain role *in some sentence or other,*
and sometimes "predicate" has been defined as that which *can*
play a certain other role *in some sentence or other.* Then, indeed,
it is a definition of "subject" that is given rather than of "subject
of a certain sentence." And then it is a definition of "predicate"
which is given, rather than of "predicate of a certain sentence."
Then the definitions tell us, *given an assortment of expressions,*

which of these are logical subjects and which are logical predicates.

Either way, however, we must try to get at two different sorts of roles which expressions can play in sentences. If we are clear on this, it makes no great difference whether we say that *a subject of a certain sentence* is what is playing a certain role in that sentence, or whether we say that *a subject* is what is capable of playing such a role in some sentence or other. Here I wish simply to announce that I shall follow the former course. I shall use the word "subjectible" for what is *capable* of functioning as a logical subject in some sentence or other, and "predicable expression" for what is *capable* of functioning as a logical predicate in some sentence or other. But in our attempt to define "subject of a certain sentence" and "predicate of a certain sentence," it will not be expressions as such, but expressions as parts of specific sentences, that we will be concerned with. The sentence will be our fundamental unit of analysis.

Let us see first, then, whether for the generally agreed on ways of analyzing sentences into subjects and predicates we can state some general rules or principles in accord with which the analysis is conducted.[1]

(a) According to the generally agreed on ways of analyzing sentences, the subject(s) and predicate of a sentence, on any given subject-predicate analysis of the sentence, must exhaustively divide the sentence. As we shall shortly see, some philosophers would hold that certain sentences admit of multiple subject-predicate analyses; others would deny this. Further, among those who deny this, there is some disagreement, concerning certain sorts of sentences, as to the proper analysis. I think, however, that all the ways of analyzing sentences conform to the rule that a subject-predicate analysis of a sentence must exhaustively divide that sentence into subject(s) and predicate.

(b) According to the generally agreed on ways of analyzing sentences, what is a subject of a sentence on a certain analysis cannot also be a predicate of that sentence on some analysis, and what is a predicate of a sentence on a certain analysis cannot also be a subject of that sentence on some analysis. However, an

1. Cf. P.F. Strawson, *Individuals* (London, 1959), chap. 5.

expression which is a subject on one analysis may be *part* of what is a predicate on another analysis.

(c) According to the generally agreed on ways of analyzing sentences, if a sentence contains just one expression which is a singular term,[2] that one functioning as its *grammatical* subject, then that expression along with its modifiers is the subject of the sentence and the rest of the sentence is the predicate. No other analysis is possible. Thus in the sentences "Socrates is wise," "Socrates is a man," and "Socrates teaches," "Socrates" is the subject of the sentence and the rest of the sentence is the predicate. It is not generally agreed, however, what is to be said about those sentences which contain a singular term functioning as grammatical subject, and which contain in addition at least one other singular term, for example, "Socrates taught Plato." Many traditional logicians would say that in this sentence, "Socrates" is the subject and "taught Plato" is the predicate. More generally, they would hold that a sentence can have only one logical subject, and that only if an expression is the grammatical subject of a sentence can it, along with its modifiers, be viewed as the logical subject of the sentence. Certain contemporary logicians would say that "Socrates" and "Plato" are both subjects in "Socrates taught Plato," "taught" being the (two-place) predicate. More generally, they would hold that whatever singular terms a sentence contains, those terms plus their modifiers are its subjects, the rest of the sentence being the predicate. Yet other logicians would say that the sentence "Socrates taught Plato" admits of multiple analyses. "Socrates" may be viewed as the subject, on which analysis "taught Plato" is the predicate; or "Plato" may be viewed as the subject, on which analysis "Socrates taught" is the predicate; or "Socrates" and "Plato" may, both together, be viewed as subjects, on which analysis "taught" is the predicate. On this view, a subject-predicate analysis of a sentence can be gotten by taking any singular term in a sentence along with its modifiers, regarding

---

2. In this paragraph, "singular term" should really be expanded thus: "singular term which is not a grammatical predicate nor an adjective nor a common noun." The concept of a singular term will be discussed in detail in chapter 2. In our discussion there, it will be noticed that certain grammatical predicates, certain adjectives, and certain common nouns, qualify as singular terms. But such singular terms are to be eliminated from consideration when, in the text above, we speak of singular terms.

this as subject of the sentence, and regarding the rest of the sentence as predicate; and also by taking any *number* of singular terms in a sentence along with their modifiers, regarding them as subjects, and regarding the rest of the sentence as predicate.

So the only thing generally agreed on as to the analysis of those sentences containing more than one singular term is that, if any such term is the grammatical subject of the sentence, then the sentence permits of an analysis according to which that term along with its modifiers is at least one of the subjects. Further, it is not generally agreed as to how we are to analyze sentences containing just one expression which is a singular term, if this term is not functioning as grammatical subject—as in "Someone gave John a book." Indeed, it is perhaps not even agreed that such sentences are susceptible to subject-predicate analysis at all. And certainly there is no general agreement as to whether sentences containing *no* singular terms—for example, "All bats are rodents"—are susceptible to subject-predicate analysis. There is, on all these matters, no rule or principle of analysis to which the results of our definitions must conform if they are to be satisfactory.

One last word should be said about these rules or principles of analysis. All we have a right to expect of any definitions of "subject of a certain sentence" and "predicate of a certain sentence" is that they yield results which conform, *for the most part,* to the rules. For our language is a supple, flexible, idiomatic instrument, and we can hardly expect an invariable conformity of it to the rules. Using the distinction between standing for what something is said about, and standing for or expressing what is said about something, all we can hope to do is find definitions which secure results that, *for the most part,* are in accord with these rules or principles of analysis.

2. What, now, is the *basis* of the distinction between subjects and predicates? Let us cite what Cook Wilson gives as a summary, up to his time, of the philosophical tradition on this matter: ". . . according to the traditional definitions of subject and predicate, the subject is what in the proposition or statement we are speaking about, and the predicate is what we say of the subject: or, in a familiar form, the subject is that about which something

is asserted, and the predicate is that which is asserted about it."[3] From this passage one gathers that the subject-predicate distinction has traditionally been based on the distinction between that about which something is said or asserted and that which is said or asserted about it.

In Cook Wilson's summary of the traditional definition, a subject is taken to be a nonlinguistic entity about which something is said or asserted and perhaps a predicate is also understood as a nonlinguistic entity, whereas we have been taking both subjects and predicates to be linguistic components of sentences. This divergence, though important to notice if we are to avoid confusion, is not serious. The usual way of resolving it is by adopting a locution to the following effect. The subject of a sentence *stands for* the entity (entities) about which something is asserted, and the predicate *stands for* (or *expresses*) what is asserted about that entity (those entities). A definition built on this pattern is to be found in H.W.B. Joseph: "The subject-word in a proposition is a sign of something thought of, for which it is said to stand, and the proposition is not about it but about what it stands for. . . . In the proposition 'Dogs bark,' 'dogs' stands for the things about which the statement is made, 'bark' both is the sign of (or expresses) what is predicated about them, and also of its being predicated. . . ."[4] Except for the distinction which Joseph draws between expressing *that* something is predicated and expressing *what* is predicated, a closely parallel set of definitions is to be found in P.T. Geach: "A *predicate* is an expression that gives us an assertion about something if we attach it to another expression that stands for what we are making the assertion about. A *subject* of a sentence S is an expression standing for something that S is about, S itself being formed by attaching a predicate to that expression."[5]

3. J. Cook Wilson, *Statement and Inference* (Oxford, 1926), 1:114.
4. H.W.B. Joseph, *An Introduction to Logic* (Oxford, 1931), pp. 16–17.
5. P.T. Geach, *Reference and Generality* (Ithaca, N.Y., 1962), p. 23. This, Geach says, is only a provisional explanation. The following, I take it, includes the necessary changes and qualifications: "A *predicable* is an expression that gives us a proposition about something if we attach it to another expression that stands for what we are forming the proposition about; the predicable then becomes a predicate, and the other expression becomes its *subject* . . ." (ibid., p. 25).

3. Some serious perplexities arise in the attempt to apply these definitions. To see what these are, as well as to provide terminology essential for much of our later discussion, we must distinguish the following five sorts of entities: sentences, utterances of sentences, meanings of sentences, assertions, and propositions.

"Sentence," as I shall use the word, will always be applied to a word or to a sequence of words which has a meaning in some language or other. And "word," in turn, will always be applied to a *pattern* of sounds and/or marks which has a meaning in some language or other. Thus sentences and words are linguistic entities—meaningful units of language. A given word can be repeatedly written down or repeatedly sounded out; so too a given sentence can be repeatedly written down or sounded out. The particular marks made or sounds produced in uttering a word or sentence on a certain occasion constitute an *occurrence* of that word or sentence. Occurrences of sentences are Peirce's *tokens*. In common speech an occurrence of a word or sentence is itself sometimes called a word or sentence. I shall apply "word" and "sentence" only to that which occurs and can reoccur, not to the occurrences. Furthermore, as I shall use the word "sentence," the same sentence may have different meanings in the same language. Difference in meaning of a sentence is perhaps most frequently indicated by difference in juncture and stress when speaking, and by difference in punctuation when writing. For example, the sentence "For sale: bed for antique lovers" has at least two different meanings. In this case the difference can be brought out in speech but not in writing. We cannot always inquire after *the* meaning of a given sentence; it may have several.

A sentence, we remarked, can be repeatedly written down or repeatedly uttered. Let us extend the meaning of the word "utterance" a bit, and call any case of writing down or uttering a particular sentence, an *utterance* of that sentence. An utterance of a sentence is always an act taking place at a particular time and place, and taking some time. No doubt the word "utterance" is also often applied to *what is uttered*. But I shall apply it only to an *act of uttering*. It is obvious that exactly the same sentence can be uttered a number of different times, both by the same and by different speakers. That is to say, uttering a given sentence is something which may be repeatedly done. It is an action, each case of which is an utterance of that sentence (so-and-so's utterance of it, on such-and-such an occasion).

Since a sentence is a meaningful word or sequence of words, we can distinguish the *meaning* or *meanings* of a sentence from the pattern or sequence of patterns of sounds and marks which have that meaning. Two distinct sentences can have the same meaning or, in other words, can be synonymous. It makes no difference whether they belong to the same language. "John loves Mary" has the same meaning as "Mary is loved by John," just as "It is raining" has the same meaning as "Es regnet." In both cases, however, the sentences are different.

Many different things can be done by uttering sentences. One can ask questions, issue commands, make assertions, express wishes, make motions, referee games, and do other things. Many, or all, of these can also be done by other means than uttering sentences. Of all these different things which can be done (actions which can be performed) by uttering sentences, I wish to concentrate on one; namely, that of making an assertion. An assertion, as I shall use the word, is some specific case of the action of making an assertion. It is an act which occurs on a particular occasion.

If a man, in uttering a sentence, claims something to be true, he has then—and only then—made an assertion. It is perhaps scarcely necessary today to point out that one can utter sentences without claiming something to be true. Assuming that the following sentences are used in normal fashion, one would not have claimed something to be true by uttering "Are all men mortal?" or "I wish that all men were mortal" or "Would that all men were mortal" or "Let all men be mortal." Also, one does not claim something to be true in christening a child, or in uttering, in a parliamentary session, the words "I move that. . . ."

When someone makes an assertion, he asserts *something—there is* something which he asserts. I shall define "a proposition," then, as whatever can be asserted. (What I call a proposition is frequently nowadays called an assertion, as well as a statement, and in earlier philosophy was frequently called a judgment. In addition, what I call an assertion, namely an act of a certain sort, is also frequently called a statement, and was in the past frequently called a judgment.) Furthermore, let it be understood that the same proposition cannot be both true and false; if what one person asserted is true and what another asserted is false, it follows that they did not assert the same proposition. This may be the case even though the two persons in question uttered the same sentence. Suppose, for example, that John is ill and Peter is healthy at a certain time; and then suppose further that both of them utter at that time "I am ill." On our understanding of "proposition," they have not asserted the same proposition, since what one asserted is true while what the other asserted is false.

In general it will not be enough to know *what* proposition a man asserted, to know what sentence he uttered; we must know the circumstances in which the utterance took place. A particular proposition is to be identified not just by reference to the sentence uttered, but also by reference to various features of the context of utterance. Of course, there are some sentences, such as "All men are mortal," which, whenever used with their normal meaning to assert a proposition, will be used to assert the same proposition no matter what the context in which they are uttered; the point is that there are others, such as "Eisenhower was President eight years ago," which will be used to assert different propositions depending on various features of the context of utterance—in this particular case, depending chiefly on the date at which the sentence is uttered.

So the same sentence with the same meaning may be used to assert different propositions. On the other hand, different sentences may be used to assert the same proposition. If someone utters assertively with its normal meaning, "All men are mortal," and someone else or he himself utters assertively with its normal meaning "Alle Menschen sind sterblich," they will have asserted the same proposition;[6] what the one man asserts cannot be true while what the other asserts is false. In this particular case, the two sentences in question have the same meaning. But two sentences with different meanings can also be used to assert the same proposition: "John is busy" and "He is busy."

We defined a proposition as what *can be* asserted. But a proposition can enter thought and discourse in other ways than by being asserted. Another way occurs when we make assertions with

6. By "assertively utters *S*," I mean makes an assertion by uttering *S*.

certain sorts of compound sentences. Suppose, for example, that I assertively utter the sentence "Either Socrates is wise or Plato is wise." I have not then asserted that Socrates is wise, even though I have introduced this proposition by asserting another proposition, namely, that either 'Socrates is wise' is true or 'Plato is wise' is true. In this case a proposition is introduced as a component in another proposition which is asserted. Propositions can also be introduced into thought and discourse without any assertion whatsoever being made or entertained. One can, for example, ask whether the proposition 'Socrates is wise' is true by uttering "Is Socrates wise?" or "Is it true that Socrates is wise?" And one can suppose that Socrates is wise; and hope that Socrates is wise; and wonder whether 'Socrates is wise' is true; and wish that 'Socrates is wise' were true; and demand that 'the door is closed' be made true; and so on. It even seems that propositions can be perceived; for one can see that it is raining, and one can assert that it is raining. Of course, only true propositions can be perceived. One cannot see that it is raining when it is not. Something sounds odd, however, in saying that propositions can be perceived; someone might respond by saying that it is a *fact* that one sees, when one sees that it is raining. But does this sound any less odd? And worse, is it even clear that facts are distinct from true propositions? After all, p is true if, and only if, it is a fact that p.

To repeat, propositions can be introduced by means of different sorts of linguistic acts. Just as some linguistic acts can be described in a manner such that a proposition is seen to be the object of an act of assertion, so other linguistic acts can be described in a manner such that a proposition is seen to be the object of some other sort of act than an act of assertion. But perhaps it is worth noting that, for the most part, only when a proposition is introduced by way of assertion is it natural to respond to the utterance with the words "That's true" or "That's false." Imagine, for example, that A says, "Suppose that Hitler had defeated Britain." It would then be bizarre for B to respond, "That's false." Or if that is putting the case too strongly, if B responded "That's false," then this would properly evoke the reprimanding counter-response from A, "I know it's false; but I didn't say it wasn't; I said, *suppose* that Hitler had defeated Britain." Quite clearly what B did in his response is pick out the proposition *that Hitler defeated*

Britain from its context of proposed supposition, saying about this proposition that it is false; and what is strange in his response is that he should thus ignore the context of linguistic act in which the proposition is embedded. Again, when a man asks, "Did Hitler defeat Britain?" the natural response is "Yes" or "No," not "That's true" or "That's false." But when a man simply says, "Hitler defeated Britain," then there is nothing at all strange in the response, "That's true," nor in the response "That's false." In all three cases propositions are put forth, the same proposition in fact. Yet in one case it is natural to respond "That's true" or "That's false," in the other cases not.

Thus whether or not it is natural to respond to a man's utterance with the words "That's true" or "That's false" cannot be determined simply by determining whether he puts forth a proposition. One must also know what he was doing with the proposition. One can, surely, in responding "That's true" or "That's false" to an assertion, be using the word "that" to stand for the proposition asserted. Yet, when the same proposition is put forth nonassertively, it is not at all natural to respond "That's true" or "That's false." It would take us too far afield to explore *why* this should be so—why it should be that, for the most part, only when one *asserts* something true or false and not when one proposes for supposition something true or false, is it natural to respond "That's true" or "That's false."

4. Let us now, after this excursus, return to the topic of subjects and predicates. We saw earlier that the concepts of *assertion about something,* and *making an assertion about something,* and *speaking about something,* and *making a statement about something,* are central in the traditional definitions of "subject" and "predicate." Let us begin our probe into some of the difficulties which arise in the application of these definitions by scrutinizing how these concepts are to be used in applying the definition of "subject."

What is it that is to be regarded as being about something? Some definitions of "subject" seem to be couched in terms of what a *proposition* is about, some in terms of what a *sentence* is about, some in terms of what an *assertion* is about. Which of these is most satisfactory?

Suppose we said that the subject of a sentence is an expression in the sentence which stands for something which a proposition asserted with the sentence is about. Would that be satisfactory?

I think not. For suppose that someone asserts the proposition *that Socrates is wise*. It would seem that this proposition can be asserted by uttering any one of at least the following three sentences: "Socrates is wise," "Wisdom characterizes Socrates," and "Socrates is characterized by wisdom." Suppose that the proposition is asserted by uttering the second of the three sentences listed. Everyone would agree that "wisdom" can be viewed as being a subject of this sentence (some would hold that "Socrates" can also be so viewed). Hence, if the definition we are now considering is to be adequate, at least "wisdom" must be regarded as standing for something which the proposition is about. Hence, the proposition itself must be regarded as being at least about wisdom.

But now suppose that the proposition *that Socrates is wise* is asserted by uttering the sentence "Socrates is wise." We have just seen that the proposition thus asserted must be regarded as being at least about wisdom if the definition we are now considering is to be satisfactory. And it would seem that "wise" can be regarded as standing for wisdom in the sentence "Socrates is wise." But if so, then on the definition we are now considering the sentence "Socrates is wise" has "wise" for a subject. But it is uniformly agreed that the sentence "Socrates is wise" has but one subject— "Socrates."

If, on the other hand, we hold that the proposition *that Socrates is wise* is about only one thing, namely Socrates, then the definition we are now considering would yield the correct result that "Socrates" is the only subject in the sentence "Socrates is wise"; but it would yield the incorrect result that "Socrates" is also the only subject in the sentence "Wisdom characterizes Socrates."

When we remind ourselves that a proposition can be asserted with a variety of different sentences, it seems unlikely that there is ever a definite and complete answer to the question, asked of a certain proposition, "What is it about?" But even if every proposition *could* correctly be regarded as being about a definite, listable number of things, the argument presented leads to the conclusion that an adequate definition of "subject" cannot be formulated in terms of what a *proposition* is about.

Suppose we said that the subject of a sentence is an expression in the sentence which stands for something which the *sentence* is about. Would this be satisfactory?

I think not. One difficulty with this definition is that, granting that one can properly speak of a sentence as being about something, for many sentences there is no one thing which each can be regarded as always being about; rather, what each is about must be conceded to vary from context to context. Similarly, though it is certainly correct to speak of certain expressions as standing for things, for many expressions there is no one thing which each always stands for; rather, what it stands for also varies from context to context. Consider, for example, the sentence "He is wise." It does not seem that "he" can be regarded as standing for something which this sentence is about. For what might that thing be? Yet it is intended that "he" be a subject in this sentence. Similarly, who is the person such that "Socrates" stands for him and the sentence "Socrates is wise" is about him? Given that many persons are named "Socrates," it seems that there is no such person.

At this point someone might suggest that though a sentence *as such* cannot in general be regarded as being about something, still a sentence *on a particular occasion of utterance* can be regarded as being about something, and that our definition of "subject" should therefore be revised as follows. The subject of a sentence is an expression in the sentence which is capable of standing for something which the sentence may be about on an occasion of utterance. But then another difficulty arises. Anyone willing to allow that sentences can be about things would no doubt readily allow that "Socrates" can stand for something which the sentence "Socrates is wise" may be about on an occasion of utterance. But isn't this sentence on some occasion of utterance as much about wisdom as it is about Socrates? If it is correct to say that the sentence on some occasion of utterance is about some person, Socrates, would it always be incorrect to say that it is also on the same or some other occasion about wisdom? It certainly seems that it would not be.[7] Since we have already agreed that "wise"

<hr/>

7. Incidentally, this also shows why one could not save the attempt to define "subject" in terms of what a proposition is about by holding the proposition "Socrates is wise" is about Socrates when asserted with the sentence "Socrates is wise" and about both Socrates and wisdom when

can be regarded as standing for wisdom, however, "wise" then qualifies as a subject of this sentence. But that again violates our original requirements.

So even if sentences on occasions of utterance can be properly regarded as being about things, they are in general about too many things to enable us to formulate an adequate definition of "subject" in terms of what a sentence is about.

Suppose, finally, that we said that the subject of a sentence is that expression in the sentence which stands for something which *assertions* made with the sentence are about. Would this be satisfactory?

Again, I think not. For though a man who assertively utters "Socrates is wise" can often be regarded as making an assertion about Socrates, it would seem that there are also cases in which he should be regarded as making an assertion about wisdom.[8] Suppose, for example, that a discussion concerning wisdom were going on, and that someone said "Socrates is wise" in answer to the question "Who has wisdom?" In such a case, it seems quite clear that the person has made an assertion about wisdom, and has asserted about it that Socrates has it. If so, then since we have already agreed that "wise" can be regarded as standing for wisdom, "wise" again qualifies as a subject in "Socrates is wise."

So the suggested definition of "subject" in terms of what an assertion is about is also not satisfactory.

5. We have thus reached a blank wall in our attempt to arrive at a definition of "subject." Obviously we have not pursued every possible line of attack; but rather than try to proceed farther in this direction, let us change course and try to arrive first at a definition of "predicate." In order to define "predicate" we shall again have to make use of the concept of *about*, and we shall again have to decide what it is that is to be regarded as being

asserted with the sentence "Socrates is characterized by wisdom." For if it is correct to hold that propositions are about certain things on given occasions of assertion, there seems no good reason for holding that the proposition 'Socrates is wise' is not as much about wisdom as about Socrates when asserted with the sentence "Socrates is wise."
8. This point is made by Wilson, *Statement and Inference*, 1:114ff; and by Strawson, *Individuals*, pp. 143ff.

about something. It will prove to be natural and convenient if, in setting up our definition, we speak only of *assertions* as being about things.

In traditional definitions of "predicate," it is assumed that if we make an assertion about some thing, then we must be *asserting something* about that thing; or, to use another phrase, we must be *saying something* about that thing. This seems to be a legitimate assumption. If an assertion has been made about some thing (things), then it seems that questions asked with these following two sentences (or equivalents thereof) will always have correct answers: "About what thing (things) has something been asserted (said)?" and "What has been asserted (said) about that thing (those things)?" Thus the subject-predicate distinction has traditionally been based on and reflective of the fact that, given an assertion about something, one can distinguish between these two things: that which something has been asserted (said) about, and that which has been asserted (said) about it.

It is worth noting that what is asserted *about* something on a given occasion is in general not to be identified with what is asserted (a proposition) on that occasion. Suppose that someone assertively utters "Napoleon was conceited" and also "Wellington was conceited." He has then asserted two different propositions. Yet what he has asserted about Napoleon, namely, that he was conceited, is the same as what he has asserted about Wellington. About each of these famous military men he has asserted (said) the same thing, namely, that he was conceited.[9]

Now suppose we said that something is a predicate of a certain sentence if, and only if, when the sentence is used to make an assertion about some thing(s), it is that word or phrase in the sentence which expresses what is asserted about that thing (those things). This would be inadequate. If the sentence "Socrates is wise" is used to make an assertion about Socrates, then we can certainly say that "is wise" expresses what is said about Socrates, namely, that he is wise. But if the same sentence is used to make an assertion about wisdom, then it seems we can equally well say that "Socrates is" expresses what is said about wisdom, namely,

9. Cf. R. Cartwright, "Propositions," in R.J. Butler, ed., *Analytical Philosophy* (Oxford, 1962), p. 85.

that Socrates has it. But then "Socrates is" would also have to be a predicate of this sentence, and that violates our original requirements.

But the word "say," and correspondingly the word "assert," have an ambiguity which is most critical in this context. Suppose that one man assertively utters the sentence "Socrates is wise," and another the sentence "Socrates has wisdom," and that they are making an assertion about the same person. Then in one sense of the word "say," these two men have said the same thing; for they have both asserted the same proposition. But in another sense of the word they have not said the same thing; for they have not uttered the same sentence, the same words. There is a corresponding ambiguity in the phrase "say about." In one sense of this phrase both the man who assertively uttered "Socrates is wise" and the man who assertively uttered "Socrates has wisdom" have said something about wisdom, and the same thing; namely, that Socrates has it. But in another sense of "say about," the former speaker did not say about *anything* that Socrates has it. For he did not use the words "Socrates has" but rather the words "Socrates is." In this sense, there is nothing at all that he said about wisdom; for he certainly did not say about wisdom that Socrates is it. To say that he said about wisdom that Socrates has it would be to evoke the response: "No he didn't. He didn't even use the word 'has'."

Now suppose that we use "say about" in the narrower sense, so that to state what has been said about something one must use the speaker's very words. Then when one answers a question of the form "What has been said about . . .?" one must use only the words actually used in the sentence uttered—with the proviso that the whole answer will take the form of a noun-clause prefaced by "that," in which relative pronouns are substituted for their antecedents (the antecedents appearing in the answer to the prior question, "What has something been said about?"). For example, if someone assertively utters "Jones is a good artist," then to the question "What has been said about Jones," the answer is this: "That he is a good artist." And the words comprising this answer, exclusive of "that he," are the very words the speaker used to make his assertion. To avoid confusion, let us henceforth use the phrase "say about" only in this narrower sense; and let us use the phrase "assert about" for the broader sense. I think it is not unreasonable to assume that those who have traditionally worked with the subject-predicate distinction have tacitly had this narrower sense in mind.

It is worth noticing that for some sentences it is the case that sometimes the very words of the sentence can be used to state what has been asserted about something, and sometimes those very words cannot be so used. Whether they can be will depend on such matters as who is stating what has been asserted about something, to whom he addresses his remark, when he speaks, and where he speaks. Suppose, for example, that a clerk in an airline ticket office assertively utters, "Flight 606 will leave here an hour from now." Anyone present at the time can use the speaker's own words to state what has been asserted by him about Flight 606: "That it will leave here an hour from now." Thus anyone present at the time can state what has been *said about* Flight 606. But someone speaking half an hour later, or in another place, cannot state what has been asserted about Flight 606 with those same words: "That it will leave here an hour from now." Or better, he can perhaps still use those same words, but they will be an extremely ambiguous means of communicating what he wishes to assert. Again, suppose that I assertively utter, "John gave me the book." Then *I* can use my very words to state what has been asserted by me about John, thus: "That he gave me the book." That is, I can state what has been *said about* John. But only I can do so. And to take but one more example: If I assertively utter, "John gave you the book," then someone who addresses the same person that I was addressing can state what has been *said about* John, thus: "That he gave you the book." But only in such a circumstance can this be done.

So suppose that someone asserts something about something. Consider then a correct answer to a question asked with the sentence (or an equivalent thereof), "What has been said about it?" where the antecedent for "it" occurs in a correct answer to a prior question asked with the sentence (or an equivalent thereof), "What has something been said about?" Let us say that all the words which appear in such an answer to such a question, exclusive of "that" (or its synonym) and the relative pronoun, are what has been *predicated* by the original speaker of what the

relative pronoun stands for. And let us say that he has *referred*
to whatever he may have predicated something of. For example,
suppose that a person assertively utters "Jones is a good artist."
Thereby it has been said by him about Jones that he (Jones) is
a good artist. And thereby he has referred to Jones and has
predicated of him "is a good artist."

We can now offer the following definition of "predicate" and
of "subject." Something is a *predicate* of a sentence on some
analysis if and only if it is a part of the sentence which can be
predicated of some thing(s); and the *subject(s)* of the sentence
on that analysis is that part (are those parts) of the sentence
which, when what is the predicate on that analysis is predicated
of something, stands (stand) for that of which it is predicated.
These definitions now, I think, achieve for the most part the
results desired.

A consequence of these definitions is that many sentences, such
as "Socrates taught Plato," are susceptible of multiple subject-
predicate analyses. In the sentence "Socrates taught Plato,"
"taught Plato" can be viewed as the predicate, on which analysis
"Socrates" is the subject ("he said, about Socrates, that he taught
Plato"); "Socrates taught" can be viewed as the predicate, on
which analysis "Plato" is the subject ("he said, about Plato, that
Socrates taught him"); and "taught" can be viewed as predicate,
on which analysis "Socrates" and "Plato" are both subjects ("he
said, about Socrates and Plato, that the former taught the latter").

Another consequence of these definitions of "subject" and
"predicate" is that the subject-predicate distinction is not applicable to every sentence which can be used to make an assertion
about something. It is sometimes held that to say (assert) something, is perforce to say (assert) something about some thing(s).[10]
If one takes "say about" in the broader of the two senses we have
distinguished, so that one need not answer the question "What has
been said about it?" by giving the very words used in the originally
uttered sentence, perhaps this is true. I shall not here discuss
whether or not it is. We have defined "subject," "predicate," "to
refer," and "to predicate" in narrower terms and, given these

10. See, for example, Gilbert Ryle, "Letters and Syllables in Plato," *Philosophical Review* (October, 1960), p. 442; and Bertrand Russell, *Principles
of Mathematics* (London, 1951 reprint), pp. 39, 43.

definitions, it is clear that one can make assertions without using subject-predicate sentences, without referring and without predicating, and without saying something about something. Assertions made with the sentences "It is raining" and "Nothing came by" are good examples. Even if one held that an assertion made with the sentence "It is raining" is about something, still nothing qualifies as that part of the sentence which is predicated of what the assertion is about, and thus nothing qualifies as the subject of the sentence. An obvious consequence of this point is that the truth of an assertion does not always consist in the predicate holding of that for which the subject stands, since many assertions are made without using any subject or predicate at all.

Further, if Russell's theory of descriptions were correct, then existential sentences would not be subject-predicate sentences. Consider, for example, such a sentence as "Socrates exists." Russell held that, though in assertively uttering this sentence we can be regarded as asserting something about some thing, it is impossible to correlate this distinction with any distinct expressions in the sentence. He also held, however, that the same proposition can be asserted with a sentence to which the subject-predicate distinction *does* apply; a sentence, moreover, which to his mind makes it clear that the assertion involved is not about Socrates, but rather about a certain concept, or a certain linguistic expression (a propositional function).[11]

6. Our definitions, if satisfactory, establish a significant difference between the function of subjects and the function of predicates. Predicates are those elements of sentences which can be predicated of things, that is, they give us what is said about some thing when coupled in a noun-clause with an expression standing for that thing; subjects are those elements of sentences which can stand for what predicates can be predicated of.

Certain writers—among them Joseph, Ryle, and Strawson—claim that there is another difference in function between subjects

11. "Existence is essentially a property of a propositional function," Russell, "Logical Atomism," in R.C. Marsh, ed., *Logic and Knowledge* (London, 1956), p. 232. Above I say, "about a certain concept, or a certain linguistic expression," because Russell never makes clear which of these he takes propositional functions to be.

and predicates than that which we have thus far singled out, a difference often indicated by saying that subjects have a certain completeness about them which predicates lack, and that, if there were this further difference, the significance of the subject-predicate distinction would be even greater than has been suggested.[12] The claim is that predicates are bearers of an *assertive clue,* whereas subjects are not. I wish, in conclusion, to consider whether this claim is correct.

First, however, it is perhaps of interest to note that from our definitions it follows that subjects do indeed have a *certain* completeness or self-sufficiency about them which predicates lack. This can be seen in the following way. The subject of a sentence not only stands for what something is said about, and thereby for what the predicate is predicated of, but it, by itself, constitutes a grammatically complete answer to the question, "What has something been said about?" (The grammatical case, however, will often be different.) Suppose, for example, that someone assertively utters "Socrates is wise." Then "Socrates" is a gramatically complete answer to the question, "What has something been said about?" and, in addition, "Socrates" is the subject of the sentence. But the predicate of this sentence, though our definitions serve to tie it up to the question, "What has been said about Socrates?" does not, by itself, constitute a complete answer to this question. It is *incomplete* for this purpose.

To answer the question, "What has been said about Socrates?" we must supplement the predicate in two ways. We must add a pronominal expression (a variable) capable of standing for that which the subject stands for. One cannot express what has been said about something without also using an expression to stand for what it has been said about, whereas one *can* express what something has been said about just by using an expression to stand for it. And secondly, we must cast the whole into a noun-

12. Frege first introduced the contrast complete-incomplete (see "Concept and Object," in P. Geach and M. Black, *Translations from the Philosophical Writings of Gottlob Frege* [Oxford, 1952]). He did not, however, associate it directly with the subject-predicate distinction, but with a distinction which he claimed to hold between those entities which can be designated by subjects and those which can be designated by predicates. The former ("objects") he holds to be complete in a certain way in which the latter ("concepts") are incomplete.

clause, thereby giving the entire answer to the question "What has been said about Socrates?" a structure obviously parallel to the expression specifying what was asserted ("that he is wise" compared to "that Socrates is wise"). No such parallel structure is necessary for the answer to "What has something been said about?"

But to return to the main question under consideration. Is it the case that the predicate of a sentence is not only what is predicated of something (in the sense explained), but that it also bears an assertive clue; in other words, that its occurrence in speech signifies that an assertion is being made? Of course, even if a predicate did have these two functions, one might cast doubt on the significance of this fact by arguing that it was a mere accident of English or of Indo-European languages. But what demands prior consideration is whether the claim is true that a predicate, even in these languages, both helps to specify *what* is asserted about something, and signifies *that* something is asserted.

The doctrine in question can be introduced by citing the following passage from Gilbert Ryle:

Russell realized, rather reluctantly, that between the statement "Brutus assassinated Caesar" and the list "Brutus, assassination, Caesar" there was some vital difference. The first tells a truth or falsehood; the second tells nothing at all, though it mentions three things. Yet surely the verbal noun "assassination" expresses the same concept as the verb "assassinated" and, if so, it ought to be able to replace the live verb in a sentence *salvo sensu*—which it patently cannot do. This little crux is of great importance. For if asked "what does 'assassinated' mean?" or "what does 'will prosecute' mean?" we see automatically that we are being asked for the elucidation of the common core of all full sentences of the pattern "Blank assassinated Blank," or "A will prosecute B." Live verbs unmistakably advertise themselves as being cores cut out of full sentences. To ask what a given live verb means is to ask what a speaker would be saying if he said something with it. Live verbs are snatches from speech, that it, from the *using* of words. Live verbs could not feature in lists. They occur only in contexts; indeed, they are the life breath of those contexts.[13]

A verb supplies the sentence in which it occurs with its asserting force and so collects the nouns and other parts of speech with itself into the telling of a unitary truth or falsehood.[14]

13. Ryle, "Letters and Syllables in Plato," pp. 447–48.
14. Ibid., p. 442.

One point which Ryle makes in this passage—and certainly a correct one—is that asserting something is not to be equated with naming two or more things. "Saying one thing in two words is not to be equated with mentioning-by-name two things."[15] But the point which is of direct interest to us here is Ryle's claim that the occurrence of a live verb in an utterance is the mark of assertion, the assertive clue. In short, what Ryle is claiming, if I understand him, and what we want to assess, is the following. The appearance of a live verb in a meaningful utterance is (normally) a sufficient condition for an assertion's being made in the making of that utterance.

This claim is mistaken. Sentences used in speech acts other than assertions also contain live verbs, so that the occurrence of a live verb in a meaningful utterance is no guarantee whatsoever that an assertion is made in the making of that utterance. Can Ryle really have overlooked this obvious fact? Possibly. On the other hand, he may, without saying so, mean his claim to hold only for *certain sorts* of live verbs. Which sort? An answer readily suggests itself: those live verbs which are capable of serving as logical predicates in some sentence or other—*predicable expressions,* in other words.

Whether or not Ryle intends his thesis to be qualified in this particular manner, it does seem quite clear that this is what H.W.B. Joseph has in mind when he says, in a passage previously cited, "In the proposition 'Dogs bark,' 'dogs' stands for the things about which the statement is made, 'bark' both is the sign of (or expresses) what is predicated about them, and also of its being predicated. . . ."

Is it the case, then, that the occurrence of a predicable expression in a meaningful utterance is a sufficient condition for an assertion's being made in the making of that utterance? Quite obviously it is not. For any sentence which is capable of being used to make an assertion can also, merely by a change of inflection, be used to ask a question. The sentence "Socrates is wise" can be used to ask whether Socrates is wise as well as to assert that he is wise. And the sentence, "The door will be closed" can be used to make an assertion, to issue a command, and to ask a

15. Ibid., p. 443.

question. Some predicable expressions, furthermore, can be used all by themselves to make an intelligible utterance, without thereby an assertion being made. For example, the predicable expression "run" can be used to issue a command. Finally, it even seems that predicable expressions can be used in lists. For example, if someone asks "What are some of the things John does in the summer?" one possible answer would be: "runs, swims, and boats."

Strawson, while thinking along the same lines as Ryle and Joseph, is yet aware of some of the difficulties. Consequently he tries to weaken the claim slightly so as to make it accurate, without thereby weakening it so much as to deprive it of all interest and significance. His claim is that the occurence of an indicative verb in an intelligible utterance is a sufficient condition for that utterance's being used to make an assertion, unless its force is weakened by addition. It will be noticed that he is not making the trivial claim that it is a sufficient condition in every case except those in which it is not. Rather, he is saying that its failure to be a sufficient condition can, at least in standard usage, be attributed to some *addition*. These are his words: ". . . the standard way of insulating a propositional form of words from that commitment as to its truth-value which consists in asserting it is to *add* to it, to add, for example, the conjunction 'that'."[16] Thus Strawson holds that the primary, though not the invariant, function of an indicative verb is to signal that an assertion is being made.

Strawson also holds that an *invariant* function of the indicative verb is to "introduce a proposition": ". . . even if we cannot say that the distinctive style in which 'is wise,' 'smokes,' etc. introduce their terms, is simply the assertive style, we can at least say that the term is introduced into something which has a truth-value."[17] So Strawson's complete view as to the function of indicative verbs, and hence predicable expressions, in normal or standard usage, is as follows. The occurrence of an indicative verb in an intelligible utterance is a guarantee that in the making of that utterance a proposition is introduced; in addition, unless some qualification is

16. Strawson, *Individuals,* p. 150.
17. Ibid.

added, it is a guarantee that in the making of that utterance an assertion is made.

I think doubts can be cast on Strawson's claim that indicative verbs are always used to "introduce propositions"; we have already seen that predicable expressions can be used to issue commands, ask questions, and give lists, and at least the last of these activities is a case of something which Strawson clearly regards as not introducing a proposition. Our immediate concern, however, is with the connection which, Strawson claims, holds between predicates and assertions. It seems to me that his claim on this point is mistaken for every predicable expression whatsoever. We have already remarked that any sentence whatsoever which can be used to make an assertion can also be used to ask a question, the difference lying wholly in the stresses and inflections (or, if we are dealing with written language, in the terminal marks). Further, this is certainly a standard way of asking questions; it is not an aberrant use of words, whose force must be gathered solely from the context, but rather is a use of words which any book on grammar or linguistics will cite. Do we then *add* something when we ask a question with a sentence which, in normal usage, can also be used to make an assertion; do we, for example, *add* an inflection, or a terminal mark? If in the making of assertions by uttering sentences, we spoke without inflection, then obviously one could hold that the question-inflection must be added if the same sentence is to be used to ask a question. But assertions are not made with inflection-less utterances; rather, such utterances have their own typical and peculiar inflection. To change an assertion-making utterance to a question-making utterance, using the same sentence, one cannot merely *add* an inflection, but must rather get rid of one and substitute another. Correspondingly, an assertion in written language is not made by leaving off all terminal marks. If one wishes to use the same sentence to ask a question rather than make an assertion, one must substitute a question mark for a period.

In conclusion, I know of no one who has succeeded in showing that predicates are in some sense the bearers of an assertive clue and that subjects are not. Further, I think it can be seen that this line of thought has no chance of success. For, in the normal case, speakers indicate that they are making assertions not just by the syntactical structure of the sentences they use but also by *the inflections,* or by *the terminal marks.* For whatever reasons, philosophers have concentrated their attention on words, and ignored the importance of inflections, periods, question marks, and the like.

We are left with this difference between the function of subjects and predicates. The predicate of a sentence on a certain analysis is what can be predicated of something, that is, it can give us what has been said about some thing(s) when coupled in a noun-clause with an expression standing for that thing (those things). A subject of a sentence on a certain analysis is what can stand for something that the predicate on that analysis can be predicated of. It can stand for what something is said about.

2

General Terms
and Singular Terms

1. Philosophers and others have thought, when they surveyed our language, that they discerned a distinction between certain expressions which are or can be related to *many* things in a way in which certain other expressions are or can be related to just *one* thing. Some expressions, it seems, can be true of, or name, or denote, many things; others, it seems, can be true of, or name, or denote, only one thing. Expressions of the former sort have been called *general terms;* expressions of the latter sort, *singular terms.* This distinction has seemed especially clear in the contrast between common nouns on the one hand, and proper names and definite descriptions on the other. The former, it has been strongly felt, can bear to many things the same semantic relation which the latter can bear to just one thing.

In what follows, I should like to discuss what there is of truth to these ideas. I shall do so by exploring various definitions of "general term" and "singular term," trying to arrive at a satisfactory definition. A satisfactory definition, I judge, must do at least two things. It must make clear what *is* this semantic relation of which it is said that some expressions can bear it to many things and some to just one. But also it must have the result that for the most part, common nouns can bear this relation to many things, whereas proper names and definite descriptions can bear it to only one thing. It must have the result, that is, that common nouns are general terms, and that proper names and definite descriptions are singular terms. For it is in the distinction between common nouns on the one hand, and proper names and definite descriptions on the other, that the distinction between those expressions which can bear a certain semantic relation to many things and those which can bear it to just one thing has been felt most sharply.

If there were no way of drawing a distinction between those expressions which can bear a certain semantic relation to many things and those which can bear it to just one, except a way which yielded the result that common nouns were not, for the most part, of the former sort, or that proper names and definite descriptions were not, for the most part, of the latter sort, then I think it would have to be allowed that there was something so seriously amiss in the traditional thought on these matters that it would be misleading to speak any more of "general terms" and "singular terms." Contrariwise, if no distinction as to how they are related to things could be found between common nouns on the one hand, and proper names and definite descriptions on the other, except a distinction quite other than that between those expressions which can bear a certain semantic relation to many things and those which can bear it to just one thing, then again I think it would have to be allowed that there was something so seriously amiss in the traditional thought on these matters that it would be misleading to speak any more of "general terms" and "singular terms."[1]

1. W.E. Johnson has a discussion of what he calls *general terms* in which the idea of being capable of bearing a certain semantic relation to more than one thing plays no role at all, and in which he limits his consideration to grammatical substantives. It seems to me misleading in such a case to speak of general terms. What Johnson is really discussing is *common nouns,* his view apparently being that common nouns are not, in general, expressions capable of bearing to many things a certain relation which other expressions can bear to only one thing. He says this: ". . . we now turn to a common characteristic in the use of an article, namely, its attachment to a *general* name. The general name has usually been differentiated by reference to number, and roughly defined as a name predicable of more than one object. In fact, however, there are general names

It is by no means the case, however, that the distinction between those expressions which can bear a certain semantic relation to many things and those which can bear it to just one thing has been regarded as present only in the contrast between common nouns on the one hand, and proper names and definite descriptions on the other. I think, though, that it will be satisfactory to test the definitions we consider against just this contrast and then, after we have found satisfactory definitions, to see how they apply to other sorts of expressions.

But it may be interesting and enlightening, before we look at any definitions, to consider how various writers have tried to state, in a more general and comprehensive fashion, which sort of expressions they regard as general terms, and which sort of expressions they regard as singular terms.[2] Quine says, on this matter, that "a singular term, e.g., 'mama', admits only the singular grammatical form and no article . . . whereas if a term admits the definite and indefinite article and the plural ending, then normally under our perfected adult usage it is a general term."[3] Later he adds that grammatical predicates are also general terms, predicate nominatives and predicate adjectives being counted as part of the predicate.[4] Thus the materials which Quine uses for stating in a general way which sort of expressions he regards as singular and which as general, are three: the grammatical concept of a predicate, the grammatical concept of an article (definite and indefinite), and the grammatical distinction between the singular and plural form of words. If in addition to

such as 'integer between 3 and 4' or 'snake in Ireland' that are predicable of *no* object, while 'integer between 3 and 5' and 'pole-star' are general names predicable of only one object. There is therefore nothing in the *meaning* of a general name which could determine the number of objects to which it is applicable. Rejecting this reference to number, we may point out that a universal characteristic of the general name is its connection with the article . . ." (Johnson, *Logic* [Cambridge, 1940], 1:90).

2. There might be a question as to the status that these writers assign to these general formulations. One possibility is that they hold that a satisfactory definition *must* yield results conforming to the general formulation. Another possibility is that they regard the formulation as only a summary of the results yielded by a prior definition. The evidence, I think, points to the conclusion that they all regard it in the latter way.

3. W.V.O. Quine, *Word and Object* (Cambridge, 1960), p. 90.

4. Ibid., p. 96.

those prefixes which are articles we also include prefixes indicating quantity, and demonstrative particles, then we have, so far as I know, all the materials in terms of which anyone has ever tried to state, in a general way, which expressions he regards as singular and which as general. The considerable differences which exist among various writers on this point arise solely from their different ways of using these common materials.

Quine uses these materials in such a way that, on his statement, a term which admits *both* of being prefixed by the definite and indefinite article, and of assuming the plural form, is normally a general term; whereas a singular term is one which admits *neither* of an article nor of a plural form. When the materials are used in this way, then a mass term, such as "furniture," turns out to be a general term. For though this term certainly admits in normal adult usage of being prefixed with a definite article, as in "The furniture in the room is Shaker," yet it does not admit of being prefixed with an indefinite article, or of the plural form. Thus, since it is not the case that it admits of neither, it is not singular. Presumably, then, it is general—a conclusion not dictated by the criterion given for a general term, but compatible with it. Again, a definite description, such as "the man who came late," admits of a plural form—"the men who came late"—but it does not admit of being prefixed with an article. Thus, since it is not the case that it admits of neither, it is not singular. Presumably, then, it is general—a conclusion which is, again, not dictated by the criterion given for a general term, but certainly is compatible with it. In fact, however, Quine regards definite descriptions as singular terms in normal usage, and mass terms he regards as singular in some normal usage and general in other. Thus his attempt to correlate the distinction between singular and general terms with a very general grammatically-based distinction between terms is, even when considered in the light of his own discussion, not especially successful.

J.N. Keynes, to summarize which expressions are singular terms and which general, says that "we may take as the test or criterion of a general name, the possibility of prefixing *all* or *some* to it with any meaning"; other names are singular.[5] On this

5. J. N. Keynes, *Formal Logic* (London, 1928), p. 12.

formulation, definite descriptions are singular terms; whereas
mass terms such as "furniture" are general, for they can be prefixed with "some," as in "Some furniture isn't worth buying."

Finally, Miss Stebbing says that a general term is one which
either has a plural form *or* admits of being prefixed with words
indicating quantity: "Any name which could be significantly used
in the plural, or prefixed with *a, any, all, some,* or with any
numerical prefix, is general"; all other names apparently are
singular.[6] On this formulation, as on Quine's, both definite descriptions and mass terms are general terms. In fact, however,
Miss Stebbing regards definite descriptions as singular terms. Thus
her attempt to correlate the distinction between singular and
general terms with a very general grammatically-based distinction
between terms is also, even when considered in the light of her
own discussion, not very successful.

So the attempts to correlate the singular term-general term
distinction with a general grammatically-based distinction between the expressions in our language are not only (in two of
the cases considered) to be judged defective in the light of what
the writer himself says, but they also yield widely differing results.
The following, and not much more, is common to the formulations cited. A term which in normal usage admits *both* of a plural
form *and* of being prefixed with articles and with words indicating
quantity, is in normal usage a general term; and a term which in
normal usage admits *neither* of being prefixed with articles or
with words indicating quantity, *nor* of a plural form, is in normal
usage a singular term. It will be observed that common nouns,
by this formula, fall into the class of general terms, and that
proper names fall into the class of singular terms. However, the
fate of definite descriptions is left undetermined by this formula,
though it is universally agreed that they are singular terms.

Before we inquire into definitions of "singular term" and "general term," we must consider another matter. What is to be meant
by "term"? Quite obviously not all linguistic expressions are terms,
as the word "term" is used in discussions on singular and general terms. For it is commonly said of terms, in such discussions,

6. L. Susan Stebbing, *An Introduction to Logic* (New York, 1961 reprint),
p. 54.

that they can be *applied to* or *affirmed of* things, and no one would regard quantifiers and numerical prefixes and logical particles as words which can be applied to or affirmed of things. Furthermore, it is quite frequently held or assumed that all terms are either singular or general. Singular terms and general terms are frequently regarded as exhaustive of the whole class of terms. But obviously not all linguistic expressions are then being regarded as terms. For no one would regard quantifiers and numerical prefixes and logical particles as either singular terms or general terms. They are not terms at all. What then is the concept of *term* which underlies these discussions?

The clue to be followed, I think, is the fact that it is commonly said of terms that they can be applied to or affirmed of things. The assumption is that such words as "or" and "if" and "all" cannot, in normal usage, be applied to or affirmed of things, and thus are not terms in normal usage. Such words as "John" and "runs" and "man" can, in normal usage, be applied to or affirmed of things, and thus are terms in normal usage. Further, I think that what is meant when it is said of some expression that it can be affirmed of (applied to) something, is probably this. An assertion can be made with a sentence whose logical subject is a demonstrative or personal pronoun standing for some thing, and whose logical predicate is the expression in question (or whose logical predicate is the expression in question supplemented by the copula, or by the copula plus the indefinite article). For example, in normal usage "This is if" could not be used to make an assertion; thus in normal usage "if" is not a term. But "This is a man" could in normal usage be used to make an assertion. Thus in normal usage "man" or "a man" or "is a man" is a term.[7] Of course, in normal usage "This is not" could, in some contexts, be used to make an assertion; when, that is, some other sentence is

7. It is not clear to me why Quine regards the expressions "which I bought" and "from which extract is made" as terms (*Word and Object,* p. 110). Elsewhere, he explains "term" thus: "It is the peculiarity of a statement to be true or false. It is the peculiarity of a term, on the other hand to be *true of* many objects, or one, or none, and false of the rest" (*Methods of Logic* [New York, 1953], p. 65). Whether, on this explanation, "which I bought" and "from which extract is made" are terms is unclear. The difficulty is that the phrase "true of," on which Quine rests his explanation, is not, in its ordinary usage, applied to words.

"understood," for example, "This is not red." Yet "not" is not meant to be a term. So when we try to decide whether a certain expression is or is not a term in normal usage, by incorporating it into a certain sort of sentence and then seeing whether the sentence can in normal usage be used to make an assertion, we should not allow, in applying these tests, some *other* sentence to be "understood."

One last introductory remark is in order. Some writers have intended the singular-general distinction to be applied only to terms which are grammatically substantive expressions. Such writers are very few. Most, by way of the examples they offer, make it clear that they intend the distinction to be applied more broadly. Further, I know of no case in which the definitions offered do not in fact have a broader applicability than just to substantive expressions. The fact that most writers do not intend to confine the distinction to substantive expressions may be obscured by the fact that many of them—for example, Keynes and Stebbing in the passages quoted—speak of *names* rather than *terms*. But it should be recalled that logicians have traditionally used the word "name" very broadly. Admittedly it is the case that in many discussions of singular and general terms, grammatical substantives have been so much the focus of attention that other sorts of terms have almost been lost from sight. This is the case in some of the grammatical formulations cited. But I shall follow what I take to be clearly the intent of almost the entire tradition by not limiting the applicability of the general term-singular term distinction to those terms which are substantives.

Finally, let us, throughout, regard the grammatically singular and grammatically plural forms of a word, not as distinct terms, but as variants on the *same* term.

2. With these preliminaries behind us, let us attempt to find a satisfactory definition of "singular term" and of "general term." We cannot do better, I think, than to begin with the definitions offered by Quine. For he has discussed the distinction between singular terms and general terms at greater length than anyone else.

Quine defines "a singular term" as one which purports to be

true of just one object, and "a general term" as one which does not purport to be true of just one object.[8] He holds that the word "purports" in these definitions is essential. "Pegasus," for example, is to be counted as a singular term; for though, in Quine's terminology, it is not true of anything at all, still it *purports* to be true of just one object. On the other hand, "natural satellite of the earth" is to be counted as a general term; for though it is true of just one object, it does not *purport* to be true of just one object. Are these definitions satisfactory?

To answer this question, it is essential that we understand the sense of the phrases "purports" and "is true of." Though Quine does not explain what he means by "is true of," I think that we can reasonably assume that "*T* is true of *a*" means the same as this: "A true proposition would be asserted if one assertively uttered a sentence whose logical subject is a pronoun standing for *a*, and whose logical predicate is *T* (or whose logical predicate is *T* supplemented by the copula, or by the copula plus the indefinite article)." (Again, in applying this definition we must not allow some *other* sentence than the one under consideration to be "understood.")

What, then, is the sense of the word "purports"? Quine's stated reasons for introducing this expression are two. First, there are some terms, he suggests, which in fact are not true of anything; still it *could* be that they are true of something, though it *could not* be that they are true of more than one thing. So "*T* purports to be true of just one object" would seem to mean the same as this: "It is possible that *T* is true of one thing and not possible that *T* is true of more than one thing." Secondly, Quine holds that some terms which are true of just one thing, and some which are true of no thing, are still such that they *could* be true of more than one thing. So "*T* does not purport to be true of just one object" would seem to mean the same as this: "It is possible that *T* is true of more than one thing."

Are Quine's definitions of "singular term" and "general term," when interpreted in this fashion, satisfactory? Consider the term "John." Is it the case that "John" purports to be true of just one object? Certainly not. "John" is, *in fact*, true of a great many

8. *Word and Object*, pp. 96–98.

objects, as, indeed, are most proper names. Yet proper names
were intended to be singular terms.

It might be replied that the existence of cases like these shows
that we have misinterpreted Quine's phrase "purports to be true
of." This may indeed be the case. Yet Quine's introduction of
the word "purports" was not designed to take care of cases like
these. It was designed to take care of the proper name which
happens not to be true of anything, rather than the proper name
which is true of several things. So there is no good reason, thus
far, to suppose that we have misunderstood Quine's intent.

3. How can we cope with the difficulty arising from the fact
that a proper name can be, and usually is, borne by more than
one thing, thus being true of more than one thing? Writings on
the topic of singular and general terms contain two standard
ways of trying to cope with this difficulty. One is to insist that
we must not apply the distinction to a term as such, but rather
to a term as used in a particular context. The other is to insist
that we must not apply the distinction to a term as such, but
rather to a term in a given sense.

The former of these devices is the one seemingly favored by
Quine; for he says, that "generality is not to be confused with
ambiguity. The singular term 'Jones' is ambiguous in that it might
be used in different contexts to name any of various persons, but
it is still a singular term in that it purports in any particular
context to name one and only one person."[9]

It might be supposed that in this passage Quine is not using the
concept *being true of,* but rather a different concept, *naming.*
Perhaps he is, but against this interpretation one must, I think,
allow the following passage: ". . . the general term does not
purport to name at all. The general term may indeed 'be true of'
each of *many* things, viz., each red thing, or each man, but this
kind of reference is not called naming; 'naming', at least as I
shall use the word, is limited to the case where the named object
purports to be unique."[10] In this passage, Quine seems to be
saying that both singular and general terms purport to be 'true of'

9. Quine, *Methods of Logic,* p. 203.
10. Ibid, p. 205.

things, that is, to refer to things; but that there are two kinds of reference, singular and multiple, with only the former to be called naming. Then it is claimed that all and only singular terms name.[11] So I propose that, first at least, we assume that Quine is still basing his distinction on the concept *true of*.

Quine's basic idea, then, would be this. Though a proper name may purport to be true of more than one thing, still that term in its use as part of a sentence used to make an assertion purports to be true of exactly one thing. Other terms, however, in their use as parts of sentences used to make assertions do *not* purport to be true of exactly one thing.

If we are to state and explain this idea we must restructure our definitions of "purports to be true of exactly one thing" and "does not purport to be true of exactly one thing." We have given an explanation of what might be meant by saying that a *term* purports or does not purport to be true of exactly one thing. But this does not provide us with an explanation of what might be meant by saying that *a term in each use as part of an assertively uttered sentence* purports or does not purport to be true of exactly one thing. We must now ask, for example, what might be meant by saying that "Socrates," in each use as part of the assertively uttered sentence "Socrates is wise," purports to be true of exactly one thing; while "wise" or "is wise," in each such use, does *not*

11. Consider the following passage: ". . . 'Pegasus' counts as a singular term though true of nothing, and 'natural satellite of the earth' counts as a general term though true of just one object. As one vaguely says, 'Pegasus' is singular in that it purports to refer to just one object, and 'natural satellite of the earth' is general in that its singularity of reference is not something *purported in the term*" (*Word and Object*, pp. 95–96). Here, quite clearly, Quine is using "is true of" and "refers to" interchangeably. But then consider this passage: "Semantically the distinction between singular and general terms is vaguely that a singular term names or purports to name just one object . . . while a general term is true of each, severally, of any number of objects" (ibid., p. 90). Here it must simply be admitted that the relation between *naming* and *being true of* is not clear. Finally, consider this passage: "Predication joins a general term and a singular term to form a sentence that is true or false according as the general term is true or false of the object, if any, to which the singular term refers" (ibid., p. 96). In this passage, it seems unlikely that the concepts *is true of* and *refers to* are really identical. In short, in *Word and Object* the relation between the concepts *is true of, names,* and *refers to,* is not made clear. What accounts for this, no doubt, is that these concepts themselves are never explained.

purport to be true of exactly one thing. Our original concept, *being true of,* was not a 'contextual' concept.

One possible way of construing these words would be in terms of the concept of predication, yielding the following definitions. A singular term is a term which, whenever used as part of an assertively uttered sentence, is predicated of exactly one thing; a general term is a term which, whenever used as part of an assertively uttered sentence, is not predicated of exactly one thing. But these definitions do not at all yield the results desired. For suppose I assertively utter "Socrates is wise." In doing this, I do not predicate "Socrates" of anything at all, whereas I predicate "is wise" of exactly one thing, Socrates.

Perhaps there is some other way of interpreting the phrase, "purports to be true of just one thing in each use of the term as part of an assertively uttered sentence"—a way which is a reasonable interpretation of these words and which gives us the results desired. But I myself see none such. So let us backtrack, and surrender our assumption that *naming,* for Quine, is one species of *being true of.* Let us rather regard "naming" as a synonym of "standing for." And let us then define "a singular term" as a term which, whenever used as part of an assertively uttered sentence, purports to stand for exactly one thing; and "general term" as a term which, whenever used as part of an assertively uttered sentence, does not purport to stand for exactly one thing.

If we were actually to adopt these definitions, an explanation of "purports" as used in this context would be required from us. But I think we can see in advance that this way of drawing the distinction also has no chance of success. For though, in assertively uttering "Socrates is wise," "Socrates" might with reason be said to stand for exactly one thing, Socrates, there seems to be nothing against our saying that "wise" in such a case also stands for exactly one thing, wisdom.

The reader may by now have concluded that we perversely intend to ignore what Quine himself offers as a clarification of his phrase, "purports to refer to." For Quine says this: "As one vaguely says, 'Pegasus' is singular in that it *purports* to refer to just one object, and 'natural satellite of the earth' is general in that its simplicity of reference is not something *purported* in the term. Such talk of purport is only a picturesque way of alluding to distinctive grammatical roles that singular and general terms play in sentences. It is by grammatical role that general and singular terms are properly to be distinguished. The basic combination in which general and singular terms find their contrasting roles is that of *predication*: 'Mama is a woman', or schematically '*a* is an *F*' where '*a*' represents a singular term and '*F*' a general term. Predication joins a general term and a singular term to form a sentence that is true or false according as the general term is true or false of the object, if any, to which the singular term refers. . . . The general term is what is predicated, or occupies what grammarians call predicative position. . . ."[12]

Quine holds—this is clear—that if a term is capable of playing the subject role, then it is singular, that is, it purports to refer to just one thing; and that if a term is capable of playing the predicate role, then it is general, that is, it does not purport to refer to just one thing. What is not decisively clear from this passage, however, is whether he also holds that if a term is singular then it is capable of playing the subject role, and if it is general then it is capable of playing the predicate role. The evidence from other passages is that he does not hold these further points. For he explicitly says that "from which extract is made" is a singular term, not only purporting to refer to just one thing but actually doing so in some cases; but quite clearly it cannot play the subject role. And he holds that "which I bought" is a general term; but quite clearly it cannot play the predicate role. Thus it seems that we are not, after all, being given a *definition* of "purports to refer to" in the passage quoted above. Quine is not saying that "purports to refer to just one thing" *means* is capable of playing the subject role; nor is he saying that "does not purport to refer to just one thing" *means* is capable of playing the predicate role. The passage should be interpreted as presupposing an understanding of "purports to refer to," and as simply remarking on some typical ways in which singular terms and general terms occur in our language. The remainder of Quine's discussion makes it absolutely clear that, in his view, such terms occur in many other ways as well.

12. Ibid., p. 96.

Even so, it is questionable whether what is said is true. It is not wholly clear whether Quine means to hold that a term is singular if it can occupy the subject *position* in a sentence, and general if it can occupy the predicate *position;* or if he means to hold that a term is singular if it can *function* as a logical subject in a sentence, and general if it can *function* as a logical predicate in a sentence. The difference between these two sorts of claims is clear. It may be that a term can occupy the subject position in a sentence without ever, in fact, being able to function as a logical subject.

So suppose we understand the claim as being this. A term is singular if it can occupy the subject position in a sentence, general if it can occupy the predicate position. Quine himself points out, or at least alludes to, the refutation of this claim. Any common noun can occupy the subject position in a sentence. For example, "a lion" does so in "A lion met me on the path." We can replace "a lion" in this sentence by "Leo," and everyone would agree that in the resulting sentence, "Leo" is not only the grammatical but also the logical subject. Thus common nouns (or, common nouns-cum-indefinite articles) can regularly occupy subject positions. Yet they are to be general terms. It is not the case that only singular terms are accessible to subject positions.[13]

Suppose, on the other hand, that we interpret Quine's claim as being this: A term is singular if it can function as a logical subject,

13. Similar difficulties arise with a formulation in *Methods of Logic* which Quine *explicitly* offers as an explanation of "purports to name one and only one object." He there says that "In terms of logical-structure, what it means to say that the singular term 'purports to name one and only one object' is just this: *The singular term belongs in positions of the kind in which it would also be coherent to use variables 'x', 'y', etc.* (or, in ordinary language, pronouns)" (p. 205). Thus, "Socrates is wise" is, according to Quine, parallel in form to the open sentence "x is wise"; and because "Socrates" can thus be substituted for the variable in this open sentence, it is a singular term. On the other hand, "general terms, in contrast to singular ones, do not occur in positions appropriate to variables. Typical positions of the general term 'man' are seen in 'Socrates is a man', 'All men are mortal'; it would not make sense to write: 'Socrates is an x', 'All x are mortal'. . . ." (p. 206). Quine's suggestion, then, is that singular terms are those which can be replaced by pronouns in sentences, general terms are those which cannot be; and no doubt the pronouns he has especially in mind are singular relative pronouns. But clearly "it" can replace "a lion" in "A lion met me on the path." Yet, to repeat, it was agreed that "a lion" was not to be a singular term.

general if it can function as a logical predicate. Consider again the sentence, "A lion met me on the path." Quine denies that "a lion" is here functioning as a genuine logical subject, apparently on the ground that "There is no one thing named by the indefinite singular term 'a lion'; no one thing even temporarily for the space of the single sentence."[14] I shall shortly argue that Quine is correct here in his contention that, normally, only singular terms can function as logical subjects. I shall also, however, argue that the reason he offers is mistaken; for "a lion" in the assertively uttered sentence "A lion met me on the path" can be regarded as standing for the single thing, class of all lions. Further, I think that Quine's contention, that a term is general if it can function as a logical predicate, is for the most part correct. We shall indeed shortly see that there are some terms which, though singular, can yet function as logical predicates, for example, "is identical with Venus." But I think the generalization holds for the most part.

    4. We have been exploring one standard way of coping with the difficulty that proper names are typically true of many things. This way consisted of stipulating that in applying the definitions of "singular term" and "general term," we must not consider terms as such, but rather terms as they are actually functioning in sentences and assertions. Let us now consider the other standard way of coping with this difficulty.

    One can see this alternative way at work in the following definition of J.S. Mill. "A general name is familiarly defined, a name which is capable of being truly affirmed, in the same sense, of each of an indefinite number of things. An individual or singular name is a name which is only capable of being truly affirmed, in the same sense, of one thing."[15] Mill would apparently admit that

14. *Word and Object*, p. 113.
15. J.S. Mill, *A System of Logic* (London, 1900), p. 32. Oddly, Mill goes on in the same paragraph to say that proper names have *no* sense: *"John* is only capable of being truly affirmed of one single person, at least in the same sense. For, though there are many persons who bear that name, it is not conferred upon them to indicate any qualities, or any thing which belongs to them in common; and can not be said to be affirmed of them in any *sense* at all, consequently not in the same sense." Cf. Joseph: "A general term is thus one that is predicable of any number of individuals in the same sense; a singular term one that is predicable of one individual

"John" is true of more than one thing; but he would hold that it is not true *in the same sense* of more than one thing. It seems reasonable to assume that Mill's phrase "is capable of being truly affirmed of one thing" means the same as our phrase "purports to be true of just one thing." Then what Mill is claiming is that, though "John" does not purport to be true of just one thing, for any *sense* of "John," "John" *does* purport *in that sense* to be true of just one thing.

A proper name does not, strictly speaking, have a sense; consequently it cannot have different senses. Yet I think it can be shown that it has something rather closely analogous to different senses, analogous enough, anyway, to enable us to make something of the idea that a proper name can be related to just one thing in a way in which a common noun can be related to many things.

Suppose that I have known a family one of whose children is named "John." Suppose, further, that after not seeing the family for a span of some years I have come back to visit them, and am greeted by the mother and a boy of approximately the size and looks that I would expect of John after those years. So I greet the mother, and then remark, "And this is John." But suppose that in fact the boy before me is a neighbor boy, who bears the name "John."

In this case, I affirmed the term "John" of someone. Further, the term "John" is true of this person. A true proposition can be asserted by uttering, "This is John," when "this" stands for the boy in question. For he does bear the name; and a necessary and sufficient condition for a proper name being true of some thing is that that thing bear that name. Yet the proposition I asserted is false. What I asserted about this person—namely, that he is

---

only in the same sense" (*Introduction to Logic*, p. 29). Also see Stebbing, *Introduction to Logic*, pp. 53–54; and Abelard, *Glosses on Porphyry*, in McKeon, ed., *Selections from Medieval Philosophers* (New York, n.d.) p. 232. In J.N. Keynes one finds a rather curious combination of both ways of avoiding the difficulty arising from the fact that proper names can be true of more than one thing: "A general name is a name which is actually or potentially predicable in the same sense of each of an indefinite number of units; a singular or individual name is a name which is understood in the particular circumstances in which it is employed to denote some one determinate unity only" (*Formal Logic*, p. 11).

John—was asserted falsely about him. Though the name "John" is true of this person, it is also false of him. Of the person before me, if I were to speak truly, I would have had to assert, 'This isn't John'. And yet, of course, he is named "John." (So the proposition I asserted when I uttered "This is John" is not equivalent to the proposition I would have asserted if I had instead uttered "This is named 'John'.") A vast number of different propositions can be asserted with the words, "This is John." And that is the case even when "this," in each instance, is used to stand for the same person.

We have here something analogous to the different *senses* of adjectives and common nouns. Consider the common noun, "a shark." There are various things in this world such that this word is both true of them and false of them. The term "a shark" is true of certain crafty financiers; that is, one could assertively utter "This is a shark," "this" standing for one of them, and thereby speak truly. In that case, what is said about one of them, namely, that he is a shark, could not be said truly about any fish. But there are also certain fish in this world of which "shark" is true. One could assertively utter "This is a shark," "this" standing for a certain fish, and thereby speak truly. In that case, what is said about one of them, namely, that it is a shark, could not be said truly about any man. Thus, for certain men and certain fish, the term "shark" is both true and false of them. And we are naturally inclined to account for all this by saying that the word "shark" has (at least) two different *senses.*

What we have seen is that in affirming a given proper name or common noun of some specific thing, different propositions can be asserted, and thereby different things can be asserted about that thing—all this even when the names and nouns are used in normal fashion. Let us say that, for each such difference in what is asserted about some thing, the term is being used with a different *import.* More generally and precisely, let us say that a term is true of one thing with the same *import* as that with which it is true of another if and only if what can be truly asserted about the one thing by affirming the term of it can also be truly asserted about the other thing by affirming the term of it.

It is clearly the case that most common nouns and adjectives can be true of more than one thing with the same import. I can affirm "is brown" of both my desk and my pen. And what I assert truthfully about the desk is the very same thing as what I assert truthfully about the pen. It is also the case that proper names and definite descriptions cannot be true of more than one thing with the same import. What I asserted about the boy who greeted me at the door can only be asserted truthfully about one thing; namely, about that son, named "John," of the family which I had once known and was now coming back to visit. What I said about the boy is that he is (identical with) John. But only one person can be identical with John. Of only one person can I truly assert that he is John (though, to repeat, "John" can be true of many persons). "John" cannot be true with the same import of more than one thing. The facts are similar for definite descriptions. Suppose that John had been the eldest son in the family, and that, upon being greeted at the door by what was in fact the neighbor boy, I assertively uttered, "So, this is the eldest son." Suppose, further, that this boy was in fact the eldest son of *his* parents. I would then have affirmed the term "the eldest son" of this person, and this term would in fact be true of him. Yet, what I asserted was false. For what I asserted about him could be truly asserted about only one person—the person who was the eldest son of the family that I was then coming back to visit. Only if I had used "this" to stand for *that* person, when I assertively uttered "This is the eldest son," would I have spoken truly. Definite descriptions are like proper names in that they too cannot be true of more than one thing with the same import.

So let us define "a singular term" as *a term which can be true of just one thing with the same import.* And let us define "a general term" as *a term which can be true of more than one thing with the same import.* And let us add to the traditional classification by defining "a contradictory term" as *a term which cannot be true of any thing.*

I think that these definitions yield the result that, for the most part, proper names and definite descriptions are singular terms, and that, for the most part, common nouns and adjectives and predicates are general terms. This is not invariable, however. "Prime number between 3 and 7" turns out to be a singular term, so does "gave birth to Napoleon," and so does "is identical with the planet Venus." Indeed, any predicate consisting of "is" followed by a singular term will itself be a singular term, the "is" in all such cases having the force of "is identical with." These results do not, however, seem to be counter-intuitive.

It is worth noting that certain word-names—for example, ' "cheese" '—are the names of both a singular term and a general term. Of many different things one can affirm truly, using "cheese" with the same import, "is a cheese." Indeed, this can be affirmed truly both of different kinds of cheese, and of different nicely-formed quantities of cheese. But on the other hand, there is only one entity in the world, a certain foodstuff, of which one can affirm truly, "is cheese." And there could not be another entity of which one could affirm this truly, using "cheese" with the same import.

5. In the remainder of this chapter, I wish to point out a difference which holds for the most part between singular terms and general terms with respect to the way in which they can function in *assertions;* and another difference with respect to the way in which they can function in *sentences.*

To see a certain difference in the way in which they can function in assertions, let us note, first, that though "is wise" can be regarded as standing, in many contexts, for wisdom, still it is not *true of* wisdom. Similarly, though "is circular" can often be regarded as standing for circularity, it is not true of circularity. On the other hand, the term "Socrates" is both true of many things and, whenever used to make an assertion, stands for one of these things. So let us, using both the concept *being true of* and the concept *standing for,* put forward for consideration this thesis. *Only a singular term can be used in an assertion to stand for some thing of which it is true; a general term cannot be so used.*

The property of standing in an assertion for something of which it is true was called *supposition* by the medievals. It will be convenient to follow this practice. Ockham offered the following explanation of the concept. " '*Suppositio*' means taking the position, as it were, of something else. Thus, if a term stands in a proposition instead of something, in such a way (*a*) that we use the term for the thing, and (*b*) that the term (or its nominative case, if it occurs in an oblique case) is true of the thing (or of a demonstrative pronoun which points to the thing), then we say that the term has *suppositio* for the thing."[16] Using the concept of supposition, the thesis to be considered can be stated thus: *only a singular term can supposit for some thing; a general term cannot.* Offhand, it appears that this generalization is grossly mistaken. For every general term which is a common noun (or common noun-cum-indefinite article) can function as a *grammatical* subject of sentences. And does this not show that every such term can supposit for some thing? Suppose, for example, that I assertively utter the sentence "A man walked in," when in fact a certain man *did* walk in, namely, Peter. In this context, does not the term "a man" supposit for some thing? It is, however, a general term. Of course, when we compare "A man walked in" with "Peter walked in" we feel that there is a significant difference between them. But isn't the difference just that in the latter case we refer *definitely* to some thing, whereas in the former case we refer *indefinitely* to some thing? And does not the grammatical subject in the latter case stand *definitely* for some thing, and in the former case *indefinitely*? Is not the difference that in the latter case we are told *exactly who* walked in, so that apart from misunderstanding there is no further room for the question, "Which one?" whereas in the former we are not told exactly who walked in? Should we not then modify the thesis under consideration, thus: only a singular term can be used in an assertion to stand *definitely* for some thing of which it is true?

First we ought to ask what "man" or "a man" in fact stands for when one assertively utters "A man walked in." In the case cited it seems natural to say that it stood (indefinitely) for Peter. But suppose that I assertively utter "A man walked in," when, though I know that someone walked in, I do not know who it was. What then could I say that "man" or "a man" stood for? Certainly if a man walked in, it was some definite nameable man; but in this case I cannot state which one it was that "man" or "a man" stood for. It might seem, however, that I could say that it stood for a man, a specific man of course, though I do not happen to know which one. But now suppose, finally, that I assertively utter "A man walked in" when in fact none did. What then does "man" or "a man" stand for?

16. William of Ockham, *Summa totius logicae,* 1, chap. 62, in P. Boehner, *Ockham: Philosophical Writings* (New York, 1959), p. 64.

Whether or not Peter walked in, I am referring to the same person, Peter, when I say "Peter walked in"; and, in either case, "Peter" stands for him. But it cannot be said that whether or not a man walked in, I am referring to the same person, a certain man, when I assertively utter "A man walked in"; and that in either case "a man" stands for him. *Which* man was I referring to, and *which* man did "a man" stand for? When one assertively utters "A man walked in" and speaks falsely, the falsehood does not lie in the predicable "walked in" failing to be true of the same entity of which it would have been true had the assertion made with this sentence been true. But when one assertively utters "Peter walked in" and speaks falsely, the falsehood does lie in this. In short, it seems impossible to say that when we assertively utter "A man walked in" and speak falsely we have made an assertion about a man, to whom we have referred indefinitely and for whom "a man" stands indefinitely—but to whom we could, if we wished, or if circumstances were right, have referred definitely. And so also when we assertively utter "A man walked in" and speak truly. In assertively uttering "A man walked in," we may have had some particular man in mind—say, Peter. But even if Peter did not walk in, and, unknown to us, someone else did, what we have asserted is true. For it is true just in case some man, it makes no difference which, walked in. When I assertively utter "A man walked in," there is no man such that if he walked in, what I asserted is true, and if he did not, what I asserted is false. So even when we assertively utter "A man walked in" and speak truly, it seems impossible to say that we have made an assertion about a man to whom we have referred indefinitely and for whom "man" or "a man" stands indefinitely—but to whom we could, if we wished, or if circumstances were right, have referred definitely. Thus our conclusion is that when one assertively utters "A man walked in," one is not referring indefinitely to some man, and "man" or "a man" does not stand indefinitely for some man. But obviously the only thing of which "man" or "a man" is true is a man. Thus our generalization is sustained. Only a singular term can supposit for some thing, a general term cannot.

But now it should be noted that our generalization does, at best, hold only for the most part. For consider the term "is a property." When this is used as a predicate in assertively uttered sentences it can be regarded as standing for *being a property*. Further, *being a property* is itself a property. Hence "is a property" can stand for something of which it is true. Yet it is a general term.

It is interesting to note that, in the main, if something is a singular term it can supposit for some thing, which is the converse of the claim we have put forth, namely, that only a singular term can supposit for some thing. There are, however, exceptions. For consider again such terms as "is identical with the planet Venus," "a prime number between 3 and 7," and "gave birth to Napoleon." By our definition of "singular term," these are all, as we saw, singular terms. But it does not seem that they can supposit for some thing. For example, "is identical with the planet Venus" is true of Venus. But it does not seem that it can, in an assertion, stand for Venus. It can, indeed, stand for the property of being identical with the planet Venus. But this, in turn, is not something of which it is true. I think that we do all find something a bit surprising in the fact that terms such as those just mentioned should turn out to be singular. Perhaps some of the source of this surprise is uncovered by noticing, as we just have, that they, unlike most singular terms, cannot supposit for some thing.

We have seen, then, a certain difference which holds for the most part between singular and general terms with respect to the way in which they can function in assertions. Let us now notice a difference which holds for the most part between them with respect to the way in which they can function in sentences. *Only singular terms can function as the logical subjects of sentences; general terms cannot.*

When a general term, for example, a common noun or a common noun with an indefinite article or quantifier prefix, occurs in a sentence, can it be regarded as a logical subject of the sentence? That is to say, can it be regarded as capable of standing for some thing of which the rest of the sentence can be predicated? P.T. Geach holds that an expression consisting of a common noun prefixed by a quantifier or an indefinite article cannot function as the logical subject of a sentence. This is what he says:

If 'some man' is a logical subject in 'Peter struck some man', what does it stand for? Not for Malchus; Peter did in fact strike Malchus, but our sentence does not say so. Nor, in fact, for any definite man; for in saying 'Peter struck some man', we are not saying of any definite man that Peter struck *him*. Nor can we say that 'some man' stands here just for some man, but not for any definite man; for it would be self-contradictory and it is certainly not what we mean, to say that Peter struck some man but not any definite man. Nor can we say that 'some man' stands for the class of all men; 'Peter struck the class of all men' is absurd. . . . If we take a true or false sentence where 'Peter struck ————' seems to be attached to a subject other than an unshared name, we get into inextricable difficulties over the question what this subject stands for.[17]

It seems to me that Geach's conclusion, that such expressions as "a man" and "some man" and "some men" and "every man" and "all men" and "no man" and "no men," and so forth, cannot function as logical subjects, is correct. I take it that he also holds that just the words "man" and "men," when occurring in such expressions, cannot function as logical subjects, and this too seems to me to be correct. The reason that Geach offers for his conclusion is that there is nothing which such expressions can be regarded as standing for when they are used to make assertions. This claim, however, seems to me to be incorrect. I think that the reason for drawing the conclusion should rather be that there is nothing which such expressions can be regarded as standing for *and which the rest of the sentence can be regarded as being predicated of.*

Consider, for example, a sentence of the traditional I form, such as "A man walked in" or "Some men walked in." It seems to me that when these sentences are assertively uttered, "man" and "men" can, *contra* Geach, be viewed as standing for the class of all men. And what the speaker asserted about the class of all men is not indeed that it walked in, but rather, that some member or some members of the class walked in. Equally, "man" and "men" can be regarded as standing for the property of being a man; and what the speaker asserted about this is that some instance or some instances of the property walked in. No doubt

---

17. Geach, "Subject and Predicate," *Mind* (1950), pp. 470–71. Consider also the following passage, part of which has already been quoted: "There is no one thing named by the indefinite singular term 'a lion'; no one thing even temporarily for the space of the single sentence. In this respect the indefinite singular term is somewhat like the relative pronoun 'which', which, though it occupies positions in relative clauses corresponding to positions of singular terms in sentences, can scarcely be said even temporarily to name anything" (Quine, *Word and Object*, p. 113).

it would be less plausible to hold that the *whole* expression, "a man" and "some men," stand for the class of all men, or the property of being a man.

But though there are, then, at least two things for which "man" and "men can be regarded as standing, we have not so far found anything of which the rest of the sentence can be regarded as being predicated. The speaker did not predicate "walked in" of the class of all men, nor of the property of being a man, nor did he predicate "a ———— walked in" of either of these, nor "some ———— walked in." Further, we have already seen that "man" and "a man" do not stand for some particular man, of which "walked in" (or "a ———— walked in") has been predicated. And the same argumentation would apply to "men" and "some men." But there seem to be no other possibilities. Further, our argument seems perfectly general in form. We could have taken any other common noun instead of "man," and any other sentence in which such a term occurs preceded by the quantifier "a" or "some," and reached corresponding conclusions.

What, then, about those cases in which a common noun is prefixed by "all" or "every" or "no"? Consider, for example, a sentence of the traditional A form, say, "Every man is mortal." Here, again, when this sentence is assertively uttered, "man" can be regarded as standing for the class of all men, and what the speaker asserted about it is that every member of it is mortal; or it can be regarded as standing for the property of being a man, and what the speaker asserted about it is that every instance of it is mortal. But is there anything for which "man" can be regarded as standing, and of which "is mortal" or "every ———— is mortal" can be regarded as being predicated; or is there anything for which "every man" can be regarded as standing, and of which "is mortal" can be regarded as being predicated?

Here, certainly, we are not even *tempted* to search for some *one* thing of which "is mortal" or "every ———— is mortal" has been predicated. It would seem that the only possibility to be considered is that "man" or "every man" stands for all the men, that is, for each and every man. Is it the case, then, that in assertively uttering "Every man is mortal" we predicate something of each and every man—of Napoleon, of Wellington, and of every other man? Is it the case that we say of Napoleon that he is mortal? Of

Wellington that he is mortal? And so on, for all the men? Perhaps it is not blatantly incorrect to say that this is the case. But certainly it is odd. And what is even more odd is the view which must go with it if the sentence "Every man is mortal" is to be a subject-predicate sentence. This is the view that "man" or "every man" stands for each and every man; that is, stands for Napoleon, and for Wellington, and for every other man. I conclude, then, that it would be extremely unnatural and forced to regard this as a subject-predicate sentence. Similar considerations will be relevant to the sentence "All men are mortal." And certainly in assertively uttering the E sentence, "No men are mortal," we cannot be regarded as predicating "are mortal" or "no ——— are mortal" of each and every man. Further, our argument seems completely general in form. We could have used any other term instead of "man," and any other sentence in which a common noun prefixed by a universal quantifier appears.

I conclude, then, that those general terms which are common nouns, and those which are common nouns prefixed by the indefinite article or by a quantifier, cannot function as logical subjects. From which it follows, of course, that sentences of the traditional A, E, I, and O forms are not, in general, subject-predicate sentences. Now our argument falls short of establishing that general terms as a whole cannot function as logical subjects, since there are other sorts than those which we have considered. But the sorts of general terms considered—common nouns—would seem to be the most plausible candidates for general terms capable of functioning as logical subjects. So I think we can conclude that, normally, only a singular term can function as a logical subject. A general term cannot so function.

I think it is also true, by and large, that if something is a singular term, then it *can* function as a logical subject, which is the converse of the claim that we have put forth, namely, that only singular terms can function as logical subjects. It is interesting to note, however, that those same terms which, though singular, can yet not supposit for something, are also such that, though singular, they can yet not function as logical subjects. For example, "is identical with Venus" is a singular term; yet obviously it cannot function as a logical subject, nor, as we saw, can it supposit for something.

This leads to one final observation. A logical subject of a sentence is an expression in the sentence capable of suppositing for some thing. And also, with few exceptions, the converse is true. An expression in a sentence which can supposit for some thing is a logical subject of that sentence.

Predicables

PART TWO

3

Predicable Entities

1. In John of St. Thomas, a devoted seventeenth-century follower of Thomas of Aquinas, one reads the following: "Everyone knows that the term 'universal' designates that which has a relation to several. . . . But because there are many ways in which something can be referred or related to several objects, 'universal' admits of several meanings. . . . The universal from the point of view of being and predication is that which is related to several things in which it has existence and of which it is predicated. . . . The universal so understood is defined 'one in many and of many.'. . . Further, the universal is said to be of many by predication."[1]

Suppose that someone assertively utters the sentence "Wilson is courageous." Given the definitions which we have developed, it can correctly be said of such a person that he has referred to Wilson and has predicated "is courageous" of him. In assertively uttering this sentence a speaker predicates a certain word or phrase of that to which he refers. He predicates the predicate "is courageous" of the person, Wilson.

1. *The Material Logic of John of St. Thomas,* tr. Simon, Glanville, and Hollenhorst (Chicago, 1955), pp. 89–91.

But when John of St. Thomas, in his explication of the concept of a universal "from the point of view of predication" speaks of things which are predicated, it is not words that he has in mind. And indeed, it is not only words and phrases—predicates—which are predicated of things. Rather, *in* and *by* predicating words and phrases of things, we also predicate nonlinguistic entities of those things. Thus the following can also correctly be said of the person who assertively utters "Wilson is courageous." He referred to Wilson and predicated of him that he is courageous. Also, he referred to Wilson and predicated courageousness of him. And, he referred to Wilson and predicated being courageous of him. In each of these cases, whatever it may be that is said to have been predicated of Wilson, certainly in no case is it a word or phrase. In every case it is something nonlinguistic.

What must be kept clearly in mind here is that in and by doing one thing a person may also be doing many other things. In and by moving a flat, steel-toothed object upright back and forth across some wood one may be sawing some boards, and also making a desk, and also getting one's exercise. Correspondingly, in and by assertively uttering "Wilson is courageous" one may be doing a great many other things as well as referring to Wilson and predicating "is courageous" of him. The fact that this is what one has done does not entail that one has not also, and thereby, referred to Wilson and predicated courage of him. And referred to Wilson and predicated of him that he is courageous. And referred to Wilson and predicated being courageous of him. Perhaps this point is utterly obvious. Yet philosophers seem frequently to have forgotten it. For one of the most striking features of so-called "theories of predication" is the exclusivity claimed for such theories.

By a "theory of predication" philosophers have usually meant a way of stating what has been done in assertively uttering a subject-predicate sentence. And repeatedly they have assumed that if a given theory of predication is correct all others are incorrect. Closely asociated with this assumption, and perhaps partially accounting for it, is the frequent assumption that each proposition has a definite number of "constituents" in a definite structure. Disagreements over theories of predication have almost always involved disagreements over the number of constituents in propositions. It remains exceedingly obscure what philosophers have meant in claiming that propositions have constituents, and I shall make no use of the concept. I think that those who have made use of the concept would agree that, if the argumentation of this chapter is correct, a given proposition has several different structures of several different sorts of constituents, and that, if the argumentation of the next chapter is correct, every proposition has an infinite number of constituents.

For the sake of convenience, let us call the predicating of anything other than words, *nonlinguistic predication.* Though it is perhaps not the case that nonlinguistic predication can be performed only in and by performing an act of linguistic predication, I shall contend in a later chapter that in performing an act of linguistic predication one always performs an act of nonlinguistic predication as well. Next, let us call all those entities which can be nonlinguistically predicated, *predicable entities.* And, following long philosophical tradition, let us call those entities which cannot be nonlinguistically predicated, *substances.*

It is to be noted that not all predicable entities can be truly predicated of more than one thing. In assertively uttering "The morning star is Venus" one predicates *being Venus* of the morning star. And, though one can predicate *being Venus* of many other things than the morning star, only of this can it be truly predicated. Thus from among predicable entities we can pick out those which can be truly predicated of many. I shall follow John of St. Thomas, and the medieval tradition generally, in calling such entities *universals.* Two ideas, then, are central in the concept of a predicable universal—predicability and generality.

I shall not, however, confine the application of the word "universal" to predicable entities. Rather, I shall eventually extend the application of the word so as to include various sorts of entities which cannot be predicated but which yet bear a close analogy to predicable universals—for example, poems, symphonies, and species. These nonpredicable universals I shall call *substance universals;* the others, when there is any chance of confusion, I shall call *predicable universals.* Thus, though the core idea in the concept of a universal is the idea of that which can be predicated of many, this concept will be expanded beyond this core idea by way of analogy.

It should be noted that, contrary to what seems often to be assumed, the idea of generality is no more sufficient by itself for defining the concept of a predicable universal than is the idea of predicability. Consider, for example, the definition of a (predicable) universal as that which can be identical in many. Often, when this definition is used, generality and not predicability receives all the emphasis. One can see this approach to universals at work in Gottfried Martin's interesting book, *An Introduction to General Metaphysics* (London, 1961). Yet it is clear that this approach hinges on the sense of the word "in" as used in the phrase "can be identical in many," not merely on a one-many contrast. For there is, for every entity, some relation such that it bears that same relation to many things; and if this sort of generality were sufficient for something's being a universal, everything would be a universal. Or, to put the matter in a different light, the one-many contrast is just as present in the fact that many universals can be associated with one identical particular as in the fact that one identical universal can be associated with many particulars. In each case it is the universal which is "in" the particular, not the particular "in" the universal. Universals can be "in" other entities; that is what helps to set them off. But the explanation of that sense of "in," according to which a universal can be "in" something and a particular not in something, will come to virtually the same thing as an explanation of the concept of predication.

It must be said that the concept of nonlinguistic predication which we shall use may differ in some ways from that used by John of St. Thomas, as well as from that of other writers on the problem of universals. I shall use the ordinary concept;[2] it is not wholly clear that this is what these others were using. This is a matter which I shall not explore in any great and systematic detail, though I shall, here and there, make comments relevant to it.

In this, and most of the succeeding chapters, I shall be discussing predicable entities generally; for most of the problems raised by those predicable entities which are universals are also

2. *Shorter Oxford English Dictionary:* "To assert or affirm as a quality, property, or attribute (*of* something)." *Webster's Third International:* "To assert or affirm as a quality, attribute, or property—used with following *of* ⟨—*s* intelligence of man⟩."

raised by those which are not universals. In this chapter I shall distinguish various sorts of predicable entities and make a few comments on what is involved in predicating one entity of another. In the next chapter, I shall counter certain claims to the effect that one is committed to a vicious regress if he holds that entities other than words can be predicated. Then in following chapters I shall explore grounds for supposing that there are predicable entities, and I shall inquire into the "nature" of such entities.

2. In referring to some thing and predicating some nonlinguistic entity of that thing, one makes a claim. Or better, one makes several different sorts of claims. One thing that one claims, of course, is that the proposition asserted is true. But more relevant to our purpose here is the fact that one also claims that one or more *relations* hold between that which is referred to and that which is predicated—relations such that they *do* hold between these entities if and only if what is asserted is true. In referring to Wilson and predicating courage of him, by assertively uttering "Wilson is courageous," one claims that a certain relation holds, or that certain relations hold, between Wilson and courage— relations such that they do hold between Wilson and courage just in case it is true that Wilson is courageous.

What are some of these relations which are claimed to hold between an entity predicated and the entity of which it is predicated, and which are such that the relation holds between these two entities just in case the proposition asserted is true? Here we must consider a variety of different cases. Discussions concerning predicable entities have often suffered from a constricted survey of the terrain. Too often it is assumed that there is just one predicative relation. But in fact there are various different ones. And by reference to these different predicative relations, we can distinguish various sorts of predicable entities.

Suppose that someone assertively utters "Wilson is courageous." Then at least the following are entities that he has predicated of Wilson:

(i)   being courageous
(ii) courage, courageousness
(iv) that he is courageous

Suppose, next, that someone assertively utters "Jumbo is an elephant." Then the following nonlinguistic entities have been predicated of Jumbo:

  (i)   being an elephant
  (iv) that he is an elephant

Again, if someone assertively utters "Wilson is teaching," then the following have been predicated of Wilson:

  (iii) teaching
  (iv)   that he is teaching

Finally, if a man says of a certain ring, "It is gold," then he has predicated at least the following of the ring:

  (i)   being (of) gold
  (iv) that it is (of) gold

It will be noticed that we have arranged our examples of entities predicated into four different groups, one group containing *being courageous, being an elephant,* and *being of gold,* another group containing *courage* and *courageousness,* a third group containing *teaching,* and a fourth group containing *that he is courageous, that he is an elephant, that he teaches,* and *that it is (of) gold.* The basis for this quadruple grouping lies in the different relations which entities predicated are claimed to bear to entities referred to. Before we look closely at these relations, it may be of interest to notice typical grammatical differences between the names of entities of these various sorts. All members cited thus far of the first class are specified by gerunds of the form 'being so-and-so' or 'being a so-and-so'. More generally, however, I think it will prove to be typically the case that what is named by a gerund derived from a verb which lacks a continuous present tense (in English) is a member of the first class. In addition to *courage* and *courageousness,* members of the second class are *felinity* and *manhood.* I think it will prove to be typically the case that what is specified by a noun form ending in '-ness,' '-ity,' or '-hood,' or by abstract singular nouns having no special grammatical form at all, such as "courage," "wisdom," and "fear," is a member of the second class. The only member cited of the third class is *teaching*. However, other members are *walking, running,* and *thinking*. All of these, it will be noticed, are also specified by gerunds, but the gerunds are in this case not derived from the copula. More generally, I think it will prove to be typically the case that what is named by a gerund derived from a verb which has a continuous present tense (in English) is a member of the third class. Finally, what is specified by a 'that' clause containing a relative pronoun, the whole capable of being used to state what is asserted about some thing, will always be a member of the fourth class.

Being courageous would seem to be a state that something can be in (alternatively, that which something can be in the state of). Accordingly, a relation which can hold between Wilson and *being courageous,* and which does hold between them just in case Wilson is courageous, is the relation of *something being in the state of something.* Wilson is in the state of *being courageous* just in case he is courageous. So also Tabby is in the state of *being ferocious* just in case she is ferocious. And Alexander is in the state of *knowing how to undo the Gordian knot* just in case he knows how to undo the Gordian knot. Thus from among predicable entities we can pick out a class of entities, including *being courageous, being ferocious,* and *knowing how to undo the Gordian knot,* such that something is a member of the class just in case it is that which something can be in the state of. It will be largely, if not wholly, in accord with common usage to call all the members of this class, *states.*

It may be noted that *being round and square* is not a member of this class, since nothing *can* be in the state of being round and square. Yet being round and square has obvious affinities with the members of this class. It can be predicated of something, for example, by assertively uttering "This is round and square." A speaker, in predicating it of some thing by uttering this sentence, is claiming that that thing is in the state of being round and square. Further, that thing *is* in the state of being round and square just in case it is round and square. It will, indeed, never be *true* to say, of some thing, that it is in the state of being round and square. Yet the words "This is in the state of being round and square" have a normal sense such that in that normal sense they can be used to assert a proposition. Thus it will be natural also to call *being round and square* a state, even though, for every thing, it is necessarily false that it is round and square. Accordingly, we shall call a predicable entity a *state* if and only if a speaker, in predicating it of something, claims that it is what that thing is in the state of. Further, let us call an expression a *state-name* just in case it designates a state and can be fitted into the context "It is in the state of . . ." with the result that the whole sequence has a normal sense such that it can be used in that normal sense to assert a proposition.

Now suppose that "being-Ø" represents state-names. What is one to say about an expression, corresponding to a given state-name, which is of the form "the state of being-Ø"? Does *it* designate a state, that is, does it designate a predicable entity such that a speaker in predicating it of something claims that it is what that thing is in the state of? Notice, as an example, that the words "that it is in the state of the state of being red" lack sense; they do not have a normal sense such that in that sense they can be used to state what someone has claimed. "The state of being red" is not a state-name. Yet it would certainly be paradoxical if "being red" designated a state, while "the state of being red" did not. Indeed, it would be paradoxical if these expressions did not designate the very same state. After all, if "Tabby" designates a cat, then "the cat Tabby" does too—the same cat, at that. Suppose, on the other hand, that we had turned our explanations in the opposite direction and had resolved to call a predicable entity a state if and only if a speaker, in predicating it of something, claims that it is what that thing is in. Then, clearly, "the state of being red" designates a state. But then the question would be whether "being red" designated a state. For the sequence "that it is in being red" lacks sense; it cannot be used in its normal sense to state what someone has claimed. Yet certainly it would be paradoxical if "being red" did not designate a state; for it is true of many things that they are in the state of being red, from which it would seem to follow that there is a state in which they are, namely, *being red*. If someone bears the name of "John," then "John" is a name.

This last example, however, can serve to show us the way out of these paradoxes. For, consider the two expressions here illustrated:

(i) "John"

(ii) the name "John"

Surely these two expressions designate the same thing, a certain name. Yet sometimes the result of substituting one of these for the other in a sentence in which it occurs is to change sense into nonsense. For example, if one replaces the former with the latter in the sentence "We gave him the name 'John' " one gets the nonsense, "We gave him the name the name 'John'." And on the other hand, if one replaces the latter with the former in the sentence "We gave him the name 'John', " one gets the nonsense, "We gave him 'John'." The former does indeed bear the property of having been given to someone. For it designates the same thing as does the latter; and certainly what the latter designates bears the property of having been given to someone. It is, then, perhaps a bit paradoxical that the sequence "We gave him 'John' " should be nonsensical. But certainly this is less paradoxical than the view that the former does not designate the same thing as the latter.

Thus the following principle should not be accepted. If two expressions designate the same thing, then in substituting the one for the other in some context one never changes sense into nonsense. If it is not accepted, then we have no good reason for doubting that "the state of being red" designates a state, on our criterion. For surely it designates the same thing as "being red." And "being red," it is agreed, designates a state. Hence "the state of being red" also does. The only reason put forward for doubting that these expressions designate the same thing is that they are not interchangeable *salvo sensu*. But this fact, it is now clear, does not yield the conclusion.

Of course, it is open for someone to claim that "being red" designates something which bears the property of being that which a speaker, in predicating it of something, claims that thing to be in the state of, whereas what "the state of being red" designates does not bear this property; and it is also open for someone to claim that "the state of being red" designates something which bears the property of being that which a speaker, in predicating it of something, claims that thing to be in, whereas what "being red" stands for does not bear this property. And if either of these claims were correct, then it would follow that "being red" and "the

state of being red" did not designate the same thing. But it is
hard to see why anyone would make these claims, in the face of
the patent implausibility of holding that, though *being red* is a
state, it is not identical with *the state of being red*. One is no
doubt tempted to appeal to what does and what does not make
sense. But such an appeal, we have just seen, is unsatisfactory.
From the fact that "He claimed that this is in the state of the
state of being red" lacks sense, it does not follow that *the state of
being red* lacks the property of being that which a speaker, in
predicating it of something, claims that thing to be in the state of.
And from the fact that "He claimed that this is in being red"
lacks sense it does not follow that *being red* lacks the property of
being that which a speaker, in predicating it of something, claims
that thing to be in.

It may be noted, finally, that such words as "readiness" and
"anxiety" also seem to be state-names, though obviously they
are not gerunds derived from verbs lacking the continuous present
tense (in English). It is interesting to note also that the sequences "It is in readiness" and "It is in the state of readiness"
both have sense; and likewise, "He is in anxiety" and "He is in
the state of anxiety."

It seems clear enough that being courageous is a state that
Wilson is in (something that Wilson is in the state of) just in
case he is courageous. What seems much less clear is that
courage is a state that Wilson is in (something that Wilson is in
the state of) just in case he is courageous. Similarly, being wise
is, clearly enough, a state that Socrates is in (something that
Socrates is in the state of) just in case he is wise. But it seems
not at all clear that, when Socrates is wise, *wisdom* is a state that
Socrates is in (something that Socrates is in the state of). Rather,
courage, and *being courageous* as well, seem to be properties or
attributes or characteristics or traits that Wilson has or possesses,
or that belong to or are of, Wilson just in case Wilson is courageous. And *wisdom*, and *being wise* as well, seem to be properties
(attributes, characteristics, traits) that Socrates has or possesses
(or that belong to, or are of Socrates) just in case Socrates is
wise. Correspondingly, it is not clear that, when someone assertively utters "Wilson is courageous," he has claimed that Wilson
is in the state of courage. But it does seem that he has claimed

that Wilson has or possesses the property (characteristic, attribute, trait) of *courage,* and also of *being courageous.* For it
would seem that a relation which holds between Wilson and
courage, and also between Wilson and being courageous, just in
case it is true that Wilson is courageous, is that of *something
possessing or having the property* (*attribute, trait, characteristic*)
of something.

So from among predicable entities we can pick out a class of
entities such that something is a member of the class if and only
if it is what a speaker, in predicating it of some thing, claims that
that thing possesses the property of. We will be following common
usage closely if we call all and only such entities, *properties.* This
class will include entities which it is *impossible* that something
should possess the property of—such as, being round and square.
Let us also call *property-names* all and only those expressions
which designate properties and can be fitted into the context "It
has or possesses the property of . . ." with the result that the
whole sequence has a normal sense such that it can be used in
that normal sense to assert a proposition.

Paradoxes similar to those which came to our attention in the
case of states are also present here. For suppose that "Ø-ness" is
used to represent property-names. There is then a question as to
what is to be said about an expression, corresponding to a given
property-name, which is of the form "the property of Ø-ness."
Does it, in every case, also designate a property, that is, does it
designate that which a speaker, in predicating it of something,
claims to be what that thing possesses the property of? For, to
take an example, the words "That it possesses the property of
the property of being wise" are just nonsensical. "The property
of being wise" is not a property-name. But it would certainly be
paradoxical if being wise were a property, while the property of
being wise was not. On the other hand, if we had defined "a
property" as that which a speaker, in predicating it of something,
claims to be what that thing has or possesses; and if we had
defined "a property-name" as an expression which can be fitted
into the context "It has or possesses . . ." with the result that
the whole sequence has a normal sense such that it can be used
in that normal sense to assert a proposition, then "the property
of being wise" would clearly designate a property, and would be

a property-name. But then the question would be whether "being wise" designated a property. The sequence "That it possesses being wise" clearly lacks sense; "being wise" would not then be a property-name. But in view of the fact that various things do possess the property of being wise, it would certainly be paradoxical if *being wise* were not a property.

In philosophical discussions, a property is customarily explained as, or assumed to be, that which something can have or possess. At the same time, paradigm examples of what philosophers mention as properties are: *being red, being an elephant,* and *being (of) gold.* But "It possesses being red" and "It possesses being an elephant" and "It possesses being (of) gold" are all ill-formed sequences of words. They have no normal meaning such that, in uttering them with that meaning, we assert a proposition. The question then is whether there is an unnoticed incoherency in the manner in which philosophers think and speak of properties.

The solution to these paradoxes is, of course, the same as that offered for those which came to light in our consideration of states. Being wise, which is a property, is identical with the property of being wise; and the fact that "being wise" and "the property of being wise" are not interchangeable *salvo sensu* does not establish the opposite. Thus, since being wise possesses the property of being that which a speaker, in predicating it of something, claims to be what that thing possesses the property of, so also does the property of being wise. And the fact that the words "He claimed that it possesses the property of the property of being wise" lack sense, does not establish the opposite. For it does not establish that the property of being wise does not have the property of being that which a speaker, in predicating it of something, claims to be what that thing possesses the property of.

It may be noted that such property-names as "ferocity," "circularity," "wisdom," and "courage" not only can be fitted into the context "It has or possesses the property of . . ." but also into the context "It has or possesses . . . ," with the result that the whole sequence has a normal sense such that it can be used in that normal sense to assert a proposition. Let us call all expressions which can be fitted into this latter context, *quality-*

names. On the other hand, many of the property-names which are also state-names—for example, "being ferocious," "being circular," "being wise," "being courageous"—cannot be fitted into this context with this result, and are thus not quality-names. There are expressions, however, designating the same entities that these state-names designate, which are quality-names. For example, "being wise" is a state-name, and we agreed that it designates the same entity as "the property of being wise." But this latter expression can be fitted into the context "It has or possesses . . ." with the result indicated; it is a quality-name. *Being wise* has the property of being something such that a speaker, in predicating it of something, claims that that thing has or possesses it, even though the sequence "He claimed that it has or possesses being wise" lacks sense.

What we have suggested thus far is that there *seem* to be properties which are not states. Our examples were courage and wisdom—the entities designated with the quality-names "courage" and "wisdom." A significant question to be considered shortly is whether there *really* are properties which are not states; and whether quality-names in general designate properties which are not states.

When we turn our attention to such predicable entities as teaching, walking, writing, and others, we find a quite different sort of case. Suppose that someone assertively utters "John is walking." By so doing he has predicated walking of John. But it is not at all clear that he has then claimed that John is in the state of walking; or that John possesses walking; or that John possesses the property of walking. Rather, what he has clearly claimed is that walking is something that John is doing. A relation which holds between walking and John just in case John is walking is this: being something that something is doing.

So from among predicable entities we can pick out a class consisting of those such that something is a member of the class if and only if a speaker, in predicating it of some thing, claims that it is something that that thing is doing. Let us call the members of this class, and only the members of this class, *actions.* On this stipulation, something may be an action even though it is not that which something can be doing; it may be an *impossible* action. Also, let us call an expression an *action-name* if and

only if it designates an action and can be fitted into the context
". . . is something that it is doing" with the result that the
whole sequence has a normal sense such that it can be used in
that normal sense to assert a proposition. Notice that though
walking, running, discovering, and the like, are things that someone may be doing, and things that someone may claim that someone is doing, the sequences "He is doing walking" and "He is
doing running" and "He is doing discovering" all lack sense. On
the other hand, one can perfectly well speak of doing *some* walking and doing *some* running—though scarcely of doing some
discovering.

As in the case of states and properties, expressions designating
the same action are not always interchangeable *salvo sensu*. For
example, the words "He is performing the action of running"
make sense; the words "He is performing running" do not. However, it does seem that both the words "Running is something
that he is doing" and the words "The action of running is something that he is doing" have sense. And it is even more clear
that "He is engaged in running" and "He is engaged in the action
of running" both have sense. It does not seem, however, that all
actions can be engaged in, or performed. Sleeping is something
which someone, in predicating it of something, claims to be something that that thing is doing; it is an action. But it scarcely
seems that sleeping is something that someone can perform or
engage in.

To complete the consideration of our initial list of examples,
we must ask what is the relation which holds between Wilson and
that he is courageous just in case Wilson is courageous; between
Jumbo and that he is an elephant just in case Jumbo is an elephant. To see what this relation is, we should first notice that
that he is courageous and *that he is an elephant* are each what
can be asserted about something. Let us accordingly call them
assertibles. Now it can clearly be seen that the relation which
holds between *that he is courageous* and Wilson, just in case
Wilson is courageous, is that of *something being truly assertible
of something* or, simply, *something being true of something*.
Wilson is courageous just in case it can be truly asserted of him
that he is courageous, or just in case it is true of him that he is

courageous. And assertively to utter "Wilson is courageous," thereby to predicate of Wilson that he is courageous, is to claim that it is true of Wilson *that he is courageous.* Obviously some assertibles are such that they cannot be true of anything. Yet every assertible is something such that a speaker, in predicating it of something, *claims* it to be true of that thing.

3. There may, of course, be predicable entities which belong to none of the sorts which we have distinguished. But rather than press further with singling out sorts of predicable entities, let us, as it were, head in the opposite direction. Let us consider whether all properties are states and let us also consider whether properties, actions, and assertibles, are or are not all distinct sorts of entities. Is not to hold that they are all distinct, to multiply entities beyond necessity?

First, is there any ground for holding that there are properties which are not states? Among the most likely candidates for such are some of the entities designated by quality-names, such as "wisdom" and "courage." If these were identical with states, the most plausible view would be that "wisdom" designated *being wise,* "courage" *being courageous,* and the like. What is to be said for or against the view that wisdom is identical with being wise, courage with being courageous, and so on?

We have already seen that being courageous as well as courage both have the property of being something which a speaker, in predicating it of something, claims to be what that thing has or possesses. Thus far, there is no difference. But what about the property of being something which a speaker, in predicating it of something, claims that that thing is in the state of? Certainly being courageous has this property. And if courage did not, it would follow that courage and being courageous were not identical. But how is one to tell whether courage and being courageous do differ in their properties? What is perhaps the case is that "He claimed that he is in the state of courage" does not have sense, whereas "He claimed that he is in the state of being courageous" does. But we agreed that two expressions may designate the same entity even though they are not interchangeable *salvo sensu.* From these linguistic facts—if facts they be—we cannot conclude that being courageous and courage differ in their properties; all we can conclude is that the expressions "being courageous" and "courage" have different uses.

Let us look for some other differences which might bear on the matter. Quality-names can regularly be accompanied by indications of quantity or amount in sentences which can be used to assert something true; but if one replaces the quality-names in such sentences with the correlative state-names, one no longer has sentences which have a normal sense such that in that sense they can be used to assert something true. For example: "He displayed a great deal of ferocity," "He has some courage but not much," "He demonstrated an amazing amount of patience," "Knowledge of the physical world has increased drastically," and "A reasonable amount of aggressiveness is a good thing." Further, the following are some random examples of sentences containing quality-names which can be used to assert something true, but which are such that if one replaces the quality-names with the correlative state-names one no longer has sentences with a normal sense such that in that sense the sentence can be used to assert something true. "Darkness, quietness, and gloom descended over the camp," "Courage is a virtue," "Circularity is a shape," "Sloth is a vice," "White is a symbol of purity," "Simple, unadulterated kindness is to be found no more in children than in adults," "Psychological security is one of man's greatest needs," "He has more tenacity than anyone I've ever known," "He displayed fierce anger and jealousy," "Uncontrollable feelings of jealousy welled up within him."

The question which demands asking, concerning each of these cases, is whether we have represented to us a difference in the properties of two entities or only a difference in the properties of a quality-name and a corresponding state-name. Either view seems tenable. And to cloud the situation still further, let us remember that earlier we agreed that the property of being courageous is identical with being courageous, and that the property of courage is identical with courage. If the property of being courageous were identical with the property of courage, it would follow that being courageous was identical with courage. But not only does it seem plausible that the property of being courageous is identical with the property of courage, the expressions "the property of being courageous" and "the property of courage" function in exactly the same way.

In short, considerations in favor of the view that properties designated by quality-names are states, are balanced by considerations in favor of the view that some at least are not. There seem to be no decisive considerations one way or the other. So, solely on the ground that it will simplify the discussion, I shall speak as if they all were states. And since entities designated by quality-names seem among the likeliest candidates for properties which are not states, I shall speak as if all properties were states.

There is, I think, very little plausibility to the view*that every property is identical with some action. What action, for example, might courage, or being courageous, plausibly be identified with? The view that every action is identical with some property—that actions are just a subclass of the larger class of properties—is not so easily dismissed. Can we not, for example, identify the action of walking with the property (state) of being something that is walking; the action of scratching with the property (state) of being something that is scratching? Some of the things true of walking are these: that it can be done by someone; that it can be done reluctantly, eagerly, haltingly; that it is the best form of exercise; and that there is an Olympic contest in it. But it seems that none of these things is true of the property of being something that is walking. Consequently, I conclude that walking is not identical with the property of being something that is walking. Admittedly, I have no cogent and decisive *reason* for holding that walking differs in its properties from being something that is walking. It is not absurd to hold the view that walking and being something that is walking are identical, and that any apparent difference between them is really only a difference between the expressions "walking" and "being something that is walking." And in general, there is no demonstrable absurdity in the view that all actions are properties. I shall, however, speak as if this view were mistaken.

Finally, what is one to say about the claim that every property and every action is identical with some assertible and every assertible with some property or action? This is the claim, for example, that being courageous and courage are identical with that it is courageous, that walking is identical with that it is walking and so forth. Here the differences seem vast. The assertibles *that it is courageous* and *that it is walking* have been asserted of things and are true of things; whereas it does not seem that this is the case for being courageous, courage, and walking, or for any other property or action. On the other hand, courage was a salient trait of Alexander, whereas it does not seem that that it is courageous was a salient trait of Alexander. Walking stimulates the heart, and is done by men and animals alike, whereas it does not seem that that it is walking stimulates the heart, nor that it is done by men and animals alike. Of course, that these identifications are unsatisfactory leaves wide open the possibility that others are satisfactory. But these do seem the likeliest ones. Consequently, I shall speak as if properties and actions were not assertibles, and as if assertibles were not properties or actions. But again, it must be said that there seem to be no *decisive* considerations in favor of this view. There is nothing absurd in the view that we have noticed only apparent differences, that *really* we have noticed nothing more than differences between property-names and action-names on the one hand and assertible-designations on the other, and that properties and actions are all assertibles, and that assertibles are all properties or actions.

For the remainder of our discussion, then, we shall speak as if, within the class of predicables, there are to be found at least these three distinct subclasses: the classes of properties, of actions, and of assertibles.

4. Thus far in our discussion we have limited our attention to predications made with sentences whose predicates are affirmative. But now that some paths have been cut through the woods, let us consider cases in which someone assertively utters a sentence containing a *negative* predicate.

Suppose that someone assertively utters "Wilson is not courageous." In so doing, he has claimed that Wilson is not in the state of being courageous; that is, he has claimed that the relation of something being in the state of something does *not* hold between Wilson and being courageous. But also, he has claimed that Wilson is in the state of *not being courageous*. Not only is there such a state as being courageous, but also there is such a state as not being courageous. And these two are related as follows. Nothing can be in the state of both, and everything must be in the state of either. They are *contradictory* states.

Suppose, on the other hand, that someone assertively utters "Peter is not walking home." He has thereby claimed that walking home is something that Peter is not doing; he has claimed that the relation of being something that something is doing does *not* hold between Peter and walking home. He has not, however, claimed that not walking home is something that Peter is doing. For *not walking home* is not something that one is doing, or can be doing; it is not an action. It is not the case that Peter is not walking home just in case not walking home is something that Peter is doing. *Not walking home* is, rather, a state. What the speaker has claimed is that Peter is in the state of not walking home. And Peter is in the state of not walking home just in case Peter is not walking home. So, for the action *walking home,* it is not the case that there is another action, *not walking home,* such that nothing can be doing both of these and everything must be doing either. Rather, we have here a state and an action related in the following way. Everything is such that either it is in the state of this state, or this action is something that it is doing; and nothing is such that it is both in the state of this state, and this action is something that it is doing. Thus also it is not the case, for every state, that there is another state, such that everything is in the state of either and nothing is in the state of both. The situation described above for the action of walking home is the same, I think, for every other action.

Quality-names function somewhat differently in this context from state-names. Suppose, again, that someone assertively utters "Wilson is not courageous." He has thereby claimed that Wilson does not possess courage. Indeed, he has claimed that Wilson lacks courage. But it does not seem that he has claimed that Wilson possesses noncourage. And the reason is not just that noncourage is not a quality—that is, not the sort of thing that, in predicating it of some thing, one claims that that thing has or possesses. "Noncourage," if it means anything at all—and certainly it is doubtful that it does—seems to be a general term true of *everything* other than courage. Not some one thing other than courage, but *everything* other than courage, seems to be a case of noncourage.

The situation for assertibles, with respect to negation, is clear and straightforward. If someone assertively utters "Wilson is not courageous," then his action can be described not only thus—he claimed that *that he is courageous* is not true of Wilson; but also thus—he claimed that *that he is not courageous* is true of Wilson. And so here we find two assertibles related in this way. Nothing is such that they are both true of it, and everything is such that one or the other is true of it.

In our discussion thus far we have also limited our attention to predications made with sentences in the simple present tense. Let us now briefly consider what is to be said when a sentence in something other than the simple present tense is used. Consider, for example, the sentences "Wilson was courageous" and "Wilson will be courageous." In assertively uttering these sentences one claims, respectively, that Wilson *was* in the state of being courageous, and that Wilson *will be* in the state of being courageous. But it does not seem that in assertively uttering either of these one predicates *being courageous,* or *courage,* of Wilson. Is there then any other state, or property, which has been predicated? It would seem that there is. For consider the state of *being someone who was courageous,* and the state of *being someone who will be courageous.* It would seem that the former of these is predicated by assertively uttering the former sentence mentioned, and the latter, by assertively uttering the latter sentence mentioned. Thus, one can also predicate states or properties by using sentences in other than the simple present tense.

Next consider the sentences "Wilson walked home" and "Wilson will walk home." In assertively uttering the former, one claims that *walking home* is something that Wilson *was* doing; and in assertively uttering the latter, one claims that *walking home* is something that Wilson *will be* doing. Yet it does not seem that in either case has one predicated *walking home* of Wilson. Indeed, it does not seem that there is any action at all which has thereby been predicated of Wilson. Rather, in each case one has predicated a state or property of him—in the first case, the state of *being someone who was walking home*; in the second case, the state of *being someone who will be walking home.* And in general, it seems that if one assertively utters a subject-predicate sentence whose tense is other than the simple present, one does not then predicate an action of what is referred to.

Finally, no matter what the tense of the predicate, in predicating a predicate of something one also predicates an assertible of it. For example, in predicating "was courageous" of Wilson one predicates of him that he was courageous; and in predicating "will walk home" of Wilson one predicates of him that he will walk home. Also, in the former case one claims that that he is courageous *was* true of Wilson; and in the latter case, that that he is walking home *will be* true of him. But it does not seem that these, in these cases, have been predicated of Wilson.

5. Relational sentences, that is, sentences containing more than one logical subject, also deserve special attention. Suppose, for example, that someone assertively utters "Romeo loves Juliet." In such a case, which nonlinguistic entities have been predicated (if any), and what is the relation claimed to hold between them and what is referred to?

A speaker, in assertively uttering "Romeo loves Juliet," does the following. He predicates *that he loves Juliet* of Romeo; he predicates *that she is loved by Romeo* of Juliet; he predicates of Romeo and Juliet *that the former loves the latter.* Thus he predicates assertibles, and the relation which he claims to hold is the relation of being true of. What he asserts is true just in case this relation does hold.

In assertively uttering "Romeo loves Juliet," a speaker also predicates *loving Juliet* (alternatively, *love for Juliet*) of Romeo, and *being loved by Romeo* of Juliet. The predicative relation in these cases is that of having or possessing the property of (as well as being in the state of). The speaker claims that Romeo has the property of love for Juliet (is in the state of loving Juliet), and that Juliet has the property of being loved by Romeo (is in the state of being loved by Romeo). And what the speaker asserts is true just in case these relations do in fact hold. Both *loving Juliet* and *being loved by Romeo,* then, are properties (states). On the other hand, if someone assertively utters "Juliet is striking Romeo," then he predicates a certain action of Juliet, namely, that of striking Romeo, and a certain property (state) of

Romeo, namely, that of being struck by Juliet. He claims that striking Romeo is something that Juliet is doing, and that Romeo is in the state of being struck by Juliet.

Thus, correlative to the "active" properties (states) of loving Juliet, loving Heloise, loving someone, we find the "passive" properties (states) of being loved by Napoleon, being loved by Caesar, being loved by someone. And correlative to the actions of striking Romeo, striking Malchus, striking somebody, we find the passive properties (states) of being struck by Moses, being struck by Dimitri, being struck by someone.

Finally, in assertively uttering "Romeo loves Juliet" a speaker has also, so it would seem, predicated some one thing of *both* Romeo and Juliet, namely, a relation. He has referred to Romeo and to Juliet, and has predicated some relation of them. Similarly, it would seem that in assertively uttering "Romeo gave the ring to Juliet," a speaker refers to Romeo, the ring, and Juliet, and predicates of them some relation. If this is correct, then from the class of predicable entities we can pick out yet another subclass—that consisting of those which are relations. And in predicating a certain relation of two or more things, a speaker claims that those things *stand in* that relation, or that that relation *holds among* those things.

It is worth noting that when a speaker predicates a relation of some things, it is not always the case that the holding of that relation among those things is a necessary and sufficient condition for the truth of what was asserted. For consider again the sentence "Romeo loves Juliet." When a speaker assertively utters this, he predicates of Romeo and Juliet the relation which holds among the members of a pair just in case at least one loves the other. But this relation can hold among Romeo and Juliet even though it is not the case that Romeo loves Juliet. It would hold if Juliet loved Romeo. The holding of this relation among these two things is a necessary, but not a sufficient, condition of the truth of the assertion. In this way, *standing in the relation of* differs from all the other predicative relations we have singled out.

6. There is a final question to be considered here. How are predicates related to entities predicable? Already, of course, we

have one answer to this question. Predicates are related to entities predicable in such a way that by (or in) predicating a predicate of some thing one predicates a nonlinguistic entity of that thing. But I think it can be said in addition that predicates *stand for* predicable entities.

In our previous chapters we singled out and explained two fundamentally different relations which words may sustain to things. They may be used either to refer to things, in which case they will *stand for* those things; or they may be *predicated of* things, in which case they may *hold of* or *be true of* those things. Both the distinction between subjects and predicates and the distinction between general terms and singular terms were associated with this fundamental distinction between reference and predication. At several points in our discussion however, we found that one or another tentative definition proved defective if the possibility was allowed of predicates also standing for things. Nowhere did we argue that predicates do *in fact* stand for things. Yet we ourselves suggested the possibility of their bearing two sorts of relation to things—*standing for* things in addition to *being predicated of things*. Even if we had not ourselves at various points suggested this possibility, it would surely have occurred to almost anyone reflecting on what was developed. For a very natural answer to the question, "What is a relation between the predicate 'is wise' and wisdom?" is this: " 'is wise' can stand for wisdom." And in general it would seem that a relationship between the predicate in a sentence used to make an assertion, and the entity predicated, is that the predicate *stands for* the entity predicated.

It is perhaps appropriate to remark here that just as we must not succumb to the notion that in doing one thing one cannot also be doing another, so too we must not succumb to the notion that each word in a sentence can be related to things in only one way—that each word in a sentence has just one semantic function. We must not succumb to a one-function fallacy for words. The fact that "is wise" functions as being predicated of Socrates in the assertion "Socrates is wise" does not militate against its also functioning as standing for wisdom in the same assertion.

Though predicates can be regarded as standing for predicable entities, one cannot say that predicable entities are those which predicates can be regarded as standing for. There are certain entities which, though predicates can be regarded as standing for them, are yet not *predicable* entities.

What I have in mind is *classes,* examples of classes being the class of all men, the class of all horses, the class of all red things, the class of all things which are courageous, and so on. Suppose that someone assertively utters "Wilson is courageous." Then it seems that we can hold that "is courageous" stands for the class of all courageous things; certainly many people, and not all of them philosophers, have held that "is courageous" does stand for this. And in this case, too, a relation is claimed to hold between what is referred to, and the class for which the predicate stands, namely, the relation of something being a member of something. Wilson is a member of the class of all courageous things just in case Wilson is courageous. Yet it seems to be false that in assertively uttering "Wilson is courageous" one refers to Wilson and predicates of him the class of all courageous things. It seems that classes cannot be predicated.

The class of predicable entities, then, and the class of entities for which predicates can stand, are not identical.

4

Objections
to Predicative Relations

1. Various philosophers, from ancient to contemporary times, have argued that there is something incoherent in the concept of one or another of the predicative relations we have distinguished, or something incoherent in the supposition that something satisfies such a concept. There is no such relation, they have said, for entities to stand in. I wish, in this chapter, to look at a few of the more influential of these objections to what we have thus far concluded. And henceforth, when some predicable, no matter of what sort, can be truly predicated of some thing, let us say that the thing *exemplifies* that predicable.

Plato was the first to make a claim along these lines, and the problem he pointed to has worried many thinkers since. This is how Plato states his perplexity in *Philebus* 15b: "Whether, when one form is in many things, we think that the form is dispersed and has become many, or that it is entire and separated from itself—which latter would seem to be the most impossible notion of all—the problem remains: How can the same one form be at the same time in one and in many things." Examples which Plato here gives of forms are The Beautiful, The Good, Man, and Ox. The same difficulty is raised by Plato in *Parmenides* 130E-131E.

There the examples Plato gives of forms are beauty, justice, largeness, and similarity. He says that if various distinct things can share (*metalambano*) one of these forms, then we are confronted with the puzzle of how one form can be in many things. Cook Wilson, rather felicitously, calls Plato's problem the problem of the unity of the universal in the plurality of its particulars.

It is perhaps disputable whether it is *always* satisfactory to substitute for Plato's phrase "the beautiful" (*to kalon*) the English "beauty," for his phrase "the good" (*to agathon*) the English "goodness," and the like. But if we compare the *Philebus* passage with the *Parmenides* passage, it is clear that Plato thinks that the problem he is confronting here can be raised as well in terms of beauty as in terms of the beautiful, as well in terms of goodness as in terms of the good. I shall, then, consider the problem in terms of properties.

We would, perhaps, not naturally speak of beauty, and goodness, and justice, as *in* things. But for Plato, in *Parmenides* 130–131, it is clearly the case that if some thing partakes of (has, possesses, shares, shares in, has a share of) justice, then justice is *in* that thing and conversely. Plato, in fact, there states his puzzlement both in terms of how it can be that many distinct things each have a share of one form, and how it can be that one form is in each of many distinct things.

Plato's question is undeniably cryptic. But quite possibly one example of the general question over which he is puzzled is this. Suppose that A and B each possess paleness and are not identical; then does A have all of paleness or part of it, and similarly, does B have all of paleness or part of it (supposing all the while that there is only one such thing as paleness)? If this is indeed an example of Plato's general question, then Plato's comment about it is that he finds both answers to this question unattractive. The worse answer, he says, is that each has all of it; how can that be? But scarcely better, to his mind, is that each has only a part.

The partisan of universals need not be embarrassed by Plato's question. Indeed it cannot be that something has only part of paleness; for paleness is not the sort of thing that can have parts. But in allowing this, we are not thereby committed to holding that if something has paleness, then it has all of it. For it is surely consistent, and plausible besides, to hold that something has paleness without either having all of it or part of it. Paleness, it is plausible to think, is not the sort of thing that something can have all of, nor the sort of thing that something can have part of, while yet being the sort of thing that something can have. Alternatively, one could hold that if something has paleness then it has all of it, but repudiate Plato's assumption that two distinct things cannot each have all of it. Why should paleness not be the sort of thing that two distinct things can each have all of?

So far as we know, Plato's puzzlement over the concept of possessing never drove him to the conclusion that there can be no cases of one thing having or possessing another. Gilbert Ryle, then, in an article on Plato's *Parmenides,* goes a step beyond Plato, for he argues that this conclusion should be drawn. Ryle states his argument as follows:

> Now what of the alleged relation itself, which we are calling 'exemplification'? Is this a Form or an instance of a Form? Take the two propositions 'this is square' and 'this is circular'. We have here two different cases of something exemplifying something else. We have two different instances of the relation of being-an-instance-of. What is the relation between them and that of which they are instances? It will have to be exemplification Number 2. The exemplification of P *by* S will be an instance of exemplification, and its being in that relation to exemplification will be an instance of a second-order exemplification, and that of a third, and so on *ad infinitum.* . . . This conclusion is impossible. So there is no such relation as being-an-instance-of. 'This is green' is not a relational proposition, and 'this is bigger that that' only mentions one relation, that of being-bigger-than.[1]

Before I try to state Ryle's argument here, let me explain by example how I shall henceforth use the word "case." I shall call *Socrates' wisdom* (alternatively expressed, *the wisdom of Socrates*) a case of wisdom; and so also I shall call *Socrates' being wise* a case of being wise. I shall call *Romeo's loving Juliet* (alternatively expressed, *the loving of Juliet by Romeo*) a case of somebody loving somebody; and so also I shall call *Romeo's love for Juliet* (alternatively expressed, *the love of Romeo for Juliet*) a case of love. Further, if *x* is a case of *y,* I shall say that *x instantiates y.*

In the passage quoted, Ryle is apparently arguing as follows.

1. G. Ryle, "Plato's 'Parmenides'," *Mind* (1939), p. 138.

Suppose, he says, that there were such a relation as exemplification. Then

    (1) This is circular
would entail
    (2) This exemplifies circularity,
which in turn would entail
    (3) There is such a case as the exemplification of circularity by this, and such a relation as exemplification, and the former exemplifies the latter,
which in turn would entail
    (4) There is such a case as the exemplification of exemplification by the exemplification of circularity by this, and such a relation as exemplification, and the former exemplifies the latter,
which in turn would entail
    . . . ad infinitum

Now, says Ryle, the relation of exemplification which the sentence used in (3) says that there is, and which "exemplifies" in the sentence used in (2) is thought to stand for, is first-order exemplification; that which the sentence used in (4) says that there is, and which "exemplifies" in the sentence used in (3) is thought to stand for, is second-order exemplification; ad infinitum. In short, if there were such a relation as exemplification, then (1) would entail the existence of an infinitely large number of different orders (kinds) of exemplification, one of these being that which the sentence used in (3) says that there is; another, that which the sentence used in (4) says that there is; and so on. But there cannot be such an infinitely large set of different orders of exemplification. So if 'This is circular' did entail the existence of an infinitely large set of different orders of exemplification, it would have to be false. But it is true. So it does not entail this infinity. But if there were such a relation as exemplification, 'This is circular' *would* entail this infinity. Hence, there is no such relation. (From which it follows, of course, that it is not a relation which, in making assertions, one claims to hold between things.)

    What must be said first about this argument is that Ryle confuses exemplification with instantiation. He begins with something which exemplifies circularity. He then moves on to the case,

exemplification of circularity by this. But this case does not
exemplify the relation of exemplification. Rather, it *instantiates* it.
It is a case of this relation. Step (3) should accordingly read:

> (3a) There is such a case as the exemplification of circularity
> by this, and such a relation as exemplification, and the
> former instantiates the latter.

And step (4) should read:

> (4a) There is such a case as the instantiation of exemplification
> by the exemplification of circularity by this, and such a
> relation as instantiation, and the former instantiates the
> latter.

If we are to interpret him charitably, what Ryle must be understood as arguing is that to suppose that one thing exemplifies
another is to commit oneself to an infinite series of different kinds
of instantiation, that this consequence is absurd, and that accordingly the original supposition is absurd.

It is not clear from our way, or from Ryle's way, of stating the
argument why he holds that the relation of instantiation which
the sentence used in (4a) says that there is, is different from that
which sentence (5a) would say that there is. What reason is
there for holding that it is not the same relation which is said,
with each of these sentences, to be, and thus for holding that
(1) entails the existence of an infinitely large set of different
orders of instantiation?

Let us speculate a bit as to what Ryle might have had in mind
here. Consider the following series of *cases*:

> (iii) The exemplification of circularity by this
>
> (iv) The instantiation of exemplification by the exemplifica-
> tion of circularity by this
>
> (v) The instantiation of instantiation by the instantiation of
> exemplification by the exemplification of circularity by
> this

And so on.

Now compare that series of cases with the following series of
relations:

(III) Exemplification of ——— by ———
(IV) Instantiation of exemplification by the exemplification
of ——— by ———
(V) Instantiation of instantiation by instantiation of exemplification by the exemplification of ——— by ———

And so on.

The relation between these two series is obvious. (iii) is a case
of (III), (iv) is a case of (IV), and so on.

It will be noticed that case (iii) is what, in (3a), is said to
exist and to instantiate something; case (iv) is what, in (4a), is
said to instantiate something, and so on. But since case (iii) is
a case of relation (III), and case (iv) is a case of relation (IV),
it immediately occurs to us that the sentences used in (3a) and
(4a) are incomplete for Ryle's purposes. For (3a) we should
substitute this:

(3a′) There is such a case as the exemplification of circularity
by this, and such a relation as exemplification of ———
by ———, and the former instantiates the latter.

And for (4a) we should substitute this:

(4a′) There is such a case as the instantiation of exemplification by the exemplification of circularity by this, and
such a relation as instantiation of exemplification by the
exemplification of ——— by ———, and the former
instantiates the latter.

And so on.

So suppose we state Ryle's argument in this way. Is it then
clear that the relation which in (4a′) is said to exist is distinct
from that which (5a′) would claim to exist? In other words, is it
clear that the relation (IV) is distinct from the relation (V)?
Granted that we now have a series of different *names* for the
relation or relations said to be; is it clear that we have a series
of different *relations?*

It seems to me that this is not at all clear. Certainly the relation
(IV) is equivalent with the relation (V), in the sense that no
two things could bear to each other the relation (IV) without also
bearing to each other the relation (V), and vice versa. Also
it seems that to claim about the members of a pair that one of

them bears the relation (IV) to the other, is to make the very same claim about them as that which one makes in claiming that one of them bears the relation (V) to the other. Whether this is sufficient ground for concluding that they are identical relations is too large a question for us to consider here. Let it simply be said that some argument for the nonidentity of relation (IV) and relation (V) seems necessary if we are to have a convincing proof that in the series of sentences used in (4a'), (5a'), and so on, an infinite number of different relations is said to be. No such argument is offered by Ryle.

We said that (iii) was a case of relation (III), that (iv) was a case of relation (IV), and so on. But now consider the following series of relations:

(III') Exemplification of ——— by ———
(IV') Instantiation of ——— by the exemplification of ——— by ———
(V') Instantiation of ——— by the instantiation of ——— by the exemplification of ——— by ———

And so on.

It seems clear that the series (iii), (iv), (v), is not only a series of cases of the relations (III), (IV), (V), but is also a series of cases of the relations (III'), (IV'), (V'). For example, (iv) is a case of (IV), but also of (IV').

Corresponding to this new series of relations, there is also the following new series of sentences:

(3a'') There is such a case as the exemplification of circularity by this, and such a relation as exemplification of ——— by ———, and the former instantiates the latter

(4a'') There is such a case as the instantiation of exemplification by the exemplification of circularity by this, and such a relation as instantiation of ——— by the exemplification of ——— by ———, and the former instantiates the latter

And so on.

Now it does seem clear that in the series (III'), (IV'), (V'), we have a series of *distinct* relations. For (III') is a two-termed relation, (IV') is a three-termed relation, (V') is a four-termed relation. Thus, in the series of sentences (4a″), (5a″), and so on, an infinite number of distinct relations is said to be. But what, now, is impossible in this situation? Certainly it is not impossible that there should be infinitely large classes, nor that a true proposition should entail the existence of an infinitely large class of things. All we have from Ryle's hand is the claim that this is impossible, without any clue as to why.

But even if one thought it impossible that there should be an infinite series of relations of the sort (III′), (IV′), (V′), one would not have to conclude that there is no such relation as exemplication. For one could hold that while (2) entails (3a), the succeeding purported entailments do not hold. In other words, one could hold that there is such a relation as exemplification, and that (1) entails (2), and that (2) entails (3a); but that (3a) does not entail (4a)—on the ground, perhaps, that though one thing can instantiate another, there is no relation of instantiation. Alternatively, one could deny that (4a) entails (5a).

In short, Ryle's argument does not offer us sufficient reason for concluding that there is no such relation as exemplification; and so, it does not offer sufficient reason for denying that in assertively uttering subject-predicate sentences one claims some relation of exemplification to hold among things.

2. In a certain passage from P.F. Strawson, the claim is made, concerning *exemplifying,* and concerning *standing in the relation of something to,* that though there are such entities, they are not relations. This is what Strawson says:

> Thus we use such forms as '. . . is an instance of . . .', '. . . is characterized by . . .', '. . . has the relation of . . . to . . .'. I shall appropriate some of these expressions, using them as the names of different kinds of asserted tie. . . . It is important that we should not think of these two- or three-place expressions as themselves the names of terms of a certain kind, *viz.* relations. Something analogous to Bradley's argument against the reality of relations may be used, not indeed to show that relations are unreal, but to show that such assertible links between terms as these are not to be construed as ordinary relations. Let us speak of them as nonrelational ties.[2]

Strawson here denies that ". . . has the relation of . . . to . . ." stands for a relation. He denies that there is any such

2. Strawson, *Individuals,* p. 167.

relation as the relation of having the relation of something to. Yet he would allow that in assertively uttering "John has the relation of loving to Mary" we claim that John and loving and Mary are "linked" or "tied" in a certain manner.

Thus, as I understand him, Strawson would hold that from 'John loves Mary' it follows that there is the relation of loving and that John has it to Mary; but he would deny that it follows further that there is the relation of having the relation of something to. He wants, in other words, to distinguish between relations in general, and *having* or *bearing* or *standing in* the relation of something to. Standing in the relation of something to, he wants to say, is not a relation, or at least, not an "ordinary relation."

Now initially one might suspect that this is all merely a verbal matter. But in fact Strawson suggests, as his reason for saying that there is no such relation as that of standing in the relation of something to, that there is some absurdity involved in holding that this is a relation, or at least, in holding that this is an ordinary relation—an absurdity pointed out or suggested by Bradley. Strawson holds similar views for what the expressions ". . . is an instance of . . ." and ". . . is characterized by . . ." stand for. These do not, he holds, stand for genuine relations. They stand rather for nonrelational ties.

Ryle and Strawson would agree that there is such a relation as loving. Ryle, however, would deny that there is any such thing as standing in the relation of something to, while Strawson would insist that though there is this, it is not a relation.[3] Russell, then, goes both Ryle and Strawson one better, by denying that there are *any* relations. It may be true, he holds, that John loves Mary; but it does not follow that John stands in the relation of loving to Mary. There is some absurdity, he holds, in supposing that there is such a thing as the relation of *loving*. This is a view which he adopts in "Logical Atomism" and *Philosophy,* and which in the latter he also attributes to Wittgenstein in the *Tractatus.* Russell says, for instance, "The first step in Bradley's regress does actually have to be taken as giving verbal expression to a relation,

3. It is unclear whether Ryle thinks that 'John loves Mary' entails 'There is the relation of loving, and John stands in it to Mary.' Quite clearly he *would* hold that there is the relation of loving.

and the word for a relation does have to be related to the words for its terms."[4] He also says, "The concept of the relation as a third term between the other two . . . must be avoided with the utmost care."[5] Russell appears to hold that one can never actually refer to any relation, and also that it is never true to say that there is such a relation as so-and-so. Russell's view says nothing against the possibility of one thing having or possessing another, but it does say that nothing ever stands in a certain *relation* to another thing. Things are related; but nothing stands in some relation to another thing. Russell's reason for denying that 'John loves Mary' entails that John stands in the relation of loving to Mary, is his conviction that there is some absurdity involved in holding that there are relations, an absurdity pointed out by Bradley's regress.

To see, then, what it is that Strawson and Russell have in mind as lending justification to their views, we must look at the argument of Bradley to which both allude. To see the point that Bradley is making, we must quote him rather extensively:

One quality, *A,* is in relation with another quality, *B.* But what are we to understand here by *is?* We do not mean that 'in relation with *B*' is *A,* and yet we assert that *A is* 'in relation with *B*'. In the same way *C* is called 'before *D*', and *E* is spoken of as *being* 'to the right of *F*'. We say all this, but from the interpretation, then 'before *D*' is *C,* and 'to the right of *F*' is *E,* we recoil in horror. No, we should reply, the relation is not identical with the thing. It is only a sort of attribute which inheres or belongs. The word to use, when we are pressed, should not be *is,* but only *has.* But this reply comes to very little. The whole question is evidently as to the meaning of *has;* and, apart from metaphors not taken seriously, there appears really to be no answer. And we seem unable to clear ourselves from the old dilemma, If you predicate what is different, you ascribe to the subject what it is *not;* and if you predicate what is *not* different, you say nothing at all.

Driven forward, we must attempt to modify our statement. We must assert the relation now, not of one term, but of both. *A* and *B* are identical in such a point, and in such another point they differ; or, again, they are so situated in space or in time. And thus we avoid *is* and keep to *are.* But, seriously, that does not look like the explanation of a difficulty; it looks more like trifling with phrases. For, if you mean that *A* and *B,* taken each severally, even 'have' this relation,

4. B. Russell, *Philosophy* (New York, 1927), p. 253.
5. B. Russell, "Logical Atomism," p. 335.

you are asserting what is false. But if you mean that *A* and *B* in such a relation are so related, you appear to mean nothing. For here, as before, if the predicate makes no difference, it is idle; but, if it makes the subject other than it is, it is false.

But let us attempt another exit from this bewildering circle. Let us abstain from making the relation an attribute of the related, and let us make it more or less independent. 'There is a relation *C*, in which *A* and *B* stand and it appears with both of them.' But here again we have made no progress. The relation *C* has been admitted different from *A* and *B*, and no longer is predicated of them. Something, however, seems to be said of this relation *C*, and said, again, of *A* and *B*. And this something is not to be the ascription of one to the other. If so, it would appear to be another relation, *D*, in which *C*, on one side, and, on the other side, *A* and *B*, stand. But such a makeshift leads at once to the infinite process. The new relation *D* can be predicated in no way of *C*, or of *A* and *B;* and hence we must have recourse to a fresh relation, *E*, which comes between *D* and whatever we had before. But this must lead to another, *F;* and so on, indefinitely. Thus the problem is not solved by taking relations as independently real. For, if so, the qualities and their relation fall entirely apart, and then we have said nothing. Or we have to make a new relation between the old relation and the terms; which, when it is made, does not help us. It either demands a new relation, and so on without end, or it leaves us where we were, entangled in difficulties.[6]

As I understand him, what Bradley points out in the last part of this passage, the part containing the explication of the infinite process, is that, for example, in uttering the sentence "John is in the relation of loving to Mary," we cannot be understood as making the claim which is the conjunction of the claims that there are the entities John, Mary, and loving; nor the claim which is the conjunction of the claims that there are the entities John, Mary, loving, and the relation, call it R, which holds between any two entities, x and y, and any relation, $\emptyset$, just in case x is in the relation of $\emptyset$ to $y;$ nor the claim which is the conjunction of the claims that there are the entities John, Mary, loving, R, and the relation, call it R′, which holds between any two entities, x and y, any relation, $\emptyset$, and the relation R, just in case x is in the relation of $\emptyset$ to $y;$ and so on, ad infinitum.

But, says Bradley, he simply does not understand what could be claimed in uttering the sentence "John is in the relation of

6. F.H. Bradley, *Appearance and Reality,* (Oxford, 1930), pp. 17–18.

loving to Mary." For he has already considered, and discarded, the only other possibilities which occur to him. One possibility he considered is that "is in ———— to" is synonymous with "is identical with"; so that "John is in the relation of loving to Mary" can be paraphrased as "John is identical with the relation of loving Mary." But patently this is not the case. The other possibility he considered is that the person who utters "John is in the relation of loving to Mary" is claiming that there is some sort of tie-up between one or both of the terms and the purported relation. Perhaps he is claiming that one or both of the terms *has* the relation (*has* the relation *to*), that the relation is an attribute of one or both of the terms. Perhaps he is *asserting* or *predicating* a relation of something, or *ascribing* a relation to something. In short, perhaps the sentence "John is in the relation of loving to Mary" can be paraphrased as "John *has* the relation of loving *to* Mary." Or perhaps as "John and Mary together have the relation of loving." But this, says Bradley, is no help. We need some explanation of "has"; but it is wholly unlikely that any satisfactory explanation will be forthcoming. For we are here confronted with the old dilemma concerning predication: "If you predicate what is different, you ascribe to the subject what it is *not;* and if you predicate what is *not* different, you say nothing at all." In short, Bradley seems to regard "John has the relation of loving to Mary" as not being a meaningful sequence of words, not a sentence which can be used to assert something.

A similar argument to this one can, of course, be given for any other sentence of the form '*x* is in the relation of Ø to *y*'. What Bradley concludes is that nothing true is asserted with such sentences. It may *appear* that something true is claimed in uttering them, but nothing is, *really*. And since Bradley quite clearly regards such a sentence as "John loves Mary" as no better than "John is in the relation of loving to Mary" he concludes that nothing is really related to anything else. "The conclusion to which I am brought is that a relational way of thought—any one that moves by the machinery of terms and relations—must give appearance, and not truth."[7]

The question to ask, now, is the following. What is there about

7. Ibid., p. 28.

the infinite process which would lead Russell to hold that, though things are related, there are no relations, and Strawson to hold that, though one thing can stand in a certain relation to another thing, standing in the relation of something to, is not a relation? What Bradley says is that in uttering "John is in the relation of loving to Mary" we are not asserting any member of the infinite sequence of conjunctions indicated. How does this have any tendency to justify either Russell's contention or Strawson's?

Russell and Strawson do not wish to accept Bradley's *general* conclusion that nothing is really related to anything else. But the fact that in uttering a sentence of the form '*x* is in the relation of Ø to y' we do not assert any of the sorts of conjunctions indicated, surely does not in any way justify the conclusion that nothing is related to anything else. Nor does Bradley think that it does. Rather, Bradley's argument is that nothing is asserted in uttering sentences of the form '*x* is in the relation of Ø to y' (or, of the form '*x* Ø y'). He makes various attempts to express what might be claimed with such sentences, but all the attempts prove unsuccessful. So far as he can see, nothing at all is claimed with them, certainly nothing true. It is from this that he concludes that nothing is related to anything else. Bradley's words strongly suggest the conclusion that his view is that the only claims he understands are identity and nonidentity claims, and existence and nonexistence claims. What he is apparently trying to do is to paraphrase affirmative relational sentences by using only affirmative and negative identity sentences, affirmative and negative existence sentences, and truth-functions of such. It is after failing in this attempt that he concludes that no claims are ever made in uttering affirmative relational sentences.

What one can say to someone who holds that nothing is ever claimed in uttering affirmative relational sentences, but that one can see that sometimes something *is* claimed in uttering such sentences, and that sometimes what is claimed is true? What else can one say, except that the person who argues that nothing is claimed in uttering affirmative relational sentences conducts his argument by uttering such sentences?

Now Russell and Strawson are clearly unimpressed with Bradley's general argument. Clearly they believe that affirmative relational sentences are often used to make genuine claims.

Further, they clearly believe that often, at least, they understand what those claims are and that often those claims are true. But why, then, does Russell contend that though things are related, there are no relations? And why does Strawson contend that, though something can stand in the relation of something to something, yet standing in the relation of something to, is not a relation? These contentions seem irrelevant to Bradley's actual argument. One can escape Bradley's conclusion without adopting either contention; and adopting either of them seems to provide us with no reply whatsoever to Bradley's actual argument.

Perhaps, though, Russell and Strawson have a somewhat different "infinite process" in mind, one suggested to them by Bradley's remarks, yet not quite the one which Bradley actually presents. Possibly they have the following sort of infinite sequence of *entailments* in mind (the letters R and R' standing for the same relations for which we had them stand above).

(a) John loves Mary
    entails
(b) John is in the relation of loving to Mary
    which in turn entails
(c) John and Mary are in the relation of R to loving
    which in turn entails
(d) John and Mary and loving are in the relation of R' to R
    and so on, ad infinitum

In this case we have a sequence of entailments: (b) is the condition of (a), (c) of (b), (d) of (c), and so on. If John is to love Mary, then he must be in the relation of loving to Mary; and if he is to be in the relation of loving to Mary, he and Mary must be in the relation of R to loving; and if he and Mary are to be in the relation of R to loving, he and Mary and loving must be in the relation of R' to R, and so on. In general, for any relation (a relation being regarded as an entity), if some entities are to be in that relation to each other, those entities plus that relation must be in a certain relation to each other. It is this principle that generates what appears to be an infinite regress. Now perhaps it is the belief of Russell and Strawson that this principle is incompatible with the proposition that some things are related to each other. And since they hold that there are in fact things related to each other, they deny the principle. Russell stops the regress by denying that there are relations and that one thing can be in a certain relation to another; he denies that (a) entails (b). Strawson stops it by denying that R, R', and so on, are relations; he denies that (b) entails (c).

Now this still leaves us with some puzzlement as to Strawson's total view. For though he holds that (b) does not entail (c), he apparently holds that (b) *does* entail 'John and Mary are in the *tie* of R to loving'. If so, do we not still have an infinite regress? And is not the distinction between ties and relations after all merely verbal? Possibly, though, Strawson's point is that there is no such entity as R'; and that 'John and Mary are in R to loving' does not entail 'John and Mary and loving are in R' to R'. If this is indeed Strawson's claim, and if furthermore it were true, then the regress would be stopped, and there would be a genuine distinction between what Strawson calls *ordinary relations* and what he calls *links*. The distinction might be put thus. Ordinary relations would be those relations which bear a relation to their terms. Links would be those relations which do not bear a relation to their terms.

But suppose that the principle enunciated does in fact generate an infinite sequence. Why should it be thought, on this account, that the principle is incompatible with the fact that there are things related to each other? If we may use an analogy, the principle that for every natural number there is a successor to that number, generates an infinite sequence; but it is not on that account at all incompatible with the fact that there are numbers.

Here again we can only speculate. But perhaps something like the following analogy is tacitly at work. Suppose that we wish to link A and B together. Suppose that A cannot be linked to B unless A is linked to the link, and B likewise. Suppose that A and B cannot be linked to the link, unless A is linked to the link which is to link it to the original link, and B likewise; and so on. If all this were true, then it is clear that one is never going to succeed in linking A and B.[8]

---

8. ". . . the relation . . . , being something itself, if it does not itself bear a relation to the terms, in what intelligible way will it succeed in being anything to them? But here again we are hurried off into the eddy of a hopeless process, since we are forced to go on finding new relations

Zeno already noticed that the movement from one place to another can also be made to look mysterious. Before one can go to B, one must go half the distance to B; but to do this, one must first go half of *that* distance; and so on. But of course there is no incompatibility here. One can consistently hold both that space is infinitely divisible, and that we sometimes move. One need not deny one or the other of these. We can traverse a stretch of space which is infinitely divisible. So too John can love Mary, even though, in so doing, he stands in the relation of loving to Mary, and he and Mary stand in the relation of R to loving, and he and Mary and loving stand in the relation of R' to R, and so on, ad infinitum. In short, I see no incompatibility between the claim that things are related, and the principle that for every relation, if some entities are to be in that relation, those entities plus that relation must be in a certain relation.

But I do not think that we have yet completely disposed of all that is perplexing about the relation of standing in the relation of something to. For clearly there can be the entities, John, loving, and Mary, even though it is not the case that John loves Mary. What then is missing? Loving was supposed to be a relation, something that related things. But there can be such a relation, as well as John and Mary, without the relation of loving doing its work of relating them. What is necessary, one wants to say, is not just that these three should exist, but that they should *stand in relation.* But there can also be this relation of standing in the relation of something to, along with John, Mary, and loving, even though it is not the case that John stands in the relation of loving to Mary. What then is missing? For again we seem to have a relation which fails to do its work of relating. It does, indeed, begin to seem futile even to speak of relations. What we need is ties which actually tie. So it seems. Or perhaps, better, all we need is things in relation—objects fitting into one another like the links of a chain.

The key to the dissolution of this perplexity seems to me to lie in the distinction between a *relation* and a *case* of that relation. We must distinguish between loving (the relation holding between

without end. The links are united by a link, and this bond of union is a link which also has two ends; and these require such a fresh link to connect them with the old" (Bradley, *Appearance and Reality,* pp. 27–28).

any two things just in case one loves the other), on the one hand, and somebody's loving somebody (the loving of somebody by somebody), on the other. Loving is a relation. Somebody's loving somebody—John's loving Mary—is a *case* of that relation. We must distinguish between standing in the relation of something to (that is, the relation holding among three things just in case one stands in the relation of another to the third), on the one hand, and something's standing in a certain relation to something (the standing in a certain relation to something by something) on the other. The former is a relation; the latter—for example, John's standing in the relation of loving to Mary—is a *case* of the relation.

We are apt to overlook the distinction between a relation and a case of that relation. We are apt to confuse the relation of loving, with somebody's loving somebody; to confuse the relation of sitting next to, with somebody's sitting next to somebody. But especially we are apt, I think, to overlook the distinction between the standing in a certain relation by something to something, and the relation of standing in the relation of something to. Then only confusion can follow. For there can be such a relation as standing in the relation of something to, in addition to there being John, loving, and Mary, without its being the case that John stands in the relation of loving to Mary. Yet there cannot be such a thing as John's standing in the relation of loving to Mary, unless it is the case that John stands in the relation of loving to Mary. So if we do not see that standing in the relation of something to, is distinct from something's standing in a certain relation to something, then we are indeed perplexed. But the perplexity is eliminated if we keep in mind the distinction between a relation and its cases. There is such a case as John's standing in the relation of loving to Mary just in case John stands in the relation of loving to Mary. But it is not true that there are such things as John, Mary, loving, and standing in the relation of something to, just in case John stands in the relation of loving to Mary. The standing in a certain relation to something by something is not a relation, in particular, not the relation of standing in the relation of something to.

A case of a relation consists of things in relation; a relation does not. To get things in relation, we do not need some nonrelational links or ties. All we need is *cases* of relations. If we just have relations and things, we do not have things in relation; but we do have things in relation if we have *cases* of relations. If all we have is the relation of love, and some persons, we do not have persons loving persons. For this, we need cases of loving. We need not, then, deny that loving is a relation, or that standing in the relation of something to, is a relation. Nor need we hold that relations are irrelevant to the phenomena of things in relation. For things in relation are just *cases* of *relations*.

5

Predicate Entailment

1. In a previous chapter we claimed that entities other than words can be predicated. We called such entities predicables; some of them, we said, are universal, that is, capable of being predicated truly of many, and some of them are not. In the course of exploring the nature of nonlinguistic predication we distinguished various sorts of predicables: states, properties, actions, assertibles, and relations. We agreed that these sorts might very well overlap and in some cases even coincide. Perhaps states and properties coincide, and it may be that properties and actions are all assertibles.

In the preceding chapter we countered various objections to our analysis of nonlinguistic predication, objections to the effect that there is something incoherent in the claim that there is such a relation as exemplification holding among entities. No doubt a more frequent objection to what we have said, however, would be that there are no such entities as those which we have said can be predicated—properties, actions, and the rest. Thus, in support of our earlier claim, I wish in this chapter to consider arguments in defense of the thesis that there are such entities as properties and actions. I shall not have much to say here directly in defense of the thesis that there are also such entities as assertibles and relations, unless of course it be the case that properties and actions are assertibles.

For a given sort of predicable, it will be convenient to have a name for the view that there are entities of that sort, and also to have a name for the view that there are *not* entities of that sort. Let us call the view that there are such entities as so-and-so's, *realism in respect to so-and-so's;* and let us call the view that there are no such entities as so-and-so's, *nominalism in respect to so-and-so's.* Thus, realism in respect to actions is the view that there are such entities as actions, and nominalism in respect to relations is the view that there are no such entities as relations.

To establish that there are such things as properties and actions, we shall try to establish that there is such a thing as wisdom, that there is such a thing as running, and so on. And we shall always state the conclusions to our arguments in sentences of the form "There is such a thing as p" rather than in sentences of the form "p exists." For it is the case at least for a great many standard designations of properties and actions, that though we get a sentence with normal sense if we substitute them for "p" in the schema "There is such a thing as p", we do not get a sentence with normal sense if we substitute them for "p" in the schema "p exists." For example, "There is such a thing as being red" has normal sense; and we can discuss whether the proposition asserted with the words used in this sense is a true one. If it is, and if the proposition 'There is such a thing as being green' is also true, then it follows that there are such things as properties, since *being red* and *being green* are both properties. But the words "being red exists" do not make sense; nor in general do we get sentences with normal sense if we insert state names into the context "——— exists."[1]

1. This is but one example of the lack of interchangeability between "there is" and "exists." For a more general discussion of this matter, see Noel Fleming and Nicholas Wolterstorff, "On 'There Is'," *Philosophical Studies* (April 1960), pp. 41–48. It should also be said that "thing," as I use it in this discussion, is the most general of all possible common nouns. Anything whatsoever is a thing. From any proposition of the form 'x is a K', where 'a K' represents a common noun, the corresponding proposition of the form 'x is a thing' follows. Furthermore, I use "entity" interchangeably with "thing."

Though I shall not *directly* concern myself, in what follows, with the being of *assertibles,* it may be noted that, for the common designations of assertibles, we do not even get sentences with normal sense if we insert them into the context "There is such a thing as ————." *That it is red* and *that it is green* are assertibles, since they can be asserted about things. Thus there are things which can be asserted about things, for example, *that it is red* and *that it is green.* From which it follows that there are assertibles. But the words "There is such a thing as that it is red" and "there is such a thing as that it is green" both seem to be nonsensical, as are the words "that it is red exists" and "that it is green exists." On the other hand, the words "there is such a thing as the assertible: that it is red" do make sense. Similar oddities surround propositions. A proposition is what can be asserted. And since there are things which can be asserted, it follows that there are such things as propositions, for example, that my pen is red. Yet the words "There is such a thing as that my pen is red" make no sense, nor do the words, "that my pen is red exists" make sense. On the other hand, *these* words do make sense: "There is such a thing as the proposition: *My pen is red.*"

In what follows I shall, for the sake of convenience, use 'f-ness' as a sign standing for designations of properties; 'f-ing', for designations of actions; 'f-ity', for designations of properties and actions; and 'is-f' for logical predicates.

In what follows I shall also on occasion speak of a subjectible term as a *correlative* of a predicate. "Running," for example, I shall speak of as a correlative of "is running"; "wisdom" as a correlative of "is wise"; and so on. In this chapter we want to see what is to be said against nominalism in respect to actions and properties. Accordingly, we cannot assume that in predicating "is wise" of something, there is some predicable which we predicate of that thing, and which "is wise" then stands for; nor can we assume that there is some predicable which "wisdom" designates. But I think the nominalist would agree that "wisdom" in its current use is a term such that, if there *were* any predicable for which "is wise" stood, it (that is, "wisdom") would designate one such. Accordingly, I shall say that a certain subjectible is a correlative of a certain predicate just in case, if there is (or were) any predicable for which the predicate stands (or stood),

the subjectible designates (or would designate) one such. If one
thought that a term could designate some predicable without there
being that predicable, and that a predicate could stand for some
predicable without there being that predicable, then the concept
of "correlative of" could be explained more simply. A subjectible
is a correlative of a certain predicate just in case it designates
some predicable for which the predicate stands.

2. The sort of argument for predicables that I wish first to
present for consideration is both ancient and modern. It is suggested already in Plato; and an example of the sort of argument
I have in mind is to be found in chapter 9 of Russell's *Problems
of Philosophy,* where he says: "If we ask ourselves what justice
is, it is natural to proceed by considering this, that, and the other
just act, with a view to discovering what they have in common.
They must all, in some sense, partake of a common nature, which
will be found in whatever is just and in nothing else."[2] Arguments
for predicables of the sort I have in mind, all appeal to some
case of things resembling each other in a certain way; on that
account I shall call them *arguments from resemblance.* They all
hold that if any things resemble each other in a certain way,
then those things share in common a certain predicable; and that
if some things share in common some predicable, then there is
such a thing as that predicable.

To speak of certain things resembling each other in a certain
way is to speak vaguely. For not only do things resemble each
other in various ways, they also resemble each other in various
sorts of ways. Suppose, for example, that my pen and my pencil
are each red. There are then at least two different ways of describing specifically how they resemble each other. They resemble
each other with respect to their redness (alternatively, with respect to their both being red); and they resemble each other in
that they are both red (alternatively, in that each is red). Which
of these modes of description shall we use in presenting the
general form of arguments from resemblance? Shall we use the
"with respect to" locution, or the "in that" locution? Or does it
make no difference?

It has frequently been said by philosophers that that which

2. Russell, *The Problems of Philosophy* (New York, n.d.), p. 143.

things resemble each other with respect to, is always a universal—
a *predicable* universal. If this were so, then every argument of
the following form would be an argument from a case of resemblance for a universal. If any things resemble each other with
respect to *a,* then those things share *a* in common. And if some
things share *a* in common, then there is such a thing as *a.* There
are some things which resemble each other with respect to *a.*
Hence there is such a thing as *a.*

Now if it were indeed clearly the case that that which things
resemble each other with respect to is always a predicable universal, then the person who holds the position of nominalism
with respect to predicable universals would presumably cast
around for some other way of describing how things resemble
each other. For him to accept this mode of description as legitimate would be to sacrifice his convictions at the very beginning.
But in fact it is clearly *not* the case that everything that things
resemble each other with respect to is a predicable universal.
That it is not, can be seen by considering the facts that two
plants can resemble each other with respect to their leaves, that
two men can resemble each other with respect to their noses,
that two books can resemble each other with respect to their
bindings. But their leaves is not a universal, nor is their noses,
nor is their bindings. Indeed, from the fact that two plants resemble each other with respect to their leaves it does not even
follow that their leaves is something which they resemble each
other with respect to; "their leaves is something which they resemble each other with respect to" is just incoherent. What
things resemble each other with respect to is not, in general,
some (one) thing or entity which they resemble each other with
respect to; and so, of course, what they resemble each other with
respect to is not, in general, some predicable universal. Further,
from the fact that two plants resemble each other with respect to
their leaves it certainly does not follow that they share their
leaves in common; from the fact that two men resemble each
other with respect to their noses it certainly does not follow that
they share their noses in common; and so on.

In these cases of the noses and the leaves, it seems that the
function of the "with respect to" locution is to get us to consider
a part of each of the things in question, thus to notice some

resemblance between the things. To notice some resemblance between the two men we are invited to consider the nose of each. To notice some resemblance between the two plants we are invited to consider the leaves of each. But, of course, the noses and the leaves are not shared in common. Now I think that there is considerable plausibility in supposing that this is always the function of the "with respect to" locution. Things, we say, resemble each other with respect to *their redness;* that is, presumably, with respect to *the redness of each.* Are we not here considering *cases* of redness rather than redness itself? Are we not considering *this thing's redness* and *that thing's redness,* that is, two distinct entities, two distinct rednesses? And *these* are not shared in common; rather, at best, *redness* is shared in common. What things resemble each other with respect to is their redness; but their redness, it is plausible to think, is not some one thing which they share in common. What two red things would share in common, if anything, would be redness; but redness, it is plausible to think, is not something that they resemble each other with respect to.

In short, I think that the person who is a nominalist with respect to predicable universals can, with considerable plausibility, hold that in using the "with respect to" locution to state how things resemble, he is not mentioning any predicable universal, but is rather using a general term which is true of what I have called *cases* of predicables. There are, however, perhaps some nominalists who would even be squeamish about using terms true of *cases.* And it is easy to see that in using the "resemble each other in that" locution, one does not even do this. Accordingly, I shall henceforth use this latter locution in stating the argument from resemblance, though I myself think that the argument could as easily and effectively be stated with the other locution as well.

In presenting the general form of arguments from resemblance, we shall use the sign *is-f* and the sign *f-ity.* In deriving an actual argument from this schema, the subjectible replacing the sign *f-ity* must be a correlative of the predicate replacing the sign *is-f.* The general form of arguments from resemblance is the following. (i) Necessarily, if any things resemble each other in that each *is-f,* then those things share *f-ity* in common (or, exemplify *f-ity* jointly). And (ii) necessarily, if some things share *f-ity* in common, then there is such a thing as *f-ity*. (iii) There are some things which resemble each other in that each *is-f*. Hence, (iv) there is such a thing as *f-ity*.[3] An example of an argument with this form is the following. If any things resemble each other in that each is courageous, then those things share courage in common (exemplify courage jointly). And if some things share courage in common, there is such a thing as courage. There are some things which resemble each other in that each is courageous. Hence there is such a thing as courage.

Let us begin our evaluation of arguments from resemblance by scrutinizing the initial premises in such arguments, those premises which are of the following form. If any things resemble each other in that each *is-f,* those things must share *f-ity* in common (must exemplify *f-ity* jointly). Suppose that Wilson is courageous and that nobody else is, so that Wilson does not resemble anyone else in that each is courageous. Would anyone wish to say that in this case Wilson can be courageous without exemplifying courage, whereas if someone else is also courageous, then Wilson as well as this other person must both exemplify courage? Of course, if Wilson alone is courageous, then Wilson does not exemplify courage *jointly* with someone else. But would it be anyone's view that if only Wilson is courageous, then Wilson can be courageous without exemplifying courage; but if someone else as well is courageous, then Wilson can no longer be courageous without exemplifying courage? In short, what role does the phenomenon of resemblance actually play in this argument and in others of the sort? *Must* there be at least two things resembling each other in that each is courageous if we are to justify the conclusion that some thing exemplifies courage? Would this not also follow from the fact that one thing is courageous?

I think that no one would hold the view that resemblance is *essential* to exemplification. No one, that is to say, would hold the view that, necessarily, for anything whatsoever, if it is courageous, then it exemplifies courage just in case something else

---

3. If we used the "with respect to" locution, the first premise, but only the first premise, would be different. It would be of this form: if any things resemble each other with respect to their *f-ity*, then those things share *f-ity* in common.

resembles it in that this other thing also is courageous. But this is not yet to say that everyone who held the view, that any things which resemble each other in that each is courageous must jointly exemplify courage, would also hold the view, that if any *one* thing is courageous then it must exemplify courage. For it is at least abstractly possible that he would instead hold the view, that if any one thing is courageous and it is *possible* that there is something else which is also courageous, then the former thing must exemplify courage. And so also, for other cases.

To see whether this is anything more than an abstract possibility, let us consider the person who gave birth to Napoleon. It is certainly not possible that something else should resemble her in that it too gave birth to Napoleon. But does it not follow from the fact that she gave birth to Napoleon, that she exemplifies having given birth to Napoleon? Or better, would not anyone who accepts arguments from resemblance hold that this does follow? Again, 5 is a prime number between 3 and 7; and it is not possible that something else should resemble 5 in that it too is a prime number between 3 and 7. But, in spite of this, will not anyone who accepts arguments from resemblance hold that 5 must exemplify being a prime number between 3 and 7?

Of course, anyone who is interested only in predicable *universals,* as opposed to predicables generally, will confine his attention to cases of actual and possible resemblance. For a predicable universal is something which *can* be predicated truly of more than one thing. But still, it seems arbitrary to hold that propositions of the form 'Necessarily if *x is-f* and it is possible that something resembles *x* in that it too *is-f,* then *x* exemplifies *f-ity'* are true; and deny that propositions of the form 'necessarily if *x is-f,* then *x* exemplifies *f-ity'* are true. For as a consequence, one would have to hold that something exemplifies *being a prime number between 3 and 9,* but could deny that something exemplifies *being a prime number between 3 and 7,* while admitting that 5 is both a prime number between 3 and 7 and a prime number between 3 and 9. Again, one would have to hold that something exemplified *having given birth to someone,* but could deny that something exemplified *having given birth to Napoleon,* while admitting that the very same person gave birth to someone and gave birth to *Napoleon*. Thus it seems that not even the *possibility* of resemblance is essential for establishing exemplification.

So it would be irrational to hold that all propositions of the form 'If any things resemble each other in that each *is-f*, then those things share *f-ity* in common' are necessarily true, and to deny that all of the form "If any one thing *is-f*, then it exemplifies *f-ity*' are necessarily true. Furthermore, each proposition of the former sort follows from some proposition of the latter sort; if it is true that any one thing exemplifies courage if it is courageous, then of course it is true that any two or more things each exemplify courage if each is courageous. Thus we will be getting at the nub of the first part of any argument from resemblance if we consider whether or not the principle of the form 'Necessarily if anything *is-f*, then it exemplifies *f-ity*' is true. *This* is the pivotal question.

In step (ii) of the argument from resemblance for the conclusion that there is such a thing as courage, the following is said. Necessarily, if some things jointly exemplify courage, then there is such a thing as courage. Here, again, it is worth asking if there is a more general principle from which this one follows and which it would be incoherent to deny if one accepts this one. Certainly no one would wish to hold that if Wilson alone exemplifies courage then it may be that there is no such thing as courage; whereas if someone else also exemplifies courage then it must be that there is such a thing as courage. Anyone who held that from the fact that Wilson and Johnson both exemplify courage it follows that there is such a thing as courage, would also hold that this follows just from the fact that Wilson exemplifies courage. In general, no one would hold that something can exemplify a certain predicable, even though there is no such thing as that predicable, just so long as there is not something else which also exemplifies it.

Nor, I think, would anyone hold the view that something can exemplify a certain predicable, even though there is no such thing as that predicable, just so long as it is not *possible* that there is something else which also exemplifies it. For this would have the bizarre consequence that 5 could exemplify *being a prime number between 3 and 7* even though there were no such thing as *being a prime number between 3 and 7,* while it could not exemplify *being a prime number between 3 and 9* unless there were such a thing as *being a prime number between 3 and 9.* Rather, anyone who held the view that every proposition of the form 'Necessarily if some things jointly exemplify *f-ity* then there is such a thing as *f-ity'* is true, would also hold the view that every proposition of the form 'Necessarily if some one thing exemplifies *f-ity* then there is such a thing as *f-ity'* is true. Further, every proposition of the former sort is entailed by one of the latter sort. So the nub in the second step of any argument from resemblance is not the proposition of the form 'Necessarily if some things jointly exemplify *f-ity* then there is such a thing as *f-ity',* but rather the corresponding and more general proposition of the form, 'Necessarily if some thing exemplifies *f-ity* then there is such a thing as *f-ity'.*

Thus, pivotal to any argument from resemblance will be two general principles, of the following forms. 'Necessarily, for anything at all, if it *is-f* then it exemplifies *f-ity'.* And, 'Necessarily, if there is something which exemplifies *f-ity,* then there is such a thing as *f-ity'.* For example, 'Necessarily, for anything at all, if it is courageous, then it exemplifies courage'. And, 'Necessarily, if there is something which exemplifies courage, then there is such a thing as courage'. The key premises in any argument from resemblance follow from the relevant principles of these forms; and though it is *possible* to hold the premises without holding these more general principles, we found that it would be arbitrary and implausible to do so. The acceptability of any argument from resemblance will hang on the acceptability of these more general principles; they are the nub of what is controversial.

Now the conjunction of two corresponding principles of the form indicated entail the corresponding principle of this form. 'Necessarily, if something *is-f,* then there is such a thing as *f-ity'.* For example, 'Necessarily, for anything at all, if it is courageous, then it exemplifies courage; and, if there is something which exemplifies courage then there is such a thing as courage' entails 'Necessarily, if something is courageous, then there is such a thing as courage.' Let us, for the sake of convenience, call any proposition of the form, 'Necessarily if something *is-f,* then there is such as thing as *f-ity,' a predicate entailment principle.*

No one could, with any plausibility, accept a given argument from resemblance and deny the corresponding predicate entailment principle. On the other hand, if one accepts such a principle, he will also, certainly, accept the first two premises of the corresponding argument from resemblance. Or, if he does not, then it is worth pointing out to him that a predicate entailment principle by itself, coupled only with the corresponding proposition of the form 'Something *is-f'*, yields as conclusion the corresponding proposition of the form 'There is such a thing as *f-ity'*— which is just the conclusion that the argument from resemblance also aimed to yield. For example, from 'Something is courageous, and necessarily if something is courageous then there is such a thing as courage', it follows that there is such a thing as courage— which is just the conclusion of the argument from resemblance for there being such a thing as courage. Further, the proposition which we must add to a given predicate entailment principle to reach the desired conclusion, namely, the proposition of the form 'Something *is-f'*, is entailed by the third premise of the corresponding argument from resemblance, namely, the premise of the form 'There are some things which resemble each other in that each *is-f'*. Thus if a given predicate entailment principle is granted, there is scarcely any point in adding the other elements necessary for constructing an argument from resemblance which leads to the very same conclusion.

So we can say that a predicate entailment principle is the nub of any argument from resemblance. No one will find an argument from resemblance acceptable unless he also finds the corresponding predicate entailment principle acceptable. And no one will find a predicate entailment principle acceptable unless he also finds the first two steps in the corresponding argument from resemblance acceptable—or, if for some reason he does not find them acceptable, the predicate entailment principle alone, coupled with something entailed by the last premise in the corresponding argument from resemblance, will yield the very same conclusion that the argument from resemblance also yields. Clearly it is predicate entailment principles that we must scrutinize.

It might justly be said that what we have seen is that predication, and not generality or resemblance, is what is pivotal and essential in arguments from resemblance.

3. Before I say whether, in my judgment, any or all predicate entailment principles are true, I wish to consider a second sort of argument for the being of predicables. For the nub of what is controversial in such other arguments is also, as it turns out, predicate entailment principles.

Arguments of the sort I have in mind all appeal to situations in which a number of distinct things can have the same term with the same import affirmed truly of them. The arguments hold that if a term can be affirmed truly with the same import of various distinct things, then those things must share a certain predicable in common—some predicable other than the property of having that term affirmable truly of each. If they did not share this predicable in common, the term could not be affirmed truly of them all. I shall call such arguments, arguments from multiple affirmability.[4]

An example of this sort of argument is the following. Necessarily if any two or more things are such that "is a wallaby" can be affirmed truly with the same import of all of them, then those

4. Frequently arguments from resemblance and arguments from multiple affirmability are run into each other. It is not perceived that they begin from different premises. Witness the following passage from Russell's *Problems of Philosophy,* part of which has already been quoted. At the beginning, we find a statement of an argument from resemblance; at the end, a statement of an argument from multiple affirmability. "If we ask ourselves what justice is, it is natural to proceed by considering this, that, and the other just act, with a view to discovering what they have in common. They must all, in some sense, partake of a common nature, which will be found in whatever is just and in nothing else. This common nature, in virtue of which they are all just, will be justice itself, the pure essence the admixture of which with facts of ordinary life produces the multiplicity of just acts. Similarly with any other word which may be applicable to common facts, such as 'whiteness' for example. The word will be applicable to a number of particular things because they all participate in a common nature or essence" (p. 143). In the following passage from Quine one also finds both sorts of arguments run together, this time by an opponent of them: "One may admit that there are red houses, roses, and sunsets, but deny, except as a popular and misleading manner of speaking, that they have anything in common. The words 'houses', 'roses', and 'sunsets' are true of sundry individual entities which are houses and roses and sunsets, and the word 'red' or 'red object' is true of each of sundry individual entities which are red houses, red roses, red sunsets; but there is not, in addition, any entity whatever, individual or otherwise, which is named by the word 'redness', nor, for that matter, by the word 'household', 'rosehood', 'sunsethood'" (*From a Logical Point of View* [Cambridge, 1953], p. 10).

things share in common being a wallaby. And necessarily if some two or more things share in common being a wallaby, then there is such a thing as being a wallaby. There are some things such that "is a wallaby" can be affirmed truly with the same import of all of them. Hence there is such a thing as being a wallaby.

Let us begin our evaluation of such arguments by considering their initial premises. Consider, for example, the claim that if any two or more things are such that "is red" can be affirmed truly of them with the same import, then those things must share the color red in common. One important thing to notice here is that the words "is red" might have had a different sense from that which in fact they do have. It is purely contingent that they have the sense which in fact they have. They might, for example, have meant the same as what our English words "is green" in fact mean. If they did mean this, it would surely not be the case that if any things are such that "is red" can be affirmed truly with the same import of them, then those things share the color red in common. Rather, if they shared anything of the sort in common, it would be the color green. To circumvent these difficulties let it be agreed that ' "is red" ' is to be understood as short for ' "is red" as currently used'; ' "is a wallaby" ' as short for ' "is a wallaby" as currently used'; and so on.

But even with this understanding, the sentences used to state the initial premises of arguments from multiple affirmability will frequently be ambiguous. If we are to evaluate these premises, we must be clear as to which proposition is meant to be asserted. Consider the word-name " 'is a bank' ". Of what predicate is this the name? It is, of course, the name of a couple of different predicates. It is the name of a predicate which can be affirmed truly of various financial institutions. But also it is the name of a predicate which can be affirmed truly of a river's verge. So suppose I assertively utter: "If any things are such that 'is a bank' can be affirmed truly with the same import of them, then those things must share *being a bank* in common." Will I then have spoken truly? Evidently not. For whatever I use "being a bank" to name—whether that property which certain commercial institutions possess, or that which a river's verge possesses—it is the case that "being a bank" as currently used can be affirmed truly of two or more things without their sharing *that* property in common. In fact, the following cannot even be said truly. "If any things are such that 'is a bank' can be affirmed truly with the same import of them, then those things must each be a bank."

This difficulty can, I think, be circumvented as follows. Let us first agree henceforth to use the word "predicate" in such a way that a given predicate consists not of a given sound- or character-sequence having *some import or other,* but rather of a given sound- or character-sequence with a given import. If predicate A and predicate B have a different sense, they are different predicates. In English there are, then, at least two different predicates whose character-sequence is as follows: *is a bank.* And the word-name " 'is a bank' " is the name of at least two different predicates and could be the name of many more. Given this use of "predicate," it can now be said, truly, that the predicate " 'is a bank' " can be affirmed truly with the same import of two or more things if and only if it can be affirmed of them and each is a bank (where the predicate *used* at the end of the sentence is the same as the one *mentioned* near the beginning). But now, *which* predicate are we to take " 'is a bank' " as naming, when we assertively utter "If any things are such that 'is a bank' can be affirmed truly with the same import of them, then those things must share being a bank in common"? Rather obviously, we are to take " 'is a bank' " as naming the predicate of which "being a bank" is a correlative.

We are now in a position to express the general form of arguments from multiple affirmability. Let it be understood that, in order to derive an actual argument from this schema, the word replacing the sign *f-ity* must be a correlative of the predicate which the word-name replacing the sign ⌜is-f⌝ is taken to designate. Then the form of arguments from multiple affirmability will be this: (i) Necessarily if any two or more things are such that ⌜is-f⌝ can be affirmed truly with the same import of all of them, then those things share *f-ity* in common. And (ii) necessarily, if some two or more things share *f-ity* in common, then there is such a thing as *f-ity.* (iii) There *are* some things such that ⌜is-f⌝ can be affirmed truly with the same import of them all. Hence (iv) there is such a thing as *f-ity.*

Now suppose it so happens that there is only one thing which is a wallaby, so that "is a wallaby" can be affirmed truly of only one thing. Would anyone who held the view, that if any two or more things are such that "is a wallaby" can be affirmed truly of them with the same import then those things must jointly exemplify being a wallaby, also hold the view that if there is only one thing of which "is a wallaby" can be affirmed truly, then "is a wallaby" can be affirmed truly of that one thing even though it does not exemplify being a wallaby? Would not the view rather be that no matter how many things "is a wallaby" can be affirmed truly of, whether one or more than one, whatever it can be affirmed truly of must exemplify being a wallaby? Is not the fact of multiple affirmability actually quite extrinsic to what is essential and controversial in arguments from multiple affirmability?

But before we conclude that anyone who accepted principles of the form, 'If any two or more things are such that ⌜is-f⌝ can be affirmed truly of them with the same import, then those things must jointly exemplify *f-ity'*, would also accept principles of the form 'If any one thing is such that ⌜is-f⌝ can be affirmed truly of it, then that thing must exemplify *f-ity'*, we ought to consider whether some would not *instead* accept principles of the following form. 'If any one thing is such that ⌜is-f⌝ can be affirmed truly of it, and if it is possible that there is something else of which ⌜is-f⌝ can also be affirmed truly, then the former thing must exemplify *f-ity'*. Now a general term is a term which can be affirmed truly with the same import of more than one thing. And the effect of this principle would be to limit the inference from the applicability of terms to the exemplification of predicables, to those cases in which the terms in question are general terms.

Would this be coherent? Consider a singular term, "gave birth to Napoleon." Would it be coherent to hold that this can be affirmed truly of someone even though she did not exemplify having given birth to Napoleon, while also holding that "gave birth to someone" cannot be affirmed truly of someone unless she exemplifies having given birth to someone? It seems to me that this is not a coherent combination of views, and that no one would wish to hold such a combination. The fact that a term is general turns out, I think, to be as irrelevant to what is essential and controversial in an argument from multiple affirmability, as is the fact that, for many terms, there are in fact many things of which they can be affirmed truly.

Thus, it would be irrational to hold that all propositions of the form 'Necessarily, if any two or more things are such that ⌜is-f⌝ can be affirmed truly of them with the same import, then those things must jointly exemplify f-ity' are true, and deny that all of the form, 'Necessarily, if any one thing is such that ⌜is-f⌝ can be affirmed truly of it, then it must exemplify f-ity' are true. If we would concentrate on the nub of what is essential and controversial in arguments from multiple affirmability, then we must take singular terms as well as general terms into our purview. Of course, if one is interested in establishing the being of only those predicables which are universal, then one will limit oneself to general terms. But we are interested in predicables generally. And we have just seen that not even general terms, let alone general terms having actual multiple affirmability, are especially relevant to what is basically at stake in arguments from multiple affirmability. What is basically at stake concerns terms generally.

So let us consider the following principle (or any other one of the same form). 'For any one thing, if it is such that "is a wallaby" can be affirmed truly of it, then it must exemplify being a wallaby'. Alternatively, let us consider the principle that any proposition of the form 'a is such that "is a wallaby" can be affirmed truly if it' entails the corresponding proposition of the form 'a exemplifies being a wallaby'. Now the predicate "is a wallaby," we observed earlier, will be one such that it can be affirmed truly of some thing if and only if it can be affirmed of that thing and that thing is a wallaby (the predicate used at the end of this sentence being understood as the same as the one mentioned near the beginning). So then, 'a is such that "is a wallaby" can be affirmed truly of it' will entail the corresponding proposition of the form, 'a is a wallaby'. Now the principle which we uncovered as pivotal to the first step of the comparable *argument from resemblance* says that any proposition of the form 'a is a wallaby' *itself* entails the corresponding proposition of the form 'a exemplifies being a wallaby'. So the rest of the content of any proposition of the form 'a is such that "is a wallaby" can be affirmed truly of it' is, it turns out, really irrelevant to our purposes. On the other hand, suppose that someone judges that propositions of the form 'a is a wallaby' do not entail the corresponding propositions of the form, 'a exemplifies being a wallaby'. It is hard to see how such a person could coherently and plausibly hold at the same time that propositions of the form '*a* is such that "is a wallaby" can be affirmed truly of it' *do* entail the corresponding propositions of the form '*a* exemplifies being a wallaby'. So I conclude that a principle of the following form is pivotal to the first part of any argument from multiple affirmability, as it was to any argument from resemblance. 'For anything at all, if it *is-f,* then it exemplifies *f-ity*'.

But the second premises in arguments from multiple affirmability are just like those in arguments from resemblance. Hence, by following a line of reasoning identical with that used earlier, we can see that predicate entailment principles are what is essential and controversial in arguments from multiple affirmability. They are the nub of all such arguments. Anyone who accepts the first two premises in such arguments will also accept such principles. And though one could accept such principles without accepting the corresponding parts of arguments from multiple affirmability, if one accepts such principles, and also accepts the last premise in the corresponding argument from multiple affirmability, then one still is led to the very same conclusion.

Let us consider one possible objection to what has preceded. We said that the predicate "is a wallaby" is such that it can be affirmed truly of some thing if and only if it can be affirmed of that thing and that thing is a wallaby (where the predicate *used* at the end of this sentence is the one *mentioned* earlier in the sentence). And similarly for all parallel cases. "Is red" can be affirmed truly of some thing if and only if it can be affirmed of that thing and that thing is red. Now it is reputed that some philosophers have denied this.[5] For it is reputed that some philosophers have held that there is never any objective justification for the correct multiple affirmability of terms to things, whereas we have contended that "is a wallaby" can be affirmed truly of something if and only if it is a wallaby. Certainly this is an objective matter. There might be wallabies even if there were no such word as "wallaby" at all.

Now of course it may be meant by the claim in question (though Bambrough does not take it as meaning this) that every

5. See R. Bambrough, "Universals and Family Resemblance," *Proceedings of the Aristotelian Society,* n.s. 61 (1960–61), pp. 207–222.

word might well have had a different use or sense from that which it does have. In the assigning of use or sense to character- and sound-sequences, considerations of truth have no relevance. But this point, though true enough, has no bearing on our contentions. So suppose the point really is that, for terms in their current use, there is no objective justification for the fact that often the same term with the same import can be affirmed truly of two or more things. Such a view staggers one with its implausibility. Is it just not the case that for every predicate ("predicate" being used here in the sense explained) which can be affirmed truly of two or more things, there is a condition, and we can state the condition, for its being affirmable truly of those things? If the predicate is "is red," then the condition is that each of the things is red (where in the clause, "The condition is that each of the things is red," we *use* the very same predicate that in the clause "the predicate is 'is red' " we mention). If the predicate is "is a bank," then the condition is that each of the things is a bank (where in the clause, "the condition is that each of the things is a bank" we *use* the very same predicate that we mention in the clause "the predicate is 'is a bank' "). And similarly, for all other terms.

It may be instructive to consider a case devised by Bambrough for the express purpose of showing that it is possible for a term to lack objective justification for its correct multiple affirmability: "The value and the limitations of the nominalist's claim that things which are called by the same name have nothing in common except that they are called by the same name can be seen if we look at a case where a set of objects literally and undeniably have nothing in common except that they are called by the same name. If I choose to give the name 'alpha' to each of a number of miscellaneous objects (the star Sirius, my fountain-pen, the Parthenon, the colour red, the number five, and the letter Z) then I may well succeed in choosing the objects so *arbitrarily* that I shall succeed in preventing them from having any feature in common, other than that I call them by the name 'alpha'."[6]

It seems to me that whether what is said here is true depends on what kind of word "alpha" is meant to be. Suppose it is meant

6. Bambrough, "Universals and Family Resemblance," p. 218.

to be a general term, that is, one which can with the same import be affirmed truly of more than one thing. Then it seems to me that the six things mentioned do not only have in common that they are called by the same name, "alpha," they have in common that they are all alphas (being an alpha). And because they are all alphas, one can correctly affirm "alpha" of them all. Of course, before "is alpha" could correctly be affirmed of them, "is alpha" had to be given some sense. And this Bambrough did by stipulating, in effect, that it is to be true of something if and only if that thing is the star Sirius or his fountain pen or the Parthenon or the color red or the number five or the letter Z. But now, this stipulation having taken place, "is alpha" can be correctly affirmed of just six things. For there are just six things which are alphas—that is, just six things which are the star Sirius or his fountain pen or the Parthenon or the color red or the number five or the letter Z. And "is alpha" can be correctly affirmed of all and only alphas.

But on the other hand, it may be that Bambrough is taking "alpha" as a proper name and then assigning this proper name to six different objects. Then, of course, all the six things named "alpha" do not have in common being alpha, or being an alpha, any more than Socrates has in common with all those named "Socrates," being Socrates. But if Bambrough is taking "alpha" as a proper name, he has not given us a genuine case in which the same term can be affirmed truly *with the same import* of two or more things. It can indeed be affirmed truly of two or more things, but only with different import.

4. What, then, about the predicate entailment principles, which we have found to be pivotal in two different sorts or arguments? Are they acceptable? Let us first consider properties, for example, the property of being red. To me it seems obviously true that if something is red, then it possesses the property of being red; and that if something possessses the property of being red, then there is such a property as being red, and then there is such a thing as being red. To me it seems plainly contradictory to allow that there are red barns and red stamps and red faces, and yet that there is no such thing as being red. Again, to me it seems obviously true that if something is wise, then it possesses wisdom;

and that if something possesses wisdom, then there is such a thing as wisdom. To me it seems plainly contradictory to allow that there are wise men and wise remarks, but that there is no such thing as wisdom. More generally, it seems to me to be the case that for every proposition of the form '*x is f*', such that there is a corresponding proposition of the form 'There is such a thing as *f-ness*', the former entails the latter. Since this general principle seems to me plainly applicable to propositions of the form '*x* is red' and '*x* is wise', and since there plainly are some red things and some wise things, I find myself forced to admit that there is such a thing as being red and such a thing as wisdom.

Secondly, the same sorts of remarks must be made about actions, for example, running. The man who holds that somebody runs, but that there is no such thing as running, seems to me plainly to contradict himself. In general, it seems to me to be the case that for every proposition of the form '*x is f*' such that there is a corresponding proposition of the form 'There is such a thing as *f-ing*', the former entails the latter. Since this general principle seems to me plainly applicable to propositions of the form '*x* runs', and since there plainly are some things that run, I find myself forced to admit that there is such a thing as running.

What is less clear to me is whether it is true that *every* proposition of the form '*x is-f*' entails a proposition of the form 'There is such a thing as *f-ity*' (whether every proposition of the form 'necessarily if something *is-f*, then there is such a thing as *f-ity*' is true). This principle might be called the general predicate entailment principle. Is it true?

One explanatory or qualifying comment must be made at once.[7]

Suppose that propositions of the form '*x* is necessarily greater than 7' are taken as equivalent to propositions of the form 'the proposition that *x* is greater than 7 is necessarily true.' Then the proposition '9 is necessarily greater than 7' is true, whereas the proposition 'The number of planets is necessarily greater than 7' is false. For the proposition '9 is greater than 7' is necessarily true, whereas the proposition 'The number of planets is greater

---

7. The need for this comment was first made clear to me by my colleague, Alvin Plantinga. See his article, "De Re and De Dicto" in *Nous* (September, 1969), pp. 235–258.

than 7' is not necessarily true. But in fact 9 is identical with the number of planets. Now suppose we regarded any proposition of the form 'x is necessarily greater than 7' as entailing that there is such a property as being necessarily greater than 7. Then we would have to allow that one and the same thing—which can be referred to with either "9" or with "the number of planets"—both has and lacks this property.

There are, though, powerful reasons for concluding that there is no such property as being necessarily greater than 7. For surely a condition of there being such a property as so-and-so is that some one thing cannot both have it and lack it. No predicate entailment principle, then, must commit us to holding that from '9 is necessarily greater than 7' it follows that there is such a property as being necessarily greater than 7.

What is to be said about this 'knot'?

Throughout our discussion in this chapter we have been speaking of propositions of subject-predicate form, and inquiring into their entailments. When we said that a proposition of the form 'x is-f' entails the corresponding proposition of the form 'there is such a thing as f-ity', it was from the beginning specified that "is-f" was standing in for logical predicates. Now suppose we regarded "is necessarily greater than 7" as a logical predicate. We would have to allow that the same predicate with the same import can be both true and false of some one thing. But that seems as impossible as that some single thing should both have and not have a certain property. Thus matters will be set aright if we keep in mind that it is a condition of, or if we take it as being a condition of, something's being a logical predicate, that it cannot, when affirmed with the same import of some one thing on two different occasions, be both true and false of that thing.

With this explanatory or qualifying comment in mind, is the general predicate entailment principle true? It seems to me that it is. My reason for thinking so, however, is not that I have any general argument *for* it, but rather that I know of no counter-examples *to* it.

But what about those philosophers who, though agreeing that there are properties, hold that there is no such thing as goodness, and those who, though agreeing that there are properties, hold that there is no such thing as existence? Can they subscribe to the general predicate entailment principle and still deny that there are such entities as goodness and existence? Yes, certainly. For it is open to them to deny that any sentences of the form 'x is good' or 'x exists' are genuine logical subject-logical predicate sentences. And I think—though there is no space here for substantiating this opinion—that all such philosophers would in fact hold this. They would not hold that though "Socrates exists" and "This lollipop is good" are genuine subject-predicate sentences, the propositions expressed with these do not entail 'There is such an entity as existence" and 'There is such an entity as goodness'. They would instead deny that these are genuine subject-predicate sentences.

5. Not only have I not offered any *positive* reason for thinking that the general predicate entailment principle is true; I have offered no reason at all for thinking that the particular predicate entailment principles cited are true. All I have done is put the principles vividly before us. For I know of no reason for believing that they are true; just as I know of no reason for believing, as I do, that somebody cannot think unless he exists. Nobody, and that includes the philosopher, can give reasons for all his beliefs.

But though all the specific predicate entailment principles which I have considered seem to me obviously true, I think there is no doubt that other philosophers would consider them all false. Why should this be? Why should it be that what seems obvious to one is denied by another?

Usually, resistance to predicate entailment principles will be grounded on the conviction that there are no properties and no actions. This conviction, in turn, may arise out of many different motivations. Let me suggest a few of them.

Perhaps some people are reluctant to admit that there is, say, such a thing as wisdom, because they think that they are thereby committing themselves to a certain view as to what wisdom is; and no doubt what most people fear is that they are thereby committing themselves to Plato's view, or to something very much like it. But in allowing that there is such a thing as wisdom, one is not committing oneself to any view *about* wisdom, to any view as to the nature of wisdom. One is indeed committing oneself to something which *is* of a certain nature, but not to propositions *about* that nature. What *is* the nature of wisdom is a matter still open for discussion. In one of the following chapters we will inquire into the nature of predicable universals, and into the force of the locution "there is such a thing as," when this is followed by a term standing for a property or action.

Another reason for reluctance to admit that there are predicable universals is adherence to the popular but puzzling dictum that we ought not to multiply entities beyond necessity. Seldom is it clear what is meant by this. What might sometimes be meant by it is that we ought not to say that there is or exists a certain entity, or that there are or exist entities of a certain sort, unless we find it necessary to do so. Or what might be meant is that we ought not to refer to entities unless we find it necessary to do so. Or what might be meant is that we ought not to commit ourselves to the being or existence of a certain entity, or of entities of a certain sort, unless we find it necessary to do so. And what we find it necessary to do is presumably to be determined by reference to some human purpose, other than the purpose of finding out and saying what there is. Whether this counsel, in any of the three versions we have suggested, is clear, and, if clear, whether it is ever good counsel to follow, are interesting questions. Just as interesting, and far more important, is the question as to what ought, in a general way, to be our human purposes. But these questions are all really irrelevant to our present consideration. For what we wish to do is find out whether there are predicable universals; whether for this or that purpose it is necessary to say that there are, or to refer to them, or to commit ourselves to them, is really quite a different matter. Or put it this way. We want to know whether, for the purpose of stating what there is, it is necessary to say that there are predicable universals. I realize, of course, that some philosophers have held that there is no objective reality against which we can test our claims—that we must all simply build for ourselves a theory which we find convenient and satisfying. The depth of our disagreement with this view will be apparent to the reader.

6

Abstraction

1. In the course of our day-to-day experience we often take note of, pay attention to, or consider, colored things, shaped things, loud things, things doing something with their hands, and so on. But we also frequently take note of or pay attention to or consider the colors of colored things, the shapes of shaped things, the loudnesses of loud things, those things which people are doing with their hands, and so on. In these latter cases, what we do is single out for attention some facet of a multifaceted thing. We abstract it from the other facets of the thing. We engage in what I shall call *abstractive attention*. It will shortly become clear why I use the rather indefinite word "facet" to state what it is that we attend to in a case of abstractive attention.

The fact that we engage in abstractive attention would seem to provide us with a new argument for the conclusion that there are properties and actions. For suppose that the thing, whose color I am abstractively attending to, is red in color. Then red is what is the color of the thing. And since what I am abstractively attending to is the color of the thing, what I am abstractively attending to is this: the color red. But the color red is a property; it is a predicable which some thing can have or possess. Hence, what I am abstractively attending to, when I abstractively attend to the color of this thing, is a property. Again, suppose that the person, such that I am abstractively attending to what he is doing with his hands, is making a model airplane with his hands. Then, making a model airplane is that which he is doing with his hands. And since what I am abstractively attending to is that which he is doing with his hands, what I am abstractively attending to is this: making a model airplane. But making a model airplane is an action; it is a predicable which something can do or engage in. Hence what I abstractively attend to, when I abstractively attend to what this person is doing with his hands, is an action. Now some property is the color of this thing only if this thing *exemplifies* that property (possesses the color). And some action is what this person is doing with his hands only if this person *exemplifies* that action (is engaged in doing that with his hands). So, in attending to the color of this thing, and what this person is doing with his hands, I am attending to an *exemplified* property, and an *exemplified* action. But from the fact that something exemplifies a certain property or a certain action, it follows, as we saw in the previous chapter, that there is such a thing as that property or that action. Hence, to repeat, the fact that we engage in abstractive attention seems to provide us with a new argument—or, better, a new set of arguments—for there being such entities as properties and actions.

It is worth noting that often we engage in abstractive attention by perceiving: by looking, by listening, by tasting, and the like. One notes the sweetness of the pie by tasting, one considers the loudness of the sound by listening, one attends to the color of the hat by looking. So if, in these and other cases, it is predicables that are the objects of abstractive attention, it follows that predicables are not merely objects of thought, but, rather, are objects which occur in our perceptual experience.

There are, of course, a number of points at which protest can be made against an argument of the sort indicated from a case of abstractive attention to the conclusion that there is a certain property or action. It seems to me that the most interesting and also the most promising is the following. In abstractively attending to something, we are not attending to a property which a certain thing has, or to an action which it is engaging in. Rather, we are attending to a *case* of a property or action. For example, in attending to the color of something red we are not attending to the color red, this being a certain property; we are attending to the redness of that thing (that thing's redness), this being a certain case of the color red. In attending to that which someone, who is making a model airplane, is doing with his hands, we are not attending to the action of making a model airplane; we are attending to a certain case of that action, the case which consists of that person's making a model airplane.

If we are to give this objection the evaluation which it deserves, we must first consider more closely what a case of a property or action is. For the recognition of such entities is almost wholly missing from modern and contemporary philosophical thought. And though, in previous chapters, we have spoken of *cases,* we have not explored the concept.

Already some examples have been provided of the distinction between a property or action, on the one hand, and a case of the property or action, on the other; this is the only way I am able to get the distinction across—by way of examples. One can distinguish between courage, and Wilson's courage (the courage of Wilson). The latter is a case of the former. One can distinguish between being courageous, and Wilson's being courageous. The latter is a case of the former. One can distinguish between walking home, and John's walking home. The latter is a case of the former. And one can distinguish between loving, and Romeo's loving Juliet. The latter is a case of the former.

These examples make it clear that if a certain property or action has a name, then normally one can get the name of a case of that property or action simply by taking the name of the property or action, plus a term designating some entity of which the property or action can be truly predicated, and putting the two together in the following fashion: "S's f-ness," or "the f-ness of S," or "S's f-ing," or "the f-ing by S." For example: "Napoleon's brashness," "the brashness of Napoleon," "Mary's coughing," "the coughing of Mary." Let us call all such expressions *abstractive descriptions.* It may be noted that color words do not seem to fit into the pattern described. One can speak of the blackness of my tire, but scarcely of the color blackness; and one can speak of the color black, but scarcely of my tire's black. So in the case of color, we seem to have words specially adapted to case designations ("blackness") and others to property designations ("black," "the color black").

Cases of *actions* are such that, for the most part, they occur (take place, happen) during (within) or at a certain stretch (duration, period) or moment of time. Bannister's running of the first four-minute mile took place during the year 1956. And Mary's coughing took place during the playing of the adagio movement of the concerto. Cases of *properties,* on the other hand, do not occur or take place or happen. They may, however, be present (last) for a stretch of time. Elroy's cockiness, for example, though it does not take place, may first appear at a certain time, be present during a stretch of time, and then disappear by a certain time and no longer be present. And also John's nervousness may be present only for a while. By no means is it *always* the case, however, that a case of a property is present in something *for a stretch of time.* Bannister's having won the first four-minute mile does not last for a time. It cannot disappear and no longer be present.

Though Socrates may have possessed wisdom, he did not possess *his* wisdom; and though Napoleon may have possessed brashness, he did not possess *his* brashness. Rather, Socrates' wisdom is that entity which stands to Socrates in the relationship of being the wisdom of him; and Napoleon's brashness is that entity which stands to Napoleon in the relationship of being the brashness of him. Schematically, S's f-ness (the f-ness of S) is that entity which stands to S in the relationship of being the f-ness of it. Similarly, though running the first four-minute mile is something that Bannister did, Bannister's running the first four-minute mile is not something that he did; and though coughing is something that Mary is doing, Mary's coughing is not something that she is doing. Rather, Bannister's running of the first four-minute mile is that entity which stands to Bannister in the relationship of being the running of the first four-minute mile by him; and Mary's coughing is that entity which stands to Mary in the relationship of being the coughing by Mary. Schematically, S's f-ing (the f-ing by S) is that entity which stands to S in the relationship of being the f-ing by it.

Socrates' wisdom is present (in him) at a certain time if and only if Socrates is wise at that time—that is, if and only if Socrates possesses wisdom at that time; and Napoleon's brashness is present (in him) at a certain time if and only if Napoleon is brash at that time—that is, if and only if Napoleon possesses brashness at that time. Schematically, S's f-ness is present (in S) at a certain time if and only if S has f-ness at that time. Similarly, Bannister's running of the first four-minute mile is taking place at a certain time if and only if Bannister is running the first four-minute mile at that time—that is, if and only if running the first four-minute mile is something that Bannister is doing at that time; and Mary's coughing is taking place at a certain time if and only if Mary is coughing at that time—that is, if and only if coughing is something that Mary is doing at that time. Schematically, S's f-ing is taking place at a certain time if and only if f-ing is something that S is doing at that time.

These observations make clear that there is a close connection between cases of predicables and true propositions. The case, Socrates' wisdom, is present (in him) if and only if the proposition 'Socrates is wise' is true; the case, Bannister's running the first four-minute mile, is taking place if and only if the proposition 'Bannister is running the first four-minute mile' is true. No doubt some readers will be inclined to go one step further and *identify* those cases which are present in some thing, and those which take place, with true propositions—that is, claim that each such case is identical with some (true) proposition. I think that this temptation should be resisted. Propositions can be asserted, and can be true or false, but it does not seem that any cases can be asserted, or that they can be true or false. Again, cases can be present or take place during a certain time, but it does not seem that any propositions can either be present or take place during a certain time. To give one specific example, Bannister's running the first four-minute mile was a great milestone in the history of sports. But it does not seem that any proposition at all is a great milestone in the history of sports.

It must be admitted, however, that these things merely *seem* to be so; it is not decisively clear that they are so. For it could be argued, along lines discussed in chapter 3, that these things which seem to be true of cases are really only reflections of what is in fact true of the language we use in speaking about cases. It might be argued, for example, that though normal usage does not permit of inserting "Socrates' wisdom" into the context "———— was asserted by someone," still Socrates' wisdom does have the property of being asserted by someone, it being identical with the proposition 'Socrates is wise'. Thus I know of no decisive arguments against the view that at least some cases are identical with true propositions. And if true propositions are in turn identical with facts—as seems plausible—then of course I also have no decisive argument against the view that at least some cases are identical with facts. Whether, conversely, *every* fact and true proposition is identical with some case or other will depend, in part, on whether such propositions as 'It is raining' and 'Nobody came by' are identical with any case. Further, it may even be that there are cases which are identical with *false* propositions. For it may be that cases can exist without being present in anything and without taking place.

It will be convenient to have some word for the relation which Socrates' wisdom bears to Socrates just when it is present in him (schematically: for the relation which S's f-ness bears to S just when it is present in it), and which Bannister's running the first four-minute mile bears to Bannister just when it is taking place (schematically: for the relation which S's f-ing bears to S just when it is taking place). Let us use the words, "is an aspect of." Socrates' wisdom is an aspect of Socrates just so long as it is present (in him); and Mary's coughing is an aspect of Mary just so long as it is taking place. Thus, when Socrates is wise, the relations between Socrates, wisdom, and Socrates' wisdom, are these. Socrates exemplifies wisdom, Socrates' wisdom is a case of wisdom, and Socrates' wisdom is an aspect of Socrates. And when Mary is coughing, the relations between Mary, coughing, and Mary's coughing, are these. Mary exemplifies coughing, Mary's coughing is a case of coughing, and Mary's coughing is an aspect of Mary.

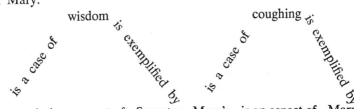

For any cases, *x* and *y,* a necessary condition of their identity is this: *x* is identical with *y* only if *x* and *y* are cases of the same predicable and aspects of the same entity. The circularity of my tire is not the same as the blackness of my hat, and Mary's sneezing is not the same as Mary's coughing.

Perhaps one thing that has hindered the recognition, in contemporary and modern philosophy, of cases (aspects) as a distinct category of entity, is the fact that abstractive descriptions can also plausibly be viewed, in many cases at least, as designating properties and actions, rather than cases of such. For example, if one has a certain brightness in mind, and has difficulty in communicating to someone just which brightness it is that he has in mind, he might try doing so with a definite description such as "The brightness of this light." In this case, the abstractive description, "the brightness of this light," would designate a property rather than a case of a property. Similarly, if one has difficulty in communicating to someone which loudness he has in mind, he might try doing so with such a definite description as "The loudness of that sound which you just heard." In this case, too, the abstractive description is used to designate a property rather than a case of a property.

The contention that abstractive descriptions can be used to designate properties and actions as well as cases of such is roundly denied by P.T. Geach. They can only be used, he holds, to stand for cases, or, as he calls them, individualized forms. This is what he says:

Let us consider phrases of the type 'the wisdom of Socrates'. . . . Philosophers try to construe this as 'wisdom that belongs to Socrates'; and then they ask what sort of entity wisdom is, and what sort of relation is here signified by 'belongs to'.
These discussions are, as Wittgenstein puts it, like barbarian misconstructions of civilized man's language. It is as though someone asked in regard to 'the square root of 4' what 'the' square root was, or how one number can be 'of', belong to, another number. Logically, we must divide the phrase thus: 'the square root of/4'; the first part of the phrase (or, better, the circumstance that this is followed by some number-expression or other) is the sign of a *function,* and the 'of' (or the genitive inflexion in other languages) does not stand for a special relation of *belonging to,* but indicates the way that the sign for a function needs completion with the sign of an *argument.* . . .
Similarly, we must divide 'the wisdom of/Socrates' in the way

shown: the first part of the phrase (or, better, the circumstance that it is followed by the name of an individual thing) is the sign of a *form;* the 'of', or the genitive inflexion, does not signify special relation, but merely indicates how the sign of a form needs completion with the sign of an object whose form it is. 'Wisdom' *tout court* means nothing in heaven or earth; wisdom is always wisdom-of—as Aquinas puts it, it is of-something (*entia*) rather than itself something (*ens*). A Platonist's belief in Wisdom is like my barbarian's wonder what The Square Root might be.

. . . A form is as it were a function that takes an individualized form as its value for a given individual as argument.[1]

Geach holds the view that the expression "the wisdom of Socrates" can be used to stand only for that individualized form which is the value of the form 'wisdom of' for the argument Socrates. He also holds that the component expression "the wisdom of" itself stands for what he calls a form—which he regards as a function-like entity. There is not, in addition to this individualized form (case) and this form *simpliciter* (function) some entity, wisdom. Clearly Geach means the same analysis to be given for all other abstractive descriptions. Further, he holds that the predicate "is wise" stands for the same thing as "the wisdom of"; and so also for all parallel cases. Thus it seems, on Geach's view, that there are no properties and actions, only function-like forms and what we have called cases (aspects). Geach compares the expression "the wisdom of Socrates" to the expression "the square root of 4." This latter, he rightly holds, designates that number which is the value of the function 'square root of' for the argument 4; and "square root of" itself stands for the function. Presumably Geach would likewise hold that the expression "the mother of Napoleon" stands for that person who is the value of the function 'mother of' for the argument Napoleon; "mother of" itself standing for the function (form) 'mother of'.

About these contentions I wish to make two comments.[2] In

1. G.E.M. Anscombe and P.T. Geach, *Three Philosophers* (Oxford, 1961), pp. 77–80.
2. Throughout these comments I shall speak, following Geach, only of functions, not of relations. However, I myself hold that, for example, if 2 is the value of the function 'square root of' for the argument 4, then 2 stands to 4 in the *relation* of being the square root of it. One suspects that Geach would disagree.

the first place, I agree that "the wisdom of Socrates" can be used to stand for that case, or individualized form, which is the value of the function 'wisdom of' for the argument Socrates. But it can also, it seems to me, be used to stand for that particular type or sort of *wisdom* which is the value of the function 'wisdom of' for the argument Socrates. This is what Geach overlooks. He argues that we must not try to divide "the wisdom of" into components. The whole phrase stands for a function-like form. To view it otherwise is, he says, to subject it to a barbarian misconception. But even if this were admitted, we can still view the whole phrase "the wisdom of Socrates" as standing for a certain property. Of course, then "wisdom of" must be viewed as capable of standing for two different functions, or forms.

But secondly, though it is quite correct to hold that "the wisdom of Socrates" can stand for that individualized form or case which is the value of the function 'wisdom of' for the argument Socrates, this, it seems to me, is nothing at all against the view that at the same time the entity it stands for is a value of the function 'case of' for the argument *wisdom*. Geach, of course, announces his view that there is no such thing as wisdom. But nothing he says constitutes a defense of this denial.

I think it is worth going on to note that though abstractive descriptions are, in form at least, definite descriptions, they differ in an interesting way from many, perhaps most, definite descriptions. Corresponding to definite descriptions of the form "The father of *a*" we have the common noun "a father." And corresponding to definite descriptions of the form "the square root of *a*" we have the common noun "a square root." In general, very often corresponding to an expression of the form "the K of *a*" we have a common noun, "a K." But this is for the most part not true of abstractive descriptions. Given that we have the phrase "the wisdom of Socrates," one would also expect the common noun "a wisdom." And further, given the ambiguity of "the wisdom of Socrates," one would expect that "a wisdom" was true both of cases of wisdom and types of wisdom. But in fact, we do not have this common noun in our speech at all. And generally, we do not have common nouns corresponding in the way indicated to abstractive descriptions. In this respect, there is resemblance between predicables and stuffs. Consider, for example, the expression "the water in this bucket." This expression is ambiguous in almost the same way that "the wisdom of Socrates" is ambiguous. It may designate either a quantity of water or a kind of water. Thus one would also expect there to be a common noun, "a water," which has two different senses—true both of quantities of water and sorts of water. But instead of being able to speak of a water, in these two different senses, we must speak of *a quantity of water,* or *a kind of water.* So too, lacking the common noun "a wisdom," we must compose a common noun for our purposes or, rather, two of them: "a case of wisdom" and "a kind of wisdom."

I have already remarked that the concept of aspects is almost wholly missing from modern and contemporary philosophical thought. It is possible, however, to find traces of it here and there, for example, in the following passage from G.F. Stout: ". . . of two billiard balls, each has its own particular roundness separate and distinct from that of the other, just as the billiard balls themselves are distinct and separate. As Jones is separate and distinct from Robinson, so the particular happiness of Jones is separate and distinct from that of Robinson."[3] This particular passage occurs in Stout's contribution to a symposium with G.E. Moore, and it is especially noteworthy that Moore finds it impossible to make anything at all of what Stout is saying. The concept can also be found in P.F. Strawson, who speaks of "particularized qualities";[4] and in D.C. Williams, who speaks of "abstract particulars."[5]

Though the concept of aspects is almost wholly absent from post-Cartesian thought, it loomed very large indeed in medieval philosophy. The medievals on this point, as on so many others, were reflecting their Platonic and Aristotelian heritage. It may be worthwhile, in concluding our attempt to make this concept clear, to cite one or two of the passages which perhaps were among their sources.

A passage from Plato in which it seems clear that he has

3. "Are the Characteristics of Particular Things Universal or Particular?" *Proceedings of the Aristotelian Society,* supp. vol. 3 (1923): 95–113.
4. *Individuals* (London, 1959), p. 168, and fn. 1, p. 168.
5. "On the Elements of Being," *The Review of Metaphysics* (September 1953), pp. 1–18, (December 1953), pp. 172–92. See also J. Cook Wilson, *Statement and Inference,* 1:349; 2:713.

aspects in mind is the following from the *Phaedo:* "Simmias is
not really taller because he is Simmias, but because of his height.
Nor again is he taller than Socrates because Socrates is Socrates,
but because of Socrates' shortness compared with Simmias' tallness. . . . Nor is Simmias shorter than Phaedo because Phaedo
is Phaedo, but because of Phaedo's tallness compared with
Simmias' shortness."[6] And again, slightly later, "It seems to me
not only that absolute greatness will never be great and small at
once, but also that greatness in us never admits smallness, and
will not be exceeded. . . . Just in the same way again smallness
in us will never become nor be great. . . ."[7] And again, this time
from the *Parmenides:* "And now tell me: have you yourself drawn
this distinction you speak of and separated apart on the one side
Forms themselves and on the other the things that share in them?
Do you believe that there is such a thing as Likeness itself apart
from the likeness that we possess, and so on with the Unity and
Plurality and all the terms in Zeno's argument that you have just
been listening to?" "Certainly I do, said Socrates."[8]

A passage from Aristotle in which the concept is quite clearly
expressed occurs at the beginning of the *Categories.* There
Aristotle distinguishes between those things which are predicable
of a subject and those things which are present in a subject. It
is the latter that here concern us. To explain what he has in
mind Aristotle says this: "By being 'present in a subject' I do
not mean present as parts are present in a whole, but being incapable of existence apart from the said subject. For instance, a
certain point of grammatical knowledge is present in the mind,
but is not predicable of any subject; or again, a certain whiteness
may be present in the body . . . yet is never predicable of anything."[9]

I trust that this concept of cases or aspects is now clearly
before us, and that we can therefore return to our original topic
of discussion. We suggested that one can abstractively attend to
properties and actions—to the loudness of a sound, the brightness of a light, the coughing by a person. We mentioned, how-

6. 102b-c (tr. F.J. Church).
7. 102d (tr. F.J. Church).
8. 130b (tr. F.M. Cornford).
9. 1a 22–30 (tr. E.M. Edghill).

ever, that an objection to this view would be that we never abstractively attend to properties and actions, but only to *cases* of these. And now the question to be considered is this: Can we somehow *show* that this objection is mistaken? Can we somehow *show* that we can and do abstractively attend to properties and actions, as well, perhaps, as to *cases* of these?

Let it first be said that there surely are some cases of abstractive attention which consist of attending to aspects (cases). Consider, for example, the sentence, "I noticed the circularity of the tire." If this sentence is used to assert something true, then "the circularity of the tire" must stand for a *case* of circularity. For suppose it were thought to stand for a certain property, namely, circularity. Something else than my tire can have this property; so, then, something else than my tire could have the circularity of my tire. But in fact it seems incoherent to hold that the circularity of my tire is also the circularity of, say, my steering wheel. If the circularity of something else *could* be the circularity of my tire, then by looking at that something else one would be able to attend to the circularity of my tire. But obviously it would just be bizarre for someone to say, when looking in the direction of my steering wheel, that he is taking note of the circularity of my tire. "The circularity of my tire" and "the circularity of my steering wheel" do not seem capable of being regarded as alternative definite descriptions of the same entity—a certain property. But the sentence, "I noticed the circularity of the tire" certainly can be used to assert something true. I conclude, then, that beyond a doubt there are cases of abstractively attending to aspects.

But on the other hand, there are surely some cases of abstractive attention which consist of attending to a property or action. For example, suppose that, pointing at a color chip on my desk, I say, "Look at that and you'll see the color of my new coat," and you do so. Or suppose that, pointing at my neighbor's car, I say to you, "Look over there and you'll see the shape of the car we're getting," and you do so. Or suppose that I am running a psycho-acoustical experiment and say to you, "Listen to this and you'll hear the loudness of the first tone I played," and you do so. In all such cases, you would be attending to properties. For you would see the color of my new coat by looking at the

paint chip; the color of the coat is also the color of the chip.
And you would see the shape of our car by looking at my neighbor's car; the shape of our car is also the shape of his. And you
would hear the loudness of the first tone by listening to the
second; the loudness of the first is also the loudness of the
second. Properties can be abstractively attended to. Similar
examples can be given for actions.

No doubt many cases of abstractive attention are such, however, that it simply is not clear whether the person is attending
to a property or an aspect; and perhaps there are also cases
in which the person is not definitely doing either the one or the
other. One test is whether what he attends to when, say, he
attends to the shape of one thing, can also be the shape of another
thing; and whether, consequently, he can also attend to it by
considering something else. But sometimes such questions cannot be asked; then it may have to remain unclear what he was
attending to. In other cases, the result of asking these questions
may be indecisive. Suppose, for example, that someone says
that he is taking note of the color of a certain sculpture. If we
then ask him whether the color of that sculpture is also the
color of this other one, he may say "Yes"; then it was a property
that he was attending to—a certain color, shared by two different things. On the other hand, he may say, "No, of course not,
the color of this sculpture cannot also be the color of that one";[10]
then it quite clearly was an aspect that he was attending to—the
particular color of that particular sculpture. But it may also be
that he hesitates to answer either Yes or No, or perhaps in the
course of a conservation he answers both. In such a case, perhaps
all that can rightly be concluded is that he is not definitely attending either to one sort or the other. And indeed, why *must* he be?
It must also be borne in mind that some properties and actions
cannot be exemplified by more than one thing.

Reflection on what we have been saying leads to the conclusion that some abstractive descriptions—"the color of my hat,"
"the shape of my car," "the color of this sculpture"—can be used
to stand either for a case or a property or action, depending
on the context. In this there is of course nothing surprising or

10. Cf. Stout, "The Characteristics of Particular Things."

puzzling. But it also leads to the conclusion that other abstractive descriptions—"the roundness of this ball," "the straightness of this line," "the circularity of my tire"—can only be used to stand for cases. And there is, I think, something surprising or puzzling in the fact that some abstractive descriptions are capable of dual function and others are not. Must we simply confess that our language is erratic at this point? Or can we spy some order and regularity in it?

I think that we *can* spy a certain degree of order and regularity here. In the first place, it seems to me that the reason such expressions as "the shape of so-and-so," "the color of so-and-so," "the wisdom of so-and-so," can all be used to stand for properties, is that there are different *sorts* of colors, of shapes, of wisdom. A person may then pick out the sort he has in mind either by naming it, or by identifying it as the sort which a given entity has. Color, shape, and wisdom are determinables with many determinants. Secondly, it seems to me that the reason such expressions as "the loudness of so-and-so," "the brightness of so-and-so," "the swiftness of so-and-so," can all be used to stand for properties is that there are different *degrees* of brightness, loudness, and swiftness. A person may then pick out the degree he has in mind by identifying it as that which a given entity has. But thirdly, there are neither sorts nor degrees of circularity and straightness and roundness.[11] It is for that reason, I think, that "the circularity of my tire" and "the straightness of this line" and "the roundness of this ball" can only be used to stand for cases. They cannot be used to pick out one from among all the sorts or degrees of circularity and straightness and roundness.

2. We have defended, against an important objection, the thesis that predicables—properties and actions—are the objects of abstractive attention. Now in abstractively attending to properties and actions, one is attending to *exemplified* properties and

11. Of course, one line can be straighter than another. But then it is more nearly *straight*. I am using the word "straight" above as it is used in its occurrence as the last word in the sentence preceding this one. What we count as straight, in this sense, will vary from situation to situation, depending on our interests. If we use the word in its other sense, then of course "the straightness of the rule" may well refer to a property—to a *degree* of straightness.

actions. But if one can abstract predicable universals from the things which exemplify them, it would seem that the predicables are there, objectively, in the things. It would seem that the phenomenon of abstractive attention is good ground not only for the conclusion that there are predicables, but also that these predicables are "in" the things of experience. But there is a long tradition of philosophical opinion which holds that though we can indeed abstract predicable universals from concrete things and make them the objects of our abstractive attention, yet it does not follow from this that there is anything at all which is universal in things. Everything outside the mind—so it is said—is individual, particular, singular; nothing is universal outside the mind. Things resemble each other outside the mind but do not share anything in common. Yet, it is possible to abstract predicable universals from the particular, singular, individual things of experience. The classic statement of this view is to be found in St. Thomas Aquinas. However, clear adumbrations of it are to be found in various of his predecessors, for example, Boethuis[12] and Abelard;[13] and the view is still clearly being espoused by John Locke.[14] We will do well to attend to St. Thomas' exposition of the view.

St. Thomas held that there is nothing at all which things jointly exemplify. It is frequently said about Aquinas that he held an *in re* theory of universals. It will be seen that in a certain sense this is correct. But certainly Aquinas did not hold that there is anything shared in common between two distinct things. For example, in *De Ente et Essentia,* chap. 3, he says: ". . . there is no commonness to be found in Socrates; whatever there is in him is individualized." And certainly this is the way that his devoted follower, John of St. Thomas, understood him.[15]

Yet, in spite of his view that there is nothing common between two distinct things, Aquinas held that there are forms and natures;

12. See "The Second Edition of the Commentaries on the Isagoge of Porphyry," in McKeon, ed., *Selections from Medieval Philosophy* (New York, 1957), 1:70–99.
13. See "The Glosses of Peter Abailard on Porphyry (Introduction)," ibid., pp. 208–58.
14. See *An Essay Concerning Human Understanding,* III, iii.
15. See *The Material Logic of John of St. Thomas,* tr. Simon, Glanville, and Hollenhorst (Chicago, 1955), pt. 2, "On the Universal," pp. 89–140.

and that these not only exist outside the mind in the singulars, but also that a given form or nature may be the form or nature of two or more distinct things. Human nature, for example, is the nature of Socrates and also the nature of Plato; it is the nature of both. And wisdom is a quality of Socrates and also a quality of Plato; it is one of the qualities of both.

We must see how Aquinas attempted to harmonize these views—that human nature and wisdom are of Socrates and of Plato both, and that there is nothing in Socrates and Plato which is common to both. Aquinas was of the view that forms and natures, when existing outside the mind, are always and necessarily "individualized" or, as he sometimes puts it, "determined to some particular existence." Human nature, as it exists outside the mind, is always the nature of some individual man. It may be the nature of Socrates, and it may also be the nature of Plato. But still, the nature of Socrates can not be identical with the nature of Plato. Of course, it is not *necessary* that human nature exist outside some mind, as the nature of some thing or things, but if it does, it must exist *individualized*. And of course it is not necessary that it exist as the nature, say, of Socrates and of Plato. But if it does, it must exist as determined to the existence of Socrates and also as determined to the existence of Plato. It must exist in Socrates as the nature of Socrates, and it must exist in Plato as the nature of Plato. That nature or form which exists in Socrates also exists in Plato. But form never exists as such. Outside the mind it always exists as individualized. Thus the nature of Socrates is not identical with the nature of Plato but, rather, is similar to it. "Forms which can be received in matter are individuated by matter . . . although form of itself, unless something else prevents it, can be received by many" (*Summa Theologica,* Ia, Q. 3, a. 2, ad 3). "Form is made finite by matter inasmuch as form, considered in itself, is common to many; but when received in matter, the form is determined to this one particular thing" (*S.T.,* Ia, Q. 7, a. 1, resp.).

Now the human mind, in confronting experience, has the power of abstraction. It can abstract one thing from another. It can attend to one thing and ignore the context of that thing. "For the intellect to abstract things which are not really abstract from one another, does not involve falsehood, as clearly appears in the case of the senses. For if we said that color is not in a colored body, or that it is separate from it, there would be error in what we thought or said. But if we consider color and its properties, without reference to the apple which is colored, or if we express in word what we thus understand, there is no error in such an opinion or assertion; for an apple is not essential to color, and therefore color can be understood independently of the apple. In the same way, the things which belong to the species of a material thing, such as a stone, or a man, or a horse, can be thought without the individual principles which do not belong to the notion of the species" (*S.T.,* Ia, Q. 85, a. 1, ad 1).

According to St. Thomas, the human mind, when it abstracts, abstracts forms and natures from their individuating circumstances. For example, it ignores the fact that human nature is determined to the singular existence of Socrates, of Plato, and the like, and simply attends to human nature. "It is proper to [the human intellect] to know form existing individually in corporeal matter, but not as existing in this individual matter. But to know what is in individual matter, yet not as existing in such matter, is to abstract the form from individual matter which is represented by the phantasms" (*S.T.,* Ia, Q. 85, a. 1, resp.). Of course, there is no necessity in human nature existing as the object of abstraction, and certainly there is no necessity in its existing this way in any particular intellect. Yet, it *can* exist in this state of abstraction in some intellect, and when it does so, it exists in the state of universality. For then it is no more determined to the existence of one man than to any other; it is "one single representation" of all. "Therefore the nature itself which suffers the act of being understood, or the act of being abstracted, or the intention of universality, exists only in individuals; but that it is understood, abstracted or considered as universal is in the intellect. We see something similar to this in the senses. For the sight *sees* the color of the apple apart from its smell. If therefore it be asked where is the color which is seen apart from the smell, it is quite clear that the color which is seen is only in the apple; but that it be perceived apart from the smell, this is owing to the sight, inasmuch as sight receives the likeness of color and not of smell. In like manner, the humanity which is understood exists only in this or that man; but that humanity be apprehended without the conditions of individuality, that is, that it be abstracted and consequently considered as universal, befalls humanity inasmuch as it is perceived by the intellect, in which there is a likeness of the specific nature, but not of the individual principles" (*S.T.,* Ia, Q. 85, a. 2, ad 2).[16]

Thus, according to Aquinas, human nature is in fact universal, and human nature in fact existed in Socrates and Plato. So there was in Socrates and Plato something which is universal. But it does not follow that it existed as universal in them. Rather, it existed as individualized in them. Similarly, human nature is in fact individualized, and human nature in fact exists in some mind. Hence there is something individualized which exists in some mind. But it does not follow that it exists as individualized in this mind. Rather, it exists as universal in this mind.

Perhaps an analogy will help us to see Aquinas' point here. Suppose that a certain person, John, is taciturn at home and voluble at work. Then, when John is at home, somebody who is voluble is at home. And, when John is at work, then somebody who is taciturn is at work. But it does not follow that John is voluble at home, or that there is somebody at home who is voluble at home. And it does not follow that John is taciturn at

16. "Now by matter the form of a thing is determined to some one thing. . . . The intellect . . . abstracts the species not only from matter, but also from the individuating conditions of matter . . ." (*S.T.,* Ia, Q. 84, a. 2, resp.). "The universal can be considered in two ways. First, the universal nature may be considered together with the intention of universality. And since the intention of universality—viz., the relation of one and the same to many—is due to intellectual abstraction, the universal thus considered is subsequent in our knowledge. . . . Secondly, the universal can be considered according to the nature itself (for instance, *animality* or *humanity*) as existing in the individual" (*S.T.,* Ia, Q. 85, a. 3, ad 1). "Our intellect cannot know the singular in material things directly and primarily. The reason for this is that the principle of singularity in material things is individual matter; whereas our intellect, as we have said above, understands by abstracting the intelligible species from such matter. Now what is abstracted from individual matter is universal" (*S.T.,* Ia, Q. 86, a. 1, resp.). "But matter is the principle of individuation, whereas the universal comes from the abstraction of the form from particular matter" (*S.T.,* Ia, Q. 86, a. 3, resp.). "For in the intellect, human nature itself has an existence that abstracts from all individualizing features; and as a consequence, it has exactly the same kind of relation to all the individuals that exist outside the soul, since it represents each of them equally and leads to a knowing of every one in so far as they are human beings" (*De Ente et Essentia,* chap. 3).

work, or that there is somebody at work who is taciturn at work. To say that John is taciturn, is incomplete; John is *taciturn at work*. And to say that he is voluble, is incomplete; he is *voluble at work*.

So also, humanity is individualized in the things and universal in the mind. Thus, when humanity is in the things, there is something which is universal which is in the things. And when humanity is in the mind, there is something which is individualized which is in the mind. But it does not follow that humanity is universal in the things, or that there is something in the things which is universal in the things. And it does not follow that humanity is individualized in the mind, or that there is something in the mind which is individualized in the mind. To say that humanity is individualized, is incomplete; it is individualized in the things. And to say that humanity is universal, is incomplete; it is universal in the mind.

According to Thomas, then, the very same forms and natures can exist both individualized and universalized—both outside the mind in the singulars, and in the mind by virtue of being abstracted from the singulars. But it does not follow from this that there is anything common in distinct entities. Of course, what is in fact universal exists *in re*—but always individualized.

This theory, ingenious as it is, suffers from a crucial and incurable ambiguity, or incoherence. Aquinas holds that human nature can be the nature of Socrates and also the nature of Plato. It can be individualized. The key question then is this. If human nature is the nature both of Socrates and of Plato, then is the nature of Socrates identical with the nature of Plato? To this question, Aquinas answers "No." But surely the answer must be "Yes" if the reference of "the nature of Socrates" and "the nature of Plato" is indeed the same as that of "human nature." If human nature is the nature of Socrates and also the nature of Plato, then the nature of Socrates is identical with the nature of Plato. On the other hand if "the nature of Socrates" and "the nature of Plato" are used to refer to different things, then neither of these phrases can be used to stand for that nature which is supposedly the nature of both. Then it is false that human nature is the nature of Socrates, and false that it is the nature of Plato, and certainly false that it is the nature of Socrates and also the nature of Plato.

It may be helpful to consider the following analogy. Water can be the stuff in this bucket, and water can be the stuff in that bucket. Suppose it is. Then, is the stuff in this bucket identical with the stuff in that bucket? Aquinas would presumably say "No." But if "the stuff in this bucket" and "the stuff in that bucket" are both used to designate water, then the answer must be "Yes." On the other hand, if these phrases are used, as they can be, to designate distinct quantities of that stuff which is water, then it is false that water is the stuff in this bucket, and false that water is the stuff in that bucket. For water is not the quantity of water in this bucket, nor is water the quantity of water in that bucket. Water is a stuff, not a quantity of stuff.

It was apparently Aquinas' view that human nature was one or many or zero in number, depending on how many men there were—one, many, or none; that wisdom was one or many or zero in number, depending on how many wise things there were— one, many, or none; and so on. Thus the number of a given form or nature was, on his view, contingent. A given form or nature is capable of being multiplied, though it need not be. And some of them are in fact multiplied, for example, human nature. Yet, Aquinas constantly refers to human nature with grammatically singular substantives—"human nature," "it," and the like. He says, for example, that "if the question is raised, 'Can this nature, looked at in this way, be called one or many?' neither of these alternatives should be admitted, because they are both outside of the concept of humanness, and either one is a possible adjunct to it. For if manyness were an essential constituent of the concept of human nature, human nature could never be a unit: although it is nevertheless a unit in as much as it is in Socrates. Similarly, if oneness were among its essential constituents, the human nature of Socrates and of Plato would in that case be one and the same, and it could never be numerically many, in several individuals" (*De Ente et Essentia*, chap. 3). And again, "In individuals it [human nature] also has a manifold existence according as these individuals are different" (*ibid*).

Now it seems to me that all this is incoherent. If there is indeed such an entity as human nature, then it is one entity, and cannot be identical with many or with none. Of course, it can have many *instances*. But quite clearly this is not what Aquinas had in mind; for the different instances of a given form or nature would have that form or nature in common. Aquinas perceived that Achilles, say, cannot be many (*S.T.*, Ia, Q. 13, a. 9, resp.). But he failed to see that human nature and wisdom also cannot be many, except in the sense of having many instances. Nothing at all, in fact, can be many. Neither forms and natures, nor anything else, are such that there can be many of each. Thus it seems that Aquinas' concept of individualized forms and natures is incoherent. If human nature is the nature both of Socrates and of Plato, then Socrates and Plato have something in common, namely, human nature. There are indeed what Geach calls individualized forms of wisdom, but there is not what Aquinas claims there is—the form wisdom, individualized.

As one might expect, the same ambiguity or incoherence appears when Aquinas speaks of abstraction. Suppose that "the nature of Socrates" and "the nature of Plato" are conceived as naming distinct things. Then one can indeed attend to the nature of Socrates without attending to Socrates and his individuating matter, and one can attend to the nature of Plato without attending to Plato and his individuating matter. One can, in short, abstract the nature of Socrates and abstract the nature of Plato. But then two distinct things have been abstracted, the nature of Socrates and the nature of Plato—not one distinct thing, human nature. On the other hand, if one can indeed abstract human nature both from Socrates and from Plato, then there must be one thing, human nature, there to be abstracted from both Socrates and Plato. And indeed, Aquinas does often speak of abstracting a given form from various distinct things. If one is abstractively attending to the nature of Plato and the nature of Socrates, then one is abstractively attending to either one thing or two things. One cannot be abstracting one thing which happens to be two—abstracting it by virtue of ignoring the fact that it is two. The activity of attending to one thing and ignoring the different accidental traits which may have accrued to it, must not be confused with the activity of attending to two similar things and ignoring their differences.

I conclude, then, that the phenomenon of abstractive attention is good ground for the conclusion that there are predicables, that they are in the things, and that some of them are such that different things may jointly exemplify them—may share them in common.

7

The Nature of
Predicable Entities

1. We have thus far been concerned to point out and establish that there are entities which can be predicated—*predicable entities,* we have called them. We have not said much as to the "nature" of such entities. But certainly in the case of universals, and predicable entities generally, this is a pressing question. For such entities seem elusive and hard to grasp. Constantly we come back to the questions "What *is* a property?" "What *is* an action?" "What *is* an assertible?" Even if it be granted that there *are* such entities, *what* are they?

We already have an answer, of sorts, to these questions. Properties, and actions, and assertibles, and relations, are, all of them, entities which can be predicated. All of them can play a role, the same role, in the human activity of predication. All of them can enter, and that in a uniform way, into this part of human life. All of them can be the *object* of the human activity of predication—that is, all of them can be *what* is predicated.

But this does not satisfy us. We do not feel that we yet know, well enough, what they are. So let us in this chapter inquire into the conditions for the *identity* and *diversity* of predicables. Let

150

us, further, try to discover conditions for the *being* of predicables. And let us briefly consider whether predicables can *act*.

Is sphericity the same property as circularity? Is courage the same property as bravery? Is being serious the same state as being solemn? Is loping the same action as running?

Under what conditions are such questions to be answered with "Yes"; and under what conditions are they to be answered with "No"? Or better, under what conditions, *if any*, are they to be answered with "Yes"; and under what, *if any*, with "No." For I do not wish to assume that there *must be* nontrivial necessary and sufficient conditions here. Some philosophers have suggested that unless we can find nontrivial necessary and sufficient conditions for the identity of predicables, we are not justified in asserting that there are such entities. I see no reason for following this suggestion. If the same demand were made of mountains, and lakes, and organisms, and persons, and symphonies, we would, so far as I can see, have to be silent as to the reality of all of these as well.

Let us begin by posing the following question. Under what conditions is that which a person predicates of something in one case of predication identical with that which he predicates of something in another case of predication? Suppose, for example, that a person predicates of someone that he is punctual, and also predicates of someone that he is prompt. Has he then predicated the same thing?

It is to be noticed, in the first place, that there is an intimate connection between the identity of properties and actions, on the one hand, and the identity of assertibles, on the other. A person predicates the same property or action of *x* and of *y* just in case he predicates the same assertible of *x* and of *y;* that is, just in case he says the same thing about *x* and about *y*. Suppose, for example, that someone says about something *that he is a brother,* and also says about something *that he is a male sibling.* In the former case he has also predicated of something the property of being a brother, and in the latter case the property of being a male sibling. And these properties are identical just in case these assertibles are identical.

The identity of assertibles, in turn, clearly has connections with the identity of propositions. It is possible, on two occasions of predication, to assert the same thing about the same thing without yet asserting the same thing, that is, without yet asserting the same proposition. If, for example, one assertively utters (in 1968) "The president of France is imperious" and also "De Gaulle is imperious," one has not then asserted the same proposition. Yet one has asserted about the same person, namely about De Gaulle, who is the president of France, the very same thing, namely, that he is imperious. But if, on two occasions, one asserts the same proposition and in so doing also asserts something about the same thing, then the same thing has been asserted about that thing; that is, then the same assertible has been predicated of it.

A condition of the identity of propositions is that it is impossible that they should be unlike in truth value. If it is possible that p is true and q false, or that p is false and q true, then p is not the same proposition as q. Correspondingly, a condition of the identity of assertibles is that it is impossible that the one be true of some thing and the other false of that thing. For any assertible x and any assertible y, if it is possible that x is true of some thing and y false of that thing, or that x is false of some thing and y true of that thing, then x is not the same assertible as y. For example, *that it is cantering* can be true of something when *that it is galloping* is not; accordingly, these are not identical assertibles. Similarly, a condition of the identity of properties is that it is impossible that something should have the one and lack the other; and a condition of the identity of actions is that it is impossible that one should be what some thing is doing and the other not be what that thing is doing. For any property x and any property y, if it is possible that something should have x and lack y, or lack x and have y, then x is not the same property as y. It is certainly possible, for example, that something should have whiteness and lack smoothness; hence these are not identical properties. And for any action x and any action y, if it is possible that x should be what something is doing while y is not something that it is doing, or if it is possible that y should be what something is doing while x is not something that it is doing, then x is not the same action as y. It is possible that *running the mile in less than five minutes* is what somebody is doing while *running the mile in less than four minutes* is not something that he is doing. Hence these are not identical actions.

It is not, however, a *guarantee* of the identity of propositions that they are necessarily alike in truth value. That every number has a successor, and that everything which thinks exists, are necessarily alike in truth value. Both are necessarily true. Yet certainly they are not the same proposition. In asserting the former, one does not assert the same thing that one does in asserting the latter. So also it is not a guarantee of the identity of assertibles that they are necessarily alike in what they are true of and what they are false of. That it has a shape and that it has a spatial size, are necessarily true and false of the same things. Yet they are not the same assertible. If someone said of something that it has a shape, and of the same thing that it has a spatial size, he would not have said or asserted the same thing about it. Similarly, it is not a guarantee of the identity of properties and actions that they are necessarily alike in their exemplifications. The property of having a shape and the property of having a spatial size are necessarily alike in this way, but they are clearly not identical properties.

Now suppose that by an *analytic* proposition, we mean one which is an instance of a law of truth-functional or quantificational logic. By this definition, 'A person is a sister if a sister' is clearly an analytic proposition, for it is a law of logic that every proposition of the form (x) $(Sx \supset Sx)$ is true. Further, it is probably also the case that the proposition 'A person is a female sibling if a sister' is analytic. For it seems likely that this is the very same proposition as 'A person is a sister if a sister'.

It is worth observing that the identity of propositions is not even guaranteed by the analyticity of the proposition claiming their equivalence. Consider, for example, the propositions 'A person is a sister if a sister' and 'A person is a brother if a brother'. Now the equivalence proposition 'A person is a sister if a sister if and only if a person is a brother if a brother' is analytic. It is an instance of the following law of logic. Every proposition of the form (x) $(Sx \supset Sx) \equiv (x)$ $(Bx \supset Bx)$ is true. Yet the proposition, 'A person is a sister if a sister' does not seem identical with the proposition, 'A person is a brother if a brother'. In asserting them, a person would not be asserting the same thing.

So also, the assertibles *that it is a sister if a sister* and *that it is a brother if a brother* are not identical; if one asserted these about something, he would be asserting two different things. Yet the following proposition is analytic. 'Everything is such that it is true of it that it is a sister if a sister, if and only if it is true of it that it is a brother if a brother'. Finally, the property of being a sister if a sister, and the property of being a brother if a brother, are not the same property; if one predicated them of something one would have predicated two different things. Yet this proposition is analytic: 'Everything is such that it has the property of being a sister if a sister, if and only if it has the property of being a brother if a brother'.

Thus far we have explored the interconnections between the identity of propositions, assertibles, properties, and actions. All of these are nonlinguistic entities. Let us now briefly reflect on how the identity of such entities is related to sentences and predicates.

We saw, in an earlier chapter, that the same propositions can be asserted with nonsynonymous sentences; synonymity of sentences is not a condition of identity of propositions. If someone, referring to the ancient Roman orator-statesman, assertively utters "Cicero is Cicero" and also "Cicero is Tully," he will, it seems, have asserted the same proposition. What he asserted in one case seems to have no entailments which what he asserted in the other case does not also have. Yet the sentence "Cicero is Cicero" does not seem to be synonymous with the sentence "Cicero is Tully." The difference between the two lies, of course, in the fact that where "Tully" occurs in the one, "Cicero" occurs in the other. But "Cicero" and "Tully" are not synonyms of each other. So also, *that he is Cicero* and *that he is Tully* seem to be the same assertible, though the predicates "is Cicero" and "is Tully" are not synonymous. And the property of being (identical with) Cicero seems to be identical with the property of being (identical with) Tully, though again, the predicates "is Cicero" and "is Tully" are not synonymous.

Not only is the synonymity of sentences not a condition of the identity of propositions, it is also not a guarantee of the identity of propositions. Indeed, as we saw in an earlier chapter, not even the identity of sentences is a guarantee of identity of propositions.

The sentence "He is ill," for example, is used to assert different propositions, depending on who is referred to and when it is uttered. Also, of course, different sentences can be used to assert the *same* proposition. If the sentence "He is ill" and the sentence "John is ill" are uttered at the same time and if the same person is referred to, then the same proposition will have been asserted.

The parallels are not at all difficult to draw out for assertibles, and for properties and actions. Consider, for example, the predicates "is giving him the book" and "is giving John the book." These are not identical predicates, nor are they synonymous. Yet a person, in predicating them of someone, may be asserting the same thing about that person, that is, predicating the same assertible of him; and he may also be predicating the same action of him. On the other hand, the single predicate "is giving him the book" may be used to assert different things about someone, in other words, to predicate different assertibles of someone. This will be the case if the predication is made at different times, or if "him" is used to stand for different persons. So also, this one predicate may be used to predicate various different actions of someone.

Thus we are led to the conclusion that the criterion for the identity of properties offered by Quine is not in fact acceptable. Quine says that "attributes . . . are individuated by this principle: two open sentences which determine the same class do not determine the same attribute unless they are analytically equivalent."[1] And again, ". . . two open sentences which determine the same class still determine distinct attributes unless they are analytically equivalent."[2] Now in Quine's usage, to say that the two open sentences 'x is a brother' and 'x is a male sibling' are analytically equivalent, is to say that the sentence "Everything is such that it is a brother if and only if it is a male sibling" is

---

1. *From a Logical Point of View*, p. 157.
2. Ibid., p. 152. Cf. Carnap: "Under what conditions properties are usually regarded as identical is less clear. It seems natural, and sufficiently in agreement with the vague customary usage, to regard properties as identical if it can be shown by logical means alone, without reference to facts, that whatever has the one property has the other and vice versa; in other words, if the equivalence sentence is not only true but L-true" (*Meaning and Necessity* [Chicago: University of Chicago Press, 1956], p. 18).

analytic. And, in turn, to say this is to say that this sentence is logically true or that it can be turned into a logically true sentence by putting synonyms for synonyms. By this criterion, the open sentences 'x gave him the book' and 'x gave John the book' are not analytically equivalent; and so also 'x is Cicero' and 'x is Tully' are not analytically equivalent. Yet we saw that, for each of these pairs, the one member of the pair may well be used to stand for the same property as the other member.

What *can* be said, however, is that predicates x and y stand for the same property or action just in case what is asserted about something by predicating x of it is the same as what is asserted about something by predicating y of it.

We said earlier that a condition, though not a guarantee, of the identity of some property, x, and some property, y, is that it be impossible for something to have x and not y, and y and not x; or, to put it the other way round, that it be necessarily true that whatever has x also has y, and whatever has y also has x. However, this claim, and the parallel claims for actions and assertibles, is subject to a possible and even rather natural misunderstanding which we ought at this juncture to guard against. Suppose, for example, that I am thinking of the property of being red. Then, obviously, the property which I am thinking of is identical with the property of being red. Yet it is not necessarily true that something has the property I am thinking of if and only if it has the property of being red; indeed, it is not necessarily true that the property I am thinking of is identical with the property of being red. For I might very well have been thinking of some other property; it is only contingently true that the property I am thinking of is the property of being red. And so, likewise, it is only contingently true that whatever has the property which I am thinking of also has the property of being red, and vice versa.

What *is* the case, however, is this. There is just one property of which I am in fact thinking, and it is necessarily true that *it* is identical with the property of being red. And similarly, the following is the case. There is just one property of which I am in fact thinking; and it is necessarily true that something has *it* if and only if it has the property of being red. So when we claim that properties are identical only if they are necessarily alike in their exemplifications, what we have in mind is a proposition of this latter sort. The property of which I am thinking is identical with the property of being red only if there is just one property of which I am thinking, and it is necessarily true that whatever has *it* also has the property of being red and vice versa. This condition may be satisfied even though it is not necessarily true that whatever has the property I am thinking of also has the property of being red and vice versa.

The example just given also makes it abundantly clear that it is not necessary that descriptive referring expressions be synonymous if they are to stand for the same predicable entities. "The property I am thinking of" and "The property of being red" are certainly not synonyms. Yet they may very well stand for the same property in a given case. It is also interesting to note that what "The property I am thinking of" stands for will seldom be the property which is predicated with the predicate "is the property I am thinking of." For the property predicated with this predicate is the property of *being the property I am thinking of.* And *being the property I am thinking of* will seldom be the property I am thinking of. Similarly, the color of my pencil may be identical with the color of this geranium. But being the color of my pencil is certainly not the same property as being the color of this geranium.

It should by no means be inferred from what has been said that empirical investigations are totally irrelevant to determining the identity of predicables. For clearly they are not. To take a simple example, let us suppose that "deep irene" is the standard name for the color which a certain species of geranium has, and that "rich crimson" is a standard name in the home-furnishings trade for a certain color of fabric. An interesting question might then be whether deep irene was the same color as rich crimson— whether being deep irene in color was the same property as being rich crimson in color. Anything other than an empirical investigation in such a case would probably be irrelevant. We know, of course, that they are the same just in case the assertible that it is deep irene is identical with the assertible that it is rich crimson. But how are we to tell whether this condition is satisfied? Again, we know that they are the same just in case what is asserted by uttering "This is deep irene" is the same as what is asserted by uttering "This is rich crimson," when "this" is used to stand for the same thing. But how are we to tell whether *this* condition is satisfied? Yet again, we know that they are *not* the same property if it is possible that something has the one and lacks the other. But how are we to tell whether *this* is the case? Quite clearly the thing to do is to bring together one of the indicated geraniums and a piece of the indicated drapery, and compare their colors. If there is no difference in color, then being deep irene in color is the same property as being rich crimson in color. Empirical investigations, in short, are often eminently relevant to determining the identity of predicables.

2. Is there such a property as being taupe in color? Is there such a property as being a 1001-sided plane figure? Is there such an action as running the mile in less than 3:50? Is there such a property as being a round square?

If a predicable, be it a universal or not, is exemplified, then there is such a thing as that predicable. A predicable cannot be exemplified and not be. But what about unexemplified predicables? Is it, or is it not, contradictory to hold that there is such-and-such a predicable but that it is unexemplified? For example, if there is such a property as being taupe in color, does it follow that something has the property of being taupe in color? And if there is such an action as running the mile in less than 3:50, does it follow that running the mile in less than 3:50 is what someone is doing? Or is it perhaps possible that there are predicables which are unexemplified? And if this is possible, is it then at least impossible that there should be predicables which *cannot* be exemplified? For example, if there is such a property as being taupe in color, does it follow that something *could* have it, though not that something *does* have it; and if there is such an action as running the mile in less than 3:50, does it follow that this is what something *could* be doing, though not that it is what something *is* doing? Or can one even hold consistently that there is such and such a predicable and that it *cannot* be exemplified? Is there, for example, such a property as being a round square even though nothing *can* have it; and is there such an action as going backwards in time even though this is something that nothing *can* do? The reader will recognize that in such questions, questions as to the criteria for the being of predicables, we have an ancient subject of controversy.

Before we make any attempt to determine the truth as to the conditions of, and the guarantees for, the being of predicables, let us delineate some alternative views on the matter.

On one possible view, the *being* of predicables is associated with the *exemplification* of predicables. This view has at least three reasonable versions. According to one version, a predicable must *now* be exemplified if it is to be. Thus, on this version, a proposition of the form 'There is such a predicable as *f-ness*' is true if and only if the corresponding one of the form 'There is now something which *is-f*' is true. For example, there is such a thing as brightness if and only if there is now something which is bright. A second version of this view differs from this first one in holding, not that a predicable must now be exemplified to be, but rather that it must now or in the past be exemplified to be. According to this version, a proposition of the form 'There is such a predicable as *f-ness*' is equivalent to the corresponding proposition of the form 'There is now or in the past something which *is-f*'. And yet a third version of this first view is the following. A proposition of the form 'There is such a thing as *f-ness*' is equivalent to the corresponding one of the form 'There is at some time or other something which *is-f*'.

Many predicables are such that it is a wholly contingent matter as to whether they are now, or now or in the past, exemplified; and many are such that it is a wholly contingent matter as to whether they are ever exemplified. Hence, on any version of this first view, it is a contingent matter, for many predicables, as to whether or not there are such predicables. Furthermore, since, according to the version first described, predicables have being just when they are exemplified, it is the case, according to this version, not only that predicables can come into being and go out of being, but even that predicables can have being intermittently; for it is clear that many predicables are such that they may at a certain time be exemplified, may later become un-exemplified, and may yet later be reexemplified. According to the second version described, however, predicables can come into being but not go out of being. And according to the third, they can neither come into nor go out of being. It is, of course, easy to conflate the three versions which we have distinguished. To do so, however, would inevitably yield confusion on the issue of whether or not predicables can come into and go out of being.

On a second possible view, the being of predicables is associated with the *possibility* of their exemplification. This view, too, has at least three reasonable versions. Suppose one characterized this view by saying that, though on this view it would be consistent to hold that there is such-and-such a predicable even though it is unexemplified, it would be inconsistent to hold that there is such-and-such a predicable and that it *cannot* (logically) be exemplified. One would then, I think, have presented an ambiguous characterization. For in using the words "It cannot be exemplified" one may mean *It cannot now be exemplified;* or one may mean *It cannot now or in the past be exemplified;* or one may mean *It cannot ever be exemplified.* Accordingly, one version of this view would be as follows. A proposition of the form 'There is such a predicable as *f-ness*' is equivalent to the corresponding proposition of the form 'It is possible that there is now something which *is-f*'. Another version of this view would be: A proposition of the form 'There is such a predicable as *f-ness*' is equivalent to the corresponding proposition of the form 'It is possible that there is now or in the past something which *is-f*'. And yet another version of this same general view would be this: A proposition of the form 'There is such a predicable as *f-ness*' is equivalent to the corresponding proposition of the form 'It is possible that there is at some time or other something which *is-f*'. That these versions yield different results can be seen from the following example. It is not possible that there is now (in 1968) something which is a space ship going to be destroyed in 1960; but it is possible that there is now or in the past, and also that there is at some time or other, something which is a space ship going to be destroyed in 1960. And it is not possible that there is now, nor that there is now or in the past, something which is a space ship constructed in 1975; but it is possible that there is at some time or other such a thing.

A consequence of either version of this second view is that whatever predicables there are, there are *necessarily*. If it is possible that there is now something which is red, or possible that there is now or in the past something which is red, or possible that there is at some time or other something which is red, then it is necessarily true that this is possible. It cannot fail to be true. Also, on the version which holds that there is such-and-such a predicable just in case it is possible that it is *sometime* exemplified, no predicables come into or go out of being. If it is ever true that it is possible that there is at some time or other something which is red, it is always true; and if it is ever false, it is always false. But on that version which holds that there is such-and-such a predicable just in case it is possible that it is *now* exemplified, predicables can come into and go out of being. For suppose that in 1956 I assertively utter: "It is possible that there is now something which is a space ship going to be destroyed in 1960." I would then have asserted something true; and so it would follow that there (then) is the property of being something which is a space ship going to be destroyed in 1960. But if I assertively utter this same sentence in any year after 1960, I would assert something false. And so it would follow that there (then) is not such a property. Finally, on the second version described, predicables can come into but not go out of being. It is, of course, easy to conflate these three different versions which we have distinguished. But, as for the previous view, to do so would be to confuse the issue as to whether or not, on this view, predicables can come into and go out of being.

On a third view, it would not even be inconsistent to hold that there is such-and-such a predicable but that it cannot possibly be exemplified—for example, that there is such a property as being a round square though nothing can possibly exemplify the property of being a round square. On this view, not only is there the property of not being a round square—a property which everything exemplifies; but also the property of being a round square—a property which nothing exemplifies, or *can* exemplify.

On this third view, there is such a predicable as being a round square just in case either there is something which is a round square or there is something which is not a round square. Can this point in some way be generalized? Can it be said that, on this third view, every proposition of the form 'There is such a predicable as *f-ness*, is true if and only if the corresponding one of the form 'There is something which *is-f* or there is something which *is-not-f*' is true? Earlier we argued that if there is something which exemplifies a certain predicable, then there is such a thing as that predicable. Is it also the case, on this third view, that if there is something which does not exemplify a certain predicable, then there is such a thing as that predicable?

I think that the answer to this must definitely be "No." For suppose that "is tove" is the predicable correlative to "the property which was last mentioned by John and which is and isn't red." And suppose we understand '*a* is tove' as true if and only if *a* exemplifies the property which was last mentioned by John and which is and isn't red; and '*a* is not tove' as true if and only if *a* does not exemplify the property which was last mentioned by John and which is and isn't red. Now, that it is true that something is not tove, seems clear enough. But it does not follow that there is such a property as being tove (that is, the property last mentioned by John and which is and isn't red). For the proposition 'There is such a thing as the property last mentioned by John and which is and isn't red' entails a contradiction, and is on that account false—necessarily false. On the other hand, by virtue of the predicate entailment principle, it does follow, from the fact that something is not tove, that there is such a thing as the property of not being tove (the property of lacking the property of being tove).

So one cannot characterize this third view as the view that every proposition of the form 'There is such a predicable as *f-ness*' is true if and only if the corresponding one of the form 'There is something which *is-f* or there is something which *is-not-f*' is true.

It is easily seen that nothing is gained if we characterize this third view as the view that every proposition of the form 'There is such a predicable as *f-ness*' is equivalent with the corresponding one of the form 'Either something *is-f* or it is not the case that something *is-f*'. It is of course true that there is something which is not red, while false that it's not the case that there is something which is red. Yet the disjunction 'Either there is something which is red or there is something which is not red' is equivalent to 'Either there is something which is red or it is not the case that there is something which is red'. The only circumstances under which these two disjunctions could vary in truth value would be that in which there was nothing at all; then the former would be false and the latter true. But this circumstance *could not* obtain, for it is impossible that there should be nothing at all.

On this third view, it is the case that there is such a property as being a round square if and only if either the property of being a round square is exemplified or the property of not being a round square is exemplified. But, as we have just seen, it is not the case that there is such a property as being tove if and only if the property of being tove is exemplified or the property of not being tove is exemplified. For the property of not being tove is exemplified; yet there is no such property as being tove. Thus, on the third view as well as on the other two views, a proposition of the form 'There is such a predicable as *non-f-ness* (*lacking f-ness*)' may be true while the corresponding one of the form 'There is such a predicable as *f-ness*' is false.

Let us explain this point more fully. One relation which holds between being a round square and not being a round square, is this: The relation such that necessarily everything exemplifies one or the other and nothing exemplifies both. Some thing does not exemplify the property of being a round square just in case it exemplifies the property of not being a round square; and some thing exemplifies the property of being a round square just in case it does not exemplify the property of not being a round square. On account of this relationship which they bear to each other, let us say that being a round square and not being a round square are *complements* of each other. And let us say of the members of *any* pair of predicables which stand in this relationship, that they are *complements* of each other. Thus the members of the pair consisting of the property of wisdom and the state of not being wise, are complements of each other. And so are the members of the pair consisting of the action of walking home and the state of not walking home. And so also are the members of the pair consisting of the assertible that it is red and the assertible that it is not red.

It should be noticed that the property of being a round square has a great many more complements than just the property of not being a round square. Consider, for example, the property of being identical with itself. Everything has this property—necessarily so. Whereas nothing can have the property of being a round square. And so these are complements of each other. Nothing can exemplify both, and everything must exemplify one or the other.

From among those pairs of predicables which are complements of each other, it is possible to pick out those which are what I shall call *negatives* of each other—the property of not being a round square is a negative of the property of being a round square, whereas the property of being identical with itself is not a negative of it. The relationship is as follows. The property of not being a round square is identical with the property of lacking the property of being a round square. And in general, some property x is the negative of some property y if and only if the property x is identical with the property of lacking the property y.

Now it might initially have been thought that, on this third view, for every predicable which there is, there is also a negative of that predicable. We have seen, however, that this is not the case. There is such a property as not being tove, but this property has no negative. Or again, consider the property of not exemplifying itself. If this property exemplifies itself, then it does not exemplify itself. And if this property does not exemplify itself, then it does exemplify itself. But that is impossible. So there can be no such property. Counter to one's intuition, it is not, for example, the case that wisdom exemplifies the property of not exemplifying itself. However, there seems no reason to deny that there is such a thing as the property of exemplifying itself. The property of being a property would seem, in fact, to exemplify it. Hence, the property of exemplifying itself has no negative.

Thus neither on this third view, nor on the other two, is it the case that there is such a thing as the predicable *f-ness* if and only if either something exemplifies *f-ness* or something exemplifies the negative of *f-ness*. It is true that there is such a property as being a round square just in case either something exemplifies being a round square or something exemplifies not being a round square. But the *general* principle cannot be accepted. It is not true that there is such a property as not exemplifying itself if and only if either something exemplifies the property of not exemplifying itself or something exemplifies the negative of it. It is agreed that nothing exemplifies this property, since there is no such property to be exemplified. But it is the case that something exemplifies its negative, the property of exemplifying itself. Accordingly, the acceptance of this general principle would commit us to holding that there is such a property as not exemplifying itself—an untenable consequence.

We are still left with the question as to whether it is possible to give any general characterization of this third view. We have seen that the view cannot be characterized as the view that every proposition of the following form is true. 'There is such a thing as *f-ness* if and only if either something *is-f* or something *is-not-f*'. And we have seen that it also cannot be characterized as the view that every proposition of the following form is true. 'There is such a thing as *f-ness* if and only if either something *is-f* or it is not the case that something *is-f*'. But if these characterizations are not satisfactory, what else would be?

The cases which we have considered of the breakdown of these principles were ones in which a proposition of the form 'There is such a thing as *f-ness*' entailed something which violated some law of logic. One is then tempted simply to attach, to either of the criteria we have considered, the proviso that the proposition of the form 'There is such a thing as *f-ness*' not entail something which violates some law of logic. The full criterion would then be the following. Every proposition of the form 'There is such a predicable as *f-ness*' which does not entail the denial of some law of logic, is true if and only if the corresponding proposition of the form 'Either something *is-f* or something *is-not-f*' is true. But now suppose that "is tuve" be used as a predicate correlative to "The property which was just mentioned by John and which thinks." It seems clear that there is no such property; for no property at all can think. Yet it is the case that there is something which is not tuve. In this case, what leads us to conclude that there is no such property as being tuve, is that the claim that there is this property entails what we recognize to be a necessary falsehood.

We naturally wonder, then, whether a person who held the third view would hold the following principle. Every proposition of the form 'There is such a thing as *f-ness*' which does not entail some necessary falsehood is true if and only if the corresponding one of the form 'Either something *is-f* or something *is-not-f*' is true. But not even this is satisfactory. For suppose that "is tave" be used as a predicate correlative to "the property mentioned on the first page of this book." Now in fact there is no property mentioned on the first page of this book, though there might have been one such. Yet it is the case that there is something which is not tave; indeed, everything is such that it is not tave.

So we have not yet found a general characterization of this third view. And in fact, I am not able to provide a general characterization of it. The lineaments of the view have been made fairly clear by way of the examples we have offered. But a general statement of this view is something which eludes me.

What, then, is the truth on the issue raised at the beginning of this section? What is the criterion for the being of predicables? Are there predicables which are now unexemplified? Are there predicables which are never exemplified? Are there predicables which cannot now be exemplified? Are there predicables which cannot *ever* be exemplified?

Which of the views that we have explored concerning such a proposition as 'There is such an action as running' is the correct one? Does such a proposition have the equivalence which one or another version of the first view claims that it has? Or does it have the equivalence which one or another version of the second view claims that it has? Or does the third view give us a correct interpretation of the logical relations of such a proposition?

When someone asks, What is the criterion, the logical equivalence, of such a proposition as 'There is such an action as running,' the best answer is, it seems to me, that it all depends on which proposition he is referring to with the name, " 'There is such an action as running'." For this name can naturally be used to refer to several different propositions; until it is made clear which one is being referred to, one cannot without confusion inquire into its logical equivalences. The words "there is," when used in speaking of predicables, are seriously ambiguous; they can be naturally used to make a variety of different claims. Hence, questions as to the criteria for the being of predicables cannot be settled until one makes it clear how one is using the words "there is," along with derivatives of these words.

The words "there is," when used in speaking of predicables, can naturally be used to assert propositions whose equivalences are correctly explicated by one or another version of the first view we have discussed. They can also be naturally used to assert propositions whose equivalences are correctly explicated by one or another version of the second view we have discussed. And they can also be naturally used to assert propositions whose equivalences are correctly explicated by the third view we discussed.

Consider, for example, the sentence, "There's no such thing as genuine humility." Such a sentence can naturally be used to make a claim equivalent to the proposition that nothing ever exemplifies genuine humility. Indeed, this is perhaps the *most* natural use of this sentence. And so also, the sentence, "There's no such thing as honest self-appraisal" can very naturally be used to make a claim whose equivalence is in accord with one or the other version of the first view we have discussed. Or again, consider such sentences as "Chastity has disappeared," "Integrity has been lost," and "Beauty, grace, and sensitivity have been destroyed by our modern mass culture." The first of these might naturally be used to assert a proposition which is true in case there are no exemplifications of chastity though once there were; the second, to assert a proposition which is true in case there are no exemplifications of integrity though once there were; and similarly for the third. Thus in such sentences we find a reflection of the first view we discussed. And yet again, the Anti-Defamation League will have succeeded in eliminating defamation just in case it eliminates all present and future exemplifications thereof; the Society for the Prevention of Cruelty to Animals will have succeeded in eradicating cruelty to animals just in case it eradicates all present and future exemplifications thereof; and the anti-poverty campaign will have succeeded in wiping out poverty just in case it wipes out all present and future exemplifications thereof.

On the other hand, consider the sentence "There's no such property as being a round square." Such a sentence might very naturally be used to make a claim equivalent to the proposition that it is impossible that something should ever be a round square. And the sentence, "There's no such action as going backward in time" might very naturally be used to make a claim equivalent to the proposition that it is impossible that something should ever go backward in time. And the sentence, "There is such a color as taupe" can certainly very naturally be used to make a claim equivalent to the proposition that it is possible that something should be taupe in color.

Lastly, consider the sentence, "There is such a property as being a round square." Such a sentence can, not unnaturally, be used to assert a proposition which is equivalent neither to the claim that it is sometime exemplified, nor to the claim that it is possibly sometime exemplified.

In short, the force of "there is," when used in the context of discussion about predicables, is ambiguous; and many disagreements as to whether or not there is such-and-such a predicable are no doubt linguistic rather than ontological in source. In particular, disagreements as to whether or not there are unexemplified predicables, and disagreements as to whether or not there are unexemplifiable predicables, seems to me to be linguistic in source. Such disputes are to be resolved by deciding whether to use words of the form "There is such a thing as the predicable x" to assert a proposition equivalent to the claim that the predicable x is now exemplified, or is now or in the past exemplified, or is sometimes exemplified, or is possibly now exemplified, or is possibly now or in the past exemplified, or is possibly sometime exemplified; or to use them to assert a proposition which does not even entail that x is possibly sometime exemplified.

If these contentions are correct, then nominalism in respect to predicables is a thoroughly untenable view. In an earlier chapter, we asserted the validity of the predicate entailment principle. We held, for example, that 'Something is wise' entails 'There is such a thing as wisdom'. It is natural now to inquire which proposition we had in mind when we used the words, "There is such a thing as wisdom"—the one whose logical relations are expressed by the first view, the one whose logical relations are expressed by the second view, or the one whose logical relations are expressed by the third view. The answer is, it makes no difference. In any case, the entailment holds. But what then are we to make of the person who holds that 'Something is wise' does not entail 'There is such a thing as wisdom'? Obviously he will have to reject all three of the views we have explored concerning the logical equivalence of 'There is such a thing as wisdom'. For if he accepted any of the three, his case would be lost. And yet, so far as I can see, invariably when people in ordinary speech use "there is" in connection with predicables, the logical relations of the proposition they mean to assert are explicated by one or the other of these three views. Thus it becomes incumbent on the nominalist to explain, if he can, what he takes to be the criteria for the being of predicables. He claims that there is no such entity as being red. Under what conditions, according to him, would his claim be false?

It is possible, however, to cast our conclusions in this chapter and in chapter 5 in quite a different light. At the beginning of chapter 5, we identified the nub of the issue between realism and nominalism (*re* predicables): the realist claims that there are predicables, the nominalist denies that there are predicables. And though we there *defined* "realism" and "nominalism," we intended that there should be considerable overlap between the class of thinkers who would be realists by our definition, and the class of thinkers who in the philosophical literature are customarily, though vaguely, called realists; and so also, considerable overlap between the class of those who are nominalists by our definition and the class of those who would customarily be called nominalists.

I think that anyone who has worked through our contentions in this present chapter has the feeling that it is 'nominalistic' in tone—that it would more readily be agreed to by those who are customarily called 'nominalists' than by those who are customarily called 'realists'.[3] And this suggests at once that there is another issue at stake between 'realists' and 'nominalists' than the one we located earlier, an issue usually not clearly differentiated from that earlier one. This is the issue as to the *force* of the claim that there are predicables, not as to its truth. Given our discussion in this chapter, it is clear that there are many different positions

3. When using the words "realist" and "nominalist" in their loose customary sense, rather than in the sense *defined* earlier, I shall put single quotes around them.

possible on this matter. All the positions we have discussed, however, probably have a 'nominalistic' ring to them. One might, then, regard a "realist"[4] as one who holds that when a sentence of the form "There is such a thing as *f-ity*" is uttered with normal sense, none of our three views explicate the equivalences of the proposition asserted. The third view does not explicate the equivalences; nor can the equivalences be explicated by reference to possible exemplifications; nor can they be explicated by reference to actual exemplifications.[5]

And now, of course, the burden is placed on the realist. It now becomes a serious obligation on his part to explain what he does take to be the criteria for the being of predicables. He approves of none of the 'nominalistic' suggestions made. Yet he claims that there is such an entity as being red. Should he not then tell us under what conditions his claim, according to him, would be false?

The upshot of the entire matter is perhaps that traditional 'realism' and 'nominalism' involve, in confused fashion, two different issues. On one of these issues we side, in chapter 5, with the 'realists'. On the other we side, in this chapter, with the 'nominalists'. Our position is that of realism and "nominalism."

Is rapprochement between two such ancient armies possible?

3. We have considered the identity and the being of predicables. Let us now briefly raise the question as to whether predicables can act and do things; whether an action can ever correctly be predicated of a predicable. Does the question "What is it doing?" or "What does it do?" asked of a predicable, ever have a correct answer? Or do predicables enter only passively into the course of history and human affairs?

I think that we all have the inclination, for whatever reason,

4. When using the words "realist" and "nominalist" in their *new, defined* sense, I shall henceforth put double quotes around them.
5. We have perhaps not considered *all* the plausible 'nominalistic' views. An additional one would be the following. Sometimes, at least, in using a sentence of the form 'There is such a thing as *f-ity*' with normal sense, one asserts a proposition equivalent to the corresponding proposition of the form 'It is *causally* possible that something is (was, will be) *f*'. Thus when I speak, in the text above, about explicating by reference to *possible* exemplifications, we should allow this word "possible" to mean either causally or logically possible.

to say that predicables cannot act and do things. Yet it would seem that we do often predicate actions of them; and in some such cases, at least, it seems that what we thereby assert is true. Consider, for example, the following sentences:[6]

Immortality has fascinated some and repelled others.
The predetermined salvation of the elect has depressed many but elated others.
Poverty often leads to warping of character.
Envy caused his lashing out at Peter.
Obesity caused his death.
Darkness, and with it quietness, decended upon the camp.
Death eventually overtakes all men.

It would seem that each of these sentences can be used to assert something true. And it would furthermore seem that in assertively uttering each of them one is predicating an action of some predicable.

However, with respect to the first two examples, the question to raise is whether the verbs "to fascinate," "to repel," "to depress," and "to elate," as these are here used, genuinely stand for actions. One is fascinated, repelled, depressed, elated, *by* something. But is it true that in every such case fascinating, repelling, depressing, and elating, are actions—things that something is doing? Repelling is of course something that one person can do with respect to someone else; it is an action that can be performed. But when an ugly sight repels me, that is, when I am repelled by an ugly sight, surely it is not at all clear that repelling is something that the ugly sight is doing with respect to me. And possibly *depressing* is one of the things that one person can do with respect to another. But it would seem that someone can depress me without his thereby performing the action of depressing me—without *depressing me* being one of the things that he is doing. It would seem that our first two examples should be understood along these lines. Though some people are depressed by the predetermined salvation of the elect, what they are depressed by does not perform the action of depressing them.

The next three examples are different. With respect to these

6. I owe the first two of these examples to my publisher's reader.

it is worth noting that what is done by the predicable is done by it just in case it is also done by some or all of its cases or instances. Poverty leads to the warping of character just in the event that *cases of poverty* lead to the warping of character. Envy caused his lashing out at Peter just in case *his envy* caused his lashing out at Peter. Obesity caused his death just in case *his obesity* caused his death.

It is not at all evident that this principle applies to the last two examples we have offered; indeed, it is evident that it does not apply to the last. It is not at all clear that darkness and quietness descend over the camp just when cases of darkness and quietness descend over the camp. And it is clearly false that death overtakes all men just in the event that some case of death overtakes every man. I think the problem here is that these sentences are metaphorical, and that the latter one, furthermore, personifies death. Do quietness and darkness literally *descend?* Does death literally *overtake?*

Thus our examples divide themselves into three groups. In some cases, it is not at all clear that it is genuinely an *action* that we have predicated. In other cases, the predicable performs the action just in case some or all of its instances or cases do so. And in yet a third sort of case, it is not really the case that some action is predicated of a predicable; it is only *metaphorically* so.

8

Identification

1. To many, predicables seem strange, mysterious, puzzling sorts of entities. And so, throughout the history of philosophical thought, there have been persistent and recurrent attempts to domesticate them. Some philosophers have claimed that they are *really* identical with one or another familiar sort of entity. Some have claimed that every concept of a predicable is identical with some concept of nonpredicables. And some have claimed that whatever can be said by referring to a predicable and by using terms true only of predicables can also be said without referring to any predicable and without using terms true only of predicables. In this and the following chapter we shall discuss these various ways of trying to make predicables "housebroken."

A recurrent suggestion in the history of philosophy has been that predicables, especially predicable universals, are all to be identified with sets (classes) of nonpredicables. A close parallel to this suggestion was already current at the time of Abelard. For Abelard says that "some hold that the universal thing is only in a collection of many. They in no manner call Socrates and Plato species in themselves, but they say that all men collected together are that species which is man, and all animals taken together that genus which is animal, and thus with the others."[1] The claim which Abelard reports as being made is that species and genera—for example, man and animal—are to be identified with sets of nonspecies and nongenera. And it is but a small step from this to the suggestion that predicable universals—whiteness and circularity, for example—are to be identified with sets of nonpredicables.

I think that, in fact, there are no classes with which any predicables are identical. For all classes except the null class have members, whereas no predicables have members. And no classes have instances or cases, whereas some predicables have instances and cases. Further, all predicables can be predicated (by definition, of course), whereas no classes can be predicated. It is true of circularity, for example, that it can be predicated of something, that my spare tire is an instance of it, and that my spare tire's circularity is a case of it. It is, however, false of circularity that my spare tire, or my spare tire's circularity, is a *member* of it. On the other hand, it is true of my spare tire that it is a member of the class of all and only circular things, and of my spare tire's circularity that it is a member of the class of all and only circularities (cases of circularity). But it is false of the class of all and only circular things that my spare tire is an *instance* of it; it is false of the class of all and only circularities that my spare tire's circularity is a *case* of it; and it is false of each of these classes that it can be *predicated* of something.

These points, however, will in all likelihood not prove persuasive to all readers, for reasons suggested by our discussion in chapter 3. Some readers will no doubt hold that it is not *really* the case that certain things which are true of sets are not true of predicables, and that certain things which are true of predicables are not true of sets. Rather, what is really the case is that there are systematic differences in the use of what may be called *class-terms* and *predicable-terms*. "Circularity" and "the class of all circularities" designate the same entity. But the latter of these expressions can with sense follow the words "is a member of," whereas the former cannot. And the former can with sense follow the words "predicated" and "is an instance of"

1. "The Glosses of Peter Abailard on Porphyry," in Richard McKeon, ed., *Selections from Medieval Philosophers* (New York, 1957), 1:228.

and "is a case of," whereas the latter cannot. Thus it is not the case that what is asserted with any sentence of the form "*S* is a member of circularity" is false, but rather that these words lack a normal sense; and likewise, it is not the case that what is asserted with any sentence of the form "*S* is an instance of the class of all circular things" is false, but that these words lack a normal sense. Classes *do* have instances; but one cannot with sense use the words "is an instance of the class of all circular things." And predicables *do* have members; but one cannot with sense use the words "is a member of circularity."

Are there then any other considerations, more decisive than these, which militate against the identification of predicables with sets?

Let us ask, With which sets are predicables to be identified? For example, with which set are we to identify *being white?* With which set, *circularity?* And with which set, *running?*

The suggestion which comes first to mind is that being white is to be identified with the class of all and only those things which are white; that circularity is to be identified with the class of all and only those things which are circular; and that running is to be identified with the class of all and only those things which are running. Or the suggestion could be stated, alternatively, by reference to the similiarities among things. Being white is to be identified with the class of all and only those things which resemble each other in that they are white; circularity is to be identified with the class of all and only those things which resemble each other in that they are circular; and running is to be identified with the class of all and only those things which resemble each other in that they are running. In short, the suggestion is that a predicable is to be identified with the set of all and only its *exemplifications,* so that its exemplifications are the members of this class.

But there is a rather obvious and decisive objection to this suggestion. Consider something which was red but is not red. This, of course, is not a member of the class of all and only those things which *are* red; nor *was* it a member of the class of all and only those things which *are* red. It is not true of the class of all and only those things which *are* red, that that thing is a member of it, nor that it *was* a member of it. It is the case, however, that that thing exemplified the property red. That is to say, it is true of red that that thing exemplified it. I conclude, then, that red is not identical with the class of all and only those things which are red. And in general, a predicable is not to be identified with the class of all and only those things which are its exemplifications.

It is not difficult to see how this particular defect can be corrected. The suggestion must be that a predicable is identical with the set of all and only the exemplifications which it *ever* has. For example, the suggestion must be that red is identical with the class of all and only its past, present, and future exemplifications.

But consider the predicables, *being a closed three-sided plane figure,* and *being a closed plane figure the sum of whose internal angles is 180°.* The suggestion is that the former of these is identical with the class of all those things which are ever closed three-sided plane figures, and that the latter is identical with the class of all those things which are ever closed plane figures the sum of whose internal angles is 180°. But if this were so, it would follow that these two predicables were identical. For whatever is a member of one of these classes is a member of the other; and since classes are identical just in case nothing is a member of one and not the other, these classes are identical. But in fact the predicable *being a closed three-sided plane figure,* and the predicable *being a closed plane figure the sum of whose internal angles is 180°,* are not identical.

This particular difficulty would of course be avoided if just one of these predicables were identified with this one class—if, for example, being a closed three-sided plane figure were identified with the class of all those things which are ever closed plane figures the sum of whose internal angles is 180° (which is also the class of all those things which are ever closed three-sided plane figures). But then, with which class could we identify the *other* predicable? It should also be noticed that a consequence of this view is that there is only one predicable which has no exemplifications, namely, the null class. Being a round square, and being a married bachelor, would have to be regarded as identical.

The difficulty in identifying a predicable with the class of all exemplifications it ever has, arises from the fact that classes are identical just in case there is nothing which is a member of one and not of the other, whereas it is not the case that predicables are identical just in case there is nothing which exemplifies one and not the other. But if it is not the case that every predicable is identical with the class of all the exemplifications it has, nor with the class of all the exemplifications it ever has, it is hard to see with which class of its exemplifications every predicable *could* be identified. If we wish to identify predicables with classes, I think that we shall have to look for something other than classes of *exemplifications* with which to identify them.

In our earlier discussions we distinguished between *exemplifications* and *cases* of predicable universals. The difficulty which has impeded us thus far is that two different predicables may have all the same exemplifications—sometimes necessarily so. But, obviously, if two different predicables have any cases at all, they will never have all the same cases. Indeed, one and the same thing can never be a case of two different predicable universals. One and the same thing may be a closed three-sided plane figure, and a closed plane figure the sum of whose internal angles is 180°. But even so, that thing's being a closed three-sided plane figure is distinct from that thing's being a closed plane figure the sum of whose internal angles is 180°. Suppose, then that it be suggested that a predicable is identical with the class of all its (past, present, and future) cases, so that its cases are the members of this class. For example, suppose it be suggested that circularity is identical, not with the class of all (past, present, and future) circular things, but rather with the class of all circularities? Is this correct?

Of every class it is true that it is impossible that it should have or should have had a different membership from that which it does in fact have. A class has its particular membership essentially. Of course, different things might have been red than those which are, and in that case the expression "the class of all those things which are red" would have designated something different from what it does designate. But whatever class it is that it does in fact designate, *that* could not have had a different membership from what it has. And the expression "The class of all the apostles" might have designated something different from what it does designate—if there had been fewer apostles, or

more, or different ones. But the class which it does in fact designate could not have had a different membership from what it
does have.

This claim, that classes have their membership essentially, is
probably not at a glance self-evident. So let us see what absurdity
is yielded if the claim is denied.

The standard criterion for the identity of classes is that any
class x is identical with any class y just in case there is nothing
which is a member of x and not of y, and also nothing which is
a member of y and not of x. Now it does not follow from *this*
that classes cannot change their membership or, more generally,
that they cannot have had different membership from that which
they do have. Perhaps this can best be seen by considering an
analogy. Possibly it is true, with respect to any physical object x
and any physical object y, that x and y are identical just in case
there is nothing which is the place of x and not of y, and nothing
which is the place of y and not of x. But even if this were true,
it would clearly not follow that physical objects cannot change
their place or, generally, that they cannot have had different
places from those they do have. In fact, it is quite possible for
nonidentical physical objects to *exchange* their places.

But why is it then that classes have their membership essentially?

Consider the class of all (currently existing) passenger pigeons
and the class of all unicorns. These classes are presumably identical, for presumably both are identical with the null class. But now
suppose there had been some (currently existing) passenger
pigeons, and suppose there had been some unicorns. What would
then have been the situation? That class which is in fact the
null class, and the class of all passenger pigeons, and the class
of all unicorns—would it then have had passenger pigeons as
its members? That is, would that class, which is the null class
and the class of all unicorns, then have had passenger pigeons
as members? Or would it then have had unicorns as members?
That is, would that class, which is the null class and the class
of all passenger pigeons, then have had unicorns as members?
Or would it then have no members? That is, would that class,
which is the class of all passenger pigeons and the class of all
unicorns, then still have had no members? If the membership of

classes could have been different from what it is, is there any reason whatsoever for preferring one of these alternatives to the other? Yet, they are incompatible.

Or consider some unit class—the class, say, whose sole member is Martin Luther King. This class is identical with the class of all civil rights leaders slain on April 4, 1968. Now suppose that there had been ten civil rights leaders slain on April 4, 1968. What would then have been the situation? That class which has Martin Luther King as its sole member and which is the class of all civil rights leaders slain on April 4, 1968—would it then still have had only Martin Luther King as its member? That is, would the class of all civil rights leaders slain on April 4, 1968, have had only Martin Luther King as its member (in spite of the fact that ten such were slain)? Or would it then have had ten members, that is, would the unit class whose sole member is Martin Luther King then have had ten members? If the membership of classes could have been different from what it is, is there any reason for preferring one of these incompatible alternatives to the other?

Finally, consider the class of all tigers and the class of all lions. And suppose that the class of all tigers is in fact identical with the class of all large striped cats. Now it would seem that tigers might not have had stripes; it may even be that over the years they will lose them. And it would seem that lions might have had stripes; it may even be that over the years they will acquire them. What would then have been the situation? That class which is in fact the class of all tigers and all large striped cats—would it then have had all large striped cats as its members? That is, would the class of all tigers then have had no tigers but only lions as its members? Or would it then have had all tigers as its members? That is, would the class of all large striped cats then have had no large striped cats but only tigers as its members? If the membership of a class could have been different from what in fact it is, is there any reason to prefer one of these incompatible alternatives to the other?

If classes did not have their membership essentially, then there would indeed be no reason to prefer one of the options we have suggested to any of its alternatives. And this would be so because there would in fact be no correct answer to the

questions we put. There would be no correct answer to the
question whether the null class would then have had no members,
or would then have had passenger pigeons as members, or would
then have had unicorns as members. In short, if it were allowed that classes did not have their membership essentially,
there would be no correct answer to the question as to what the
membership of this class would be. And if this were so, then of
course questions of class identity across possible worlds would
also have no correct answer. "Would what is now the null class
be identical with what would then be the null class, or with what
would then be the class of all passenger pigeons, or with what
would then be the class of all unicorns?" To this question, there
would be no correct answer. But there must be *some* correct
answer to such a question, or there would be no sense to the
supposition that this class might have had different membership.
For this supposition is just the supposition that this class, re-
maining the *same identical class,* might have had a different
membership. So the supposition that this class might have had a
different membership, is an incoherent supposition. And a comparable argument can be given for any other class.

It is certainly not true, however, of every predicable that it
is impossible that it should have had different cases from those
it does have. For example, it is true of the class of all circularities that it is impossible that it should have had a different
membership from that which it has; but it is not true of circularity
that it is impossible that it should have had different cases from
those it has. Consequently, circularity cannot be identified with
the class of all circularities.

Further, there are many distinct predicables which have no
exemplifications at all, and thus no cases. But the class of all
cases of any one such will be identical with the class of all cases
of any other such. It will, of course, be the null class. Thus,
though there may be various distinct unexemplified predicables,
the class of all cases of any one such will be identical with the
class of all cases of any other such. For example, *being a round
square* and *having more than two mothers* are both predicables
which lack cases. Thus, the class of all cases of *being a round
square* is identical with the class of all cases of *having more*

than two mothers. It is the null class. Yet these predicables are distinct.

Thus it cannot be held that every predicable is identical with the class of all the cases it ever has, any more than it can be held that every predicable is identical with the class of all the exemplifications it has, or with all the exemplifications it ever has. But I know of no other suggestion as to which sort of class every predicable is to be identified with. Admittedly, the arguments we have presented do not show that there is *no* predicable which is identical with the class of all the exemplifications it ever has, or that there is *no* predicable which is identical with all the cases it ever has. All that we have succeeded in *showing* is that such identifications cannot be made *generally.*

2. It is quite another matter, however, to hold that the *concept* of circularity is identical with the *concept* of circularities; that the *concept* of running is identical with the *concept* of runnings; and in general, that a concept of what we have called a *predicable* is identical with the concept of what we have called *cases* of that predicable. There is nothing absurd, on the face of it, in this suggestion. It is, I think, under a charitable interpretation of their words, the view of most or all of those in that long tradition of philosophers who have held that universals are concepts or ideas. A less charitable, albeit more straight-forward, interpretation of their view would be that every predicable is identical with some concept or idea, some mental entity. But that would yield such absurdities as that some of our concepts are colors, some are shapes, some are virtues, and the like. For the predicable red is a color, the predicable triangularity is a shape, the predicable wisdom is a virtue.

One of the most subtle, plausible, and thorough statements of the view that the concept of a predicable is identical with the concept of its cases, is to be found in William of Ockham. So let us consider what Ockham says on the matter. We may begin by noticing Ockham's distinction between singular and universal concepts. All concepts, Ockham holds, are of singular, individual, things. But some concepts are each "proper to" just one singular thing. They are of such a nature as to signify, and to be capable of suppositing for, just one certain thing, and no other. Such concepts Ockham calls *singular concepts*. Examples are the concept of Socrates and the concept of Plato. The concept of Socrates is *of* just one particular thing, namely Socrates. It is proper to him. It signifies him and him alone, and for him and him alone is it capable of suppositing when put into a sentence.[2]

There are other concepts which are not each proper to just one singular thing. They are each, on the contrary, (possibly) common to many things, no more proper to one particular thing of a sort than another of the sort. They are of such a nature as (possibly) to signify, and to be capable of being predicated truly of (and thus suppositing for) many things. Such concepts Ockham calls universal concepts. Examples of such are the concept of man and the concept of animal. The concept of man is not a concept of, and proper to, some one singular thing. It is not a concept proper to, let us say, Socrates. Nor is it proper to some one single entity designated in English by the word "man" and in Latin by the word "homo." Rather, says Ockham, it is a concept of all men, that is, a concept of each and every man. It is a concept of all those things which resemble each other in that they are men (in that each is a man). It is no more proper to one man than to another. It is common to all men, signifying them all; it is capable of being predicated truly of (suppositing for) each and every man when put into a proposition.[3]

Ockham holds that singular *terms* are associated with singular *concepts,* not in that the terms signify the concepts, but rather in that each singular term signifies, by convention, the very same thing that a singular concept signifies by its nature. And he holds that general *terms* (he calls them universal terms) are associated with universal *concepts,* not, again, in that each of these terms signifies the concept, but rather in that each of them signifies, by convention, the very same things that a universal concept signifies by its nature.[4]

It is Ockham's view that, apart from universal terms and uni-

2. P. Boehner, ed., *Ockham: Philosophical Writings* (New York, 1959), pp. 32–34, 43–45.
3. *Ibid.;* ". . . the concept of *man* which signifies all men and can stand for them and be part of a proposition . . ." ("William of Ockham: The Seven Quodlibeta," in McKeon, *Medieval Philosophers,* 2:387).
4. Boehner, *Ockham,* pp. 32–34, 43–45.

versal concepts, there is nothing which is universal, that is, nothing which can be (truly) predicated of many. He holds that there is nothing, apart from certain natural and certain conventional signs, which is a universal.

There is, of course, no inconsistency in holding this view along with the view that there are such entities as those which we have claimed to be predicable universals; for one could hold that there are such entities but deny, for whatever reason, that they can be truly predicated of many. Possibly some philosophers have held this combination of views. But this is quite clearly not Ockham's intent. He wishes, for example, not merely to deny that whiteness can be truly predicated of many, but also to deny that there is any such distinct entity as whiteness at all.

What might very well give the reader of Ockham some pause in accepting this interpretation of his view is the fact that Ockham holds that there are two ultimate sorts of entities, substances and qualities; and that he regards man, for example, as a substance, and whiteness, for example, as a quality. Now if Ockham holds that whiteness is a quality, can he really be denying that there is such an entity as whiteness—that there is some one thing such that it is identical with whiteness? Further, not only does Ockham hold that whiteness is a quality, he clearly holds that it is an *extramental* quality. It is not a concept, or any other sort of mental entity. And he says such things as this: ". . . the proposition 'Socrates is white' denotes that Socrates is *that* thing, which has whiteness; and for that reason the predicate stands for that thing which has whiteness."[5] And again, ". . . nothing is white unless it is by whiteness, nor warm unless it is warm by warmth."[6] It would seem that Ockham could scarcely be saying anything other than that, though there is such an entity as whiteness, it cannot be predicated; and is, consequently, not a universal.

The key to Ockham's actual view is that what he calls *qualities* are—all of them—the same as what we have called *cases* and *aspects*. Ockham, however, would not be willing to call them cases; for, on his view, there is nothing for them to be cases of. Rather, he describes them, adapting Aristotle, as entities signified

5. Boehner, *Ockham,* p. 65.
6. McKeon, *Medieval Philosophers,* 2:392.

by terms *present in* a subject.[7] That he should thus follow Aristotle is already some indication that he calls qualities what we have called cases; for, as we have seen in an earlier chapter, Aristotle's word for cases is *entities present in.* And what makes it decisively clear that this is what Ockham has in mind is his frequent use of such expressions as "whiteness," "this whiteness," "the whiteness of this thing," and the like. For example, on one page we find all these expressions: "this whiteness," "two whitenesses," "whitenesses," and "those whitenesses."[8] And, to cite just one other passage, on page 51 of Boehner's *Ockham: Philosophical Writings,* we find the expression "every whiteness." But if "whiteness" were used by Ockham as the proper name of some predicable, all these expressions would be unintelligible. Indeed, so foreign is it to Ockham's thought to regard qualities as universals that in considering whether any extramental entities are universals he discusses only whether any extramental *substances* are universals.

It is perhaps worth pointing out, however, that not everything that would by us be regarded as a *case* of something would by Ockham be regarded as a quality, that is, as an entity signified by a term present in a subject. For example, Ockham would not regard Socrates' humanity as a quality of Socrates, but rather as identical with him.[9]

We are ready to consider the final, and perhaps most ingenious, link in Ockham's view. According to Ockham, the concept of whiteness is not a singular concept of the predicable entity, whiteness. Rather, it is a universal concept of all the whitenesses. The concept is a universal, but it is not a concept of something which is a universal. The concept of whiteness is the concept of all whitenesses. Similarly, the concept of man is not a singular concept, but is rather a universal concept of all the men; the concept of man is the concept of all men. And the concept of humanity is the concept of all humanities, that is, of all men. Accordingly, to claim that whiteness is a color and a quality, is not to claim that there is some one thing which is identical with

7. Cf. E.A. Moody, *The Logic of William of Ockham* (New York, 1965). pp. 128, 131.
8. McKeon, *Medieval Philosophers,* 2:416.
9. Moody, *The Logic of Ockham,* pp. 60–63.

whiteness and is such that it is a color and a quality; but is rather to claim that whitenesses are colors and qualities. And to claim that man is an animal and a substance, is not to claim that there is some one thing which is identical with man and is such that it is an animal and a substance; but is rather to claim that men are animals and substances.

Parallel remarks are to be made concerning terms. The word "man" is a general term signifying all men, and capable of suppositing for all men if used in a sentence. The word "whiteness" is likewise a general term, signifying all whitenesses, and capable of suppositing for all whitenesses if used in a sentence. And the word "humanity" is a general term signifying all men, and capable of suppositing for all men if used in a sentence.

Possibly this view has a certain surprise for us which it would not have for someone speaking Latin. For English, unlike Latin and unlike Greek, has an indefinite article. Thus, when such a term as "man" is used in the singular without a definite article, as in "Man is an animal," we are inclined to regard it as functioning quite differently from how it functions when it is prefaced with an indefinite article; we are inclined to view it as a singular term. But Latin would yield no such inclination at all. Where we would say "Whiteness is a quality and a color," the Latin would say what corresponds to "Whiteness is color and quality." And where we would say "Man is an animal and a substance," the Latin would say what corresponds to "Man is animal and substance." So also, where we would say "Socrates is a man," the Latin would say what corresponds to "Socrates is man." And then it is but a natural step to interpret what corresponds to "This is whiteness" as saying what we would express as "This is a whiteness."

Ockham, then, would deny that whiteness can be predicated; for he would interpret this as the claim that *whitenesses* can be predicated, and this, he and we are both agreed, is false. Also he denies that whiteness is a concept; for this he understands as the claim that *whitenesses* are concepts, and this too is false. He might possibly allow that from 'This is white' it follows that there is such a thing as whiteness. But if so, he would understand this as equivalent to the claim that there are such entities as whitenesses, rather than as equivalent to the claim that there is some one thing which is identical with whiteness.

One facet of Ockham's theory of universals which certainly merits critical scrutiny is his description of the universal concept, that is, of the concept associated with a general term. The concept of man, according to Ockham, is the concept of all men (each man); the concept of whiteness is the concept of all whitenesses (each whiteness). He says, for example, that "just as the spoken word 'man' does not signify Socrates more than Plato, and hence does not stand more for Socrates than Plato, so it would be with an act of intellect which does not relate to Socrates any more than to Plato or any other man."[10] And again: "And so it could be said that one and the same cognition refers to an infinite number of singulars without being a cognition proper to any one of them, and this is so because of some specific likeness between these individuals that does not exist between others."[11]

In thus regarding the concept associated with a general term as a one-of-all sort of thing, Ockham is not at all unusual. Abelard, for example, says: ". . . let us distinguish between the understandings of universals and particulars. These are separated in that that which is of the universal noun conceives a common and confused image of many things, whereas that which the particular word generates, holds to the proper and as it were the particular form of one thing, that is, restricts itself to only one person. Whence when I hear *man* a certain figure arises in my mind which is so related to individual men that it is common to all and proper to none."[12] Descartes says that "Universals arise merely from our making use of one and the same idea in thinking of all individual objects between which there subsists a certain likeness; and when we comprehend all the objects represented by this idea under one name, this term likewise becomes universal."[13] Locke says, "Words become general by being made the signs of general ideas; and ideas become general by separating from them the circumstances of time and place, and any other ideas that may determine them to this or that particular existence. By this way of abstraction they are made capable of representing more individuals than one; each of which, having in it a conformity to

10. Boehner, *Ockham*, p. 44.
11. Ibid., p. 45.
12. "Glosses on Porphyry," in McKeon, *Medieval Philosophers*, 1:240.
13. *The Principles of Philosophy*, Part I, lix.

that abstract idea, is (as we call it) of that sort."[14] And Berkeley says that "an idea which, considered in itself, is particular, becomes general by being made to represent or stand for all other particular ideas of the same sort."[15] From these citations it is clear that there is a great deal of agreement on the view that a general or universal concept—a concept associated with a general term—is a one-of-all sort of thing.

There is, however, far less agreement as to just what such a concept may be. It would take us much too far astray to consider all the different views which have been held on this matter. Let us just consider the two views which Ockham held, one earlier in his career and one later.

Ockham's earlier view was that a concept is a mental picture which resembles the things of which it is a picture. Thus the concept of Socrates, for example, is a mental picture of Socrates; and the concept of man is a mental picture of all men. "And this can be called a universal, because it is a pattern and related indifferently to all the singular things outside the mind. Because of the similarity between its being as a thought-object and the being of like things outside the mind, it can stand for such things."[16]

But how can *one* mental picture be a picture of all men? Just what is the difference between that sort of picture which is a singular concept and that sort of picture which is a universal concept? There is an interesting passage in Abelard in which he addresses himself to these questions: "To show the nature of all lions, one picture can be made representing what is proper to no one of them, and on the other hand another can be made suitable to distinguish any one of them, which would bring out certain individual characteristics, as if it were painted limping or mutilated or wounded by the spear of Hercules. Just as, therefore, one figure of things is painted common, another particular, so too, are they conceived one common, another proper."[17]

There can be little doubt, however, that this will not do. Suppose, for example, that we try, following Abelard's instructions,

14. *An Essay Concerning Human Understanding,* III, 3, vi.
15. *Principles of Human Knowledge,* Introduction, section 12.
16. Boehner, *Ockham,* p. 41.
17. In McKeon, *Medieval Philosophers,* 1:241–42.

to draw a picture of all lions. What features must find representation in this picture? Shall we portray a tail on the lion? But not
all lions have tails; some have lost theirs. So we cannot represent
a tail. Four feet? But some lions have lost their front left foot.
So we cannot portray a left front foot. And some have lost their
rear right foot. So we cannot portray a rear right foot. And so
forth, for eyes, ears, mane. It is unlikely that, if we followed
Abelard's instructions, there would be enough left to give us
anything that could reasonably count as a lion-picture.

But if one sets out to draw a picture of every lion according
to Abelard's prescription, can one then *omit* the representation
of a tail? Abelard suggests that if a given lion has the peculiarity
of limping, then to picture him in all his peculiarities we must
somehow picture him as limping. Now it is a peculiarity of some
lions that they lack tails. How are we to convey this peculiarity
with a picture? Obviously by omitting the representation of a tail
in our pictures of all such lions. If things are to be pictured in
their peculiarities, then we must allow that not representing some
feature in our picture of a thing (when it *can* be represented) is
an indication that the thing lacks that trait. Now the universal
picture is said to differ from the singular in portraying only what
is common. But lacking a tail is not common to all lions. This
is a peculiarity of some. Consequently our universal picture must
not include an indication of this peculiarity. But this peculiarity
is indicated by not representing a tail. Hence, in our picture of
every lion, we shall have to represent a tail. But, as we saw
above, we must also *omit* the representation of a tail. It would
seem that Abelard's instructions for making a picture of every
lion cannot be followed.

It was considerations something like these, provoked by some
statements of Locke that are either preposterous or obscure, which
led Berkeley to locate the difference between general and singular
mental pictures (ideas) in the different uses to which the pictures
are put, rather than in some difference inherent in the pictures.
I think one can see, however, that this line of thought has no
more chance of success than does that of Abelard. For there is
something inscrutable in the very notion of one picture being a
picture of every lion. Would not a picture of each lion be a complex picture, containing as many lion-representations as there are

lions? Again, suppose that one has a picture which is a picture of each student in a class of twenty. Could this be anything other than a complex picture containing twenty representations? Can it be anything other than such a picture, if it is a picture no more of one student in the class than of any other? How could one student-representation be a picture of each of twenty students, not a picture of one of them any more than it is of any other? A picture of a specific student in the class will be a picture such that there is a correct answer to the question: "Of which student is this a picture?" And a picture of each student in the class will be a picture containing a number of student-representations, such that of each of them there is a correct answer to the question: "Of which student is this a picture?"

There are other sorts of pictures as well. It is possible to draw a picture of a lion without there being any correct answer to the question: "Of which lion is this a picture?" The words "This is a picture of a lion" can be used to assert a proposition which does not entail that there is some lion of which this is a picture. One can just draw a picture of a lion, without there being any lion of which it is a picture. And the pattern of color-on-surface which makes up such a picture need not differ in any way at all from the pattern which makes up a picture of some specific, particular lion. It need not be more sketchy, or more hazy, or more confused. Further, one can draw a picture of *some* lions, even though it is not the case that there are some lions of which one has drawn a picture. There may be no particular lions at all which one has thereby pictured. One cannot, however, draw a picture of every lion without its being the case that every lion, then, is such that it is pictured; "a picture of every lion" does not have the ambiguity which "a picture of a lion" and "a picture of some lions" have. Finally, one can draw a picture of the lion, and a picture of the robin, and the like. For example, among Audubon's drawings of the North American birds one finds a picture of the robin. The pattern of color-on-surface which is Audubon's picture of the robin might also have been put forth by someone as a picture of a robin, and might also have been the result of some-one trying to picture some particular robin. Similarly, a pattern of colors-on-surface put forward by the police as a picture of last night's burglar might also be used by a museum director as a picture of the Celtic stock of the Caucasian race. If a picture of a lion, however, in either of the senses of "picture of a lion," includes the portrayal of certain traits which are not *typical* of lions, it will not do as a picture of *the* lion.

Surely, then, it would be more plausible to describe the concept associated with the general term "lion" as a mental picture of a lion (understanding this so that it does not follow that there is some lion of which it is a picture), rather than as a mental picture of every lion. But what would be a picture, mental or nonmental, of a wisdom? And what would be a picture of a hotness? If one is going to regard concepts as mental pictures, then it seems clear that universal concepts, those associated with general terms, should not be described as pictures of every so-and-so, but rather as pictures of a so-and-so. But how is one to picture an *aspect*—what Ockham called a *quality?*

Let us, then, consider Ockham's later view as to the nature of concepts and, thus, as to the nature of universal concepts. In his later writings, Ockham renounces the view that a concept is some sort of mental object, and holds instead that a concept is just an act of knowing. That is to say, each concept is what he would call a *quality* of the intellect—my knowing so-and-so, your knowing so-and-so. It is an intellection (*intellectio*) or cognition (*cognitio*) of something.[18]

It is not wholly clear, however, what Ockham's view here is. Is he saying that to have a concept of Napoleon is to know Napoleon? Unless the word "know" is given some unusual force, this seems false. It is far more plausible to hold that to have a concept of Napoleon is to know *who Napoleon is*. Accordingly, this is how I shall understand what Ockham is saying.

One can know who or what some specific thing is. One can know what Bucephalus is, who Napoleon is, what Pike's Peak is, and the like. Such knowings are, by Ockham, identified with singular concepts, these being the concepts associated with singular terms. But also, according to Ockham, one can know what each thing of a certain sort is. One can know what each lion is, what each robin is, and so on. Such knowings are, by Ockham, identified with universal concepts, these being the concepts associated with general terms.

18. Boehner, *Ockham,* pp. 43–45.

This notion of knowing what every lion is, is surely just as puzzling as the notion of one lion-representation being a picture of every lion. In principle it is of course possible to know each lion. But the concept associated with the general term "lion" cannot be regarded as a knowing of every lion; for, if it were, it would in all likelihood be the case that no one has the concept. But what it might be to know *what* each lion is, is thoroughly obscure. One can of course know who Mary is, who Paul is, who Ralph is, who Valery is, who Stephen is; and these may be all the students that there are in the room. In that way, one can know who every student in the room is. But this is just to have a 'singular cognition' of each student in the room. It is not to have the concept associated with the general term, "student in the room."

But not only can one know who or what some particular thing is. One can also know what a so-and-so is, and what so-and-so's are. One can know what Pike's Peak is, but also one can know what a mountain is and what mountains are. And this corresponds nicely to the fact that not only can one have the concept of this particular thing and the concept of that particular thing, but also one can have the concept of a so-and-so, and the concept of so-and-so's. One can have the concept of Pike's Peak, but also one can have the concept of a mountain and the concept of mountains. Now from the fact that I know what a lion is, it does not follow that there is some lion such that I know what it is. There is no correct answer to the question, Of which lion is it the case that I know what it is? And from the fact that I know what lions are, it does not follow that there are some lions such that of each of them it is the case that I know what it is. Similarly, from the fact that I have the *concept* of a lion, it does not follow that there is some lion of which I have the concept. 'I have the concept of a lion' does not entail that there is some lion such that I have the concept of it. And I can have the concept of lions, without there being some lions such that I have the concept of each of them.

Thus it would have been better if Ockham had said, not that the concept of whiteness is the concept of each whiteness, but rather that it is the concept of a whiteness; and this, in turn, would have been better described as the knowing what a white-

ness is, rather than as the knowing what each whiteness is. To
have the concept of whiteness, Ockham should have said, is to
know what a whiteness is. He could scarcely have said this, however, since Latin, as already remarked, lacks the indefinite article.
He could have said that the concept of whiteness is the concept
of whiteness*es;* and this, it would seem, comes to the same thing.

So now, finally, is it correct that the concept of whiteness is
the concept of a whiteness (of whitenesses), that the concept of
circularity is the concept of a circularity (of circularities), and
so on? Several of our earlier conclusions are incompatible with
the view that the concept of whiteness is the concept of *a* whiteness (whiteness*es*); and here it will be satisfactory simply to
remind ourselves of some of these.

The concept of whiteness is the concept of that which something can have or possess, which several distinct things can have
or possess, which can be predicated, which has being even though
it has no exemplifications and cases, and which has being necessarily. The concept of *a* whiteness, however, is not the concept
of something which something can have or possess, which several
distinct things can have or possess, which can be predicated,
which has being even though it has no exemplifications and cases,
and which has being necessarily. The concept of a whiteness is,
rather, the concept of that which is a case of whiteness, which
is present in some thing but not in more than one, and which is
present in something for a stretch of time.

Furthermore, is it not possible to have the concept of whiteness while lacking the concept of a whiteness? Is it not in fact
the case, for most people, that they know what whiteness is but
do not know what a whiteness is?

And it is perfectly possible that the color of my tie should be
the color of my hat; the shape of my car the shape of yours. But
if so, we cannot view the color of my tie and the color of my
hat as *two* distinct cases. We have no choice but to view the
color of my tie and the color of my hat as *one* property shared
by two things. (Cf. chapter 6, pp. 139–40.)

It must be allowed that by a convinced Ockhamist none of
these points would be granted. For example, Ockham himself
would simply deny this last point. He would deny that the color
of my tie can be the color of my hat. This is readily gathered

from the following passage: "It may be objected that the proposition 'This plant grows in my garden' is true, yet the subject has no discrete *suppositio*. To this we have to say that the proposition taken as it stands is false. However, what is understood by it is the proposition 'A plant of this kind (*talis herba*) grows in my garden'."[19]

19. Ibid., pp. 70–71.

9

Reduction

1. It seems clear that at least one of the propositions which can be asserted with the sentence "Socrates had the property of being wise," used in a normal sense, can also be asserted with the sentence "Socrates was wise," used in a normal sense. And in case it is the great Greek philosopher who is being referred to, what would be asserted with these two different sentences would be true. It would be a fact. Now in using the sentence first mentioned, we refer to the property of being wise. In using the sentence next mentioned, we do not refer to the property of being wise. Thus, in this case, a fact which can be stated by referring to some predicable can also be stated without referring to that predicable, or indeed to any other. Once we notice this, we are naturally led to wonder whether this is true generally. Can every fact which can be stated by referring to some predicable also be stated without referring to any predicable? Is referring to predicables a wholly dispensable stylistic device for stating facts?

It also seems that at least one of the propositions which can be asserted with the sentence "This carpet has a harsh color," used in a normal sense, can as well be asserted with the sentence "This carpet's color is harsh," used in a normal sense. And, obviously, these sentences too can be used so that what is asserted is true. They can be used to state one and the same fact. Now in using the sentence first mentioned, we do not refer to any predicable. We refer to some indicated carpet, but carpets are not predicables. And though colors are predicables, we do not, in the sentence indicated, refer to any color. For we discovered, in chapter 2, that a condition of referring to something is that we use a singular term to stand for it; and a "a harsh color" is not a singular, but rather a general, term. It is worth noticing, though, that "a harsh color," as used in the sentence mentioned, is a term such that only if it is true of some predicable can the sentence containing it be used to state the fact; whereas in the second sentence mentioned, there is no such term. "This carpet's color" is the subject of this second sentence; and this sentence can be assertively uttered so that its subject is used to stand for a *case* of a predicable. Thus a fact, which can be stated by using a term which must be true of some predicable if the sentence containing it is to be used to state the fact, can also be stated without using any such term. And once we notice this, we are naturally led to wonder whether this too is true generally. Can every fact which can be stated by using a term which must be true of some predicable if the sentence containing it is to be used to state the fact, also be stated without using such a term?

Suppose that every fact which can be stated by making reference to some predicable, or by using some term which must be true of some predicable if the sentence containing it is to be used to state the fact, can also be stated without making reference to any predicable and without using any term which must be true of some predicable if the sentence containing it is to be used to state the fact. In that case, let us say that predicables are *reducible*. If, furthermore, some of the replacement sentences are such that in using them we make reference to a nonpredicable, or such that they contain some term which must be true of some nonpredicable if the sentence containing it is to be used to state the fact, then let us say that predicables are *reducible to nonpredicables*.

Two questions spring at once to mind. One is: Are predicables *in fact* reducible? The other is: What, if anything, would be the ontological significance of the fact if they *were* reducible; and what, if they were *not* reducible? And more specifically, what, if anything, would be the ontological significance of the fact if they were reducible to nonpredicables; and what, if they were not reducible to nonpredicables?[1]

Let us first consider whether predicables are in fact reducible. Consider, for example, the necessary fact that courage is a virtue. This fact can be stated with the sentence "Courage is a virtue." In so stating it, we refer to the predicable *courage* with the word "courage"; and we use the general term, "virtue," this being a term which must be true of some predicable (namely, courage) if the sentence containing it is to be used to state the fact in question. Now, can this fact also be stated *without* referring to any predicable, and without using any term which must be true of some predicable if the sentence containing it is to be used to state the fact in question?

A sentence which comes at once to mind is the normal English sentence:

A. All courageous things are virtuous.

This sentence can, in normal use, be used to assert two different propositions. It can be used to assert a proposition which entails that there exists at least one courageous thing, and also to assert a proposition which does not entail this. It is the latter use that is of concern to us here. For the necessary fact that courage is a virtue does not entail that there exists at least one courageous thing. If it did entail this, it would be necessarily true that some courageous entity existed—assuming that only necessary truths are entailed by necessary truths. But it does not seem to be necessarily true that some courageous entity exists.

1. Perhaps here is the place to remark that sometimes what goes under the rubric of a "program of reduction" has been attempted, not because it was thought that it itself, in its success or failure, had some ontological import, but rather, to provide a linguistic reflection of a previously accepted ontology. Usually when a program of reduction is undertaken in this spirit, more conditions are laid down for the sought-for language than we have laid down. It is required in addition that the language be more illuminating than the original, that in its structure it 'show' the accepted ontology, that by virtue of its structure it not tempt us into certain mistaken inferences as to how things are, and so on. Our inquiry here is along different lines. Our aim is not to devise a language which, in some sense or other, adequately 'reflects' the ontology we have in previous chapters argued for. Rather, our aim is to discover whether the reducibility or nonreducibility of predicables has any ontological import for predicables.

It is clear, however, that even when used in this latter way, (A) will not serve our purposes. For what is claimed in using (A) thus is that no courageous things are nonvirtuous. And while this may be true, it is certainly not necessarily true. It is eminently possible that there be somewhere a thoroughly vicious man who in spite of his viciousness has a virtue, just one—the virtue of courage. Whereas, to repeat, it is the necessary truth that courage is a virtue which we are trying to state.

A closely similar difficulty hinders the proposal to state the fact that being in love is a state much admired by Americans, with the sentence, used in a normal sense, "Everybody in love is admired by Americans." This sentence can be used, in a normal sense, to assert that everybody is admired by Americans if in love; and this does not entail that everybody is in love. But though it is not necessarily true that being in love is a state much admired by Americans, still, it might be true that being in love is a state much admired by Americans and false that everybody is admired by Americans if in love. For it may be that some people who are in love are, for the rest, very nonadmirable people, so that they are in fact not admired by Americans. And it may also be that some people in love are not known to any Americans, and are consequently not admired by any. Hence the sentence "Everybody in love is admired by Americans," when used in a normal sense, is not satisfactory as a replacement for the sentence "Being in love is a state much admired by Americans." For a similar reason, the sentence "Everything yellow is a favorite of mine," when assertively uttered in a normal sense, will not serve to state the fact that yellow is my favorite color. Hence, when used in a normal sense it is not satisfactory as a replacement for "Yellow is my favorite color."

Thus far, in our attempt to find replacements for those sentences in whose assertive utterance we make reference to some predicable, we have used general terms true of *exemplifications* of the predicable in question. But in an earlier chapter we distinguished exemplifications from *cases* of predicables. And in many circumstances the desired replacement sentences can be found with ease if we use general terms true of cases. For example, the fact that courage is a virtue can, it would seem, be stated with this sentence, used in a normal sense:

B. Everything which is a courage is a virtue.

This sentence can, no doubt, be naturally used to assert a proposition which entails that there is a courage (that is, a case of courage), as well as one which does not entail that there is a courage. Again, it is the latter use which is of interest to us here; for the fact that courage is a virtue does not entail that there is a courage. So though the sentence *need not*, in every case of normal use, be used to assert the proposition that courage is a virtue, still it seems that it *can*, in normal use, be used to assert that courage is a virtue.

The use of terms true of cases gives us ready replacements for a number of other sentences which would otherwise give trouble. For example, several sentences which Arthur Pap discusses, and concludes to be difficult or impossible of replacement, are handily dealt with.[2] His example, "Red resembles orange more than blue" can be replaced with "Every red resembles some orange more than any blue." And his example, "I like the smell of roses," has, as a replacement, "I like the smells of roses." Identity sentences which would otherwise give great difficulty are also easily dealt with. For example, "Magenta is the same color as fuchsia" can be replaced with "Every magenta is identical with some fuchsia and every fuchsia is identical with some magenta." And "Having a shape is not identical with having a size" can be replaced with "It is not true that every case of having a shape is identical with some case of having a size and every case of having a size is identical with some case of having a shape."

It is not clear whether "All yellows are favorite colors of mine" will do as a replacement for "Yellow is my favorite color." And it is even less clear, I judge, whether "All cases of being in love are much admired by Americans" will do as a replacement for "The state of being in love is much admired by Americans."

Thus far our search for replacement sentences has been confined to more or less ordinary English sentences as normally used. But there is, of course, no reason thus to limit ourselves. Perhaps normal Frisian, or Greek, or Celtic, would readily provide us with the desired way of stating the fact that yellow is my favorite

2. "Nominalism, Empiricism, and Universals—I," *Philosophical Quarterly* 9, no. 37 (October 1959).

color, or the fact that the state of being in love is much admired by Americans.

Further, there is no reason to limit ourselves to languages as they current exist. If the desired replacement sentences can not be formed from words already present in some language, there is no reason why we should not expand these languages by creating new words for the purpose, either by introducing new sound and/or character sequences, or by giving new uses to old sound and/or character sequences. For example, rather than searching about through languages as they currently exist for a satisfactory replacement for "Courage is a virtue," we could have *introduced* the predicate "is a virt," explaining it as a predicate true of a case of a certain predicable just in the event that "is a virtue" is true of the predicable. Then the sentences "Courage is a virtue" and "Every (case of) courage is a virt" could, when used in a normal fashion, be employed to assert the same proposition (they could also be employed to assert different ones; for example, by using the latter to assert a proposition which entails that there is a case of courage). And rather than trying to find in some currently existing language a satisfactory replacement for Quine's example, "Humility is rare," we could create one, by stipulating that the words "is a rare" are true of a case of some predicable just in the event that "is rare" is true of the predicable. Then "Humility is rare" and "Every (case of) humility is a rare" could, when used in normal sense, be employed to assert the same proposition. And in general, it would seem that for every sentence containing singular terms standing for predicables, one can easily produce, as replacement, a sentence containing general terms true of *cases* of predicables. All references to predicables can be eliminated.

Certain sentences containing terms which must be true of predicables if the sentences containing them are to be used to state facts are a bit more recalcitrant. For example, suppose that "is a virt" be used as true of some thing just in the event that that thing is a case of a predicable of which "is a virtue" is true. Then "All virtues are admirable," used in a normal sense, can be used to assert what "All virts are admirable," used in normal fashion, can also be used to assert. But "Some virts are admirable" will

not do as a satisfactory normal replacement for "Some virtues
are admirable." For it may be that some cases of a virtue are
admirable without that virtue being admirable, that is, without *all*
its cases being admirable. Similarly, it is far from obvious that
introducing terms true of cases of predicables will help us in
producing a satisfactory normal replacement for "Joe and John
have all the same facial features."

But at this juncture there are still a number of strategies
available. One might, for example, try producing the desired
translations by using terms true of *classes of exemplifications;* or
if that fails, of *classes of cases.* But if even that fails, one can
always fall back on one or the other of two strategies which cannot fail. One can use existing sentences in abnormal ways, or one
can introduce a sequence of sounds and/or characters which *as a
whole* is to be used as the replacement for some sentence. Thus
far we have tried to find a replacement for the sentence "Courage
is a virtue" by trying to find a sentence consisting of words which
can also be used in other sentences—these words being either
currently existing words, in English or some other language, or
words produced for the purpose. But one can also accomplish
the purpose by stipulating that, for example, when the sound and
character sequence *ciav* is used, the person using it is to be
regarded as asserting that courage is a virtue. Then whether one
assertively utters "Courage is a virtue" or whether one uses
"ciav," the same fact will be stated. And "ciav" is obviously
satisfactory for our purposes, since it contains no term at all, nor,
in using it, does one refer to anything. Or, if one prefers, one can
simply use the sentence "Everything courageous is virtuous" to
assert that courage is a virtue. One can, that is, use this sentence,
by stipulation or otherwise, in what is now an abnormal way.

It is clear that similar strategies can be resorted to whenever
we find the need for them. If the desired replacements cannot be
found in languages as they presently exist and as they are normally used, we can either use existing sentences abnormally, or
we can expand these languages, by introducing individual words
or entire sentences, so as to *make* the desired replacements
available. It is a purely contingent fact that some of the desired
replacements are to be found among the normally used sentences

of languages as presently constituted and that some are not. It might have been that all were—or that none were.

In short, there seems to be no doubt at all but that predicables are reducible.

2. It should be noted that the reducibility of predicables can also be maintained along lines quite different from any we have thus far suggested.

For one thing, it may be held that there *are* no facts which can be stated by referring to predicables.

Consider, for example, the sentence "Red is a color." It is open to someone to maintain that, contrary to appearances, this sentence itself provides us with a way of stating the fact that red is a color without referring to red or to any other predicable. And in general, the reducibility of predicables can be maintained by holding that, though many expressions appear to be logical subjects standing for predicables, none of them can in fact be such. This view would most naturally—though not necessarily— be grounded on the dual conviction that we can refer only to things that there are, and that there are no predicables. Someone who held these convictions could allow that it is a fact that red is a color, but deny that there is such a thing as the color red. And on this ground he could simply deny that in using the sentence "Red is a color" to state the fact that red is a color, we are referring to red, or to any other predicable. He could insist that "red," as it occurs in such a sentence, is no more than an *apparent* logical subject. He could deny that it is a term at all, and insist that it is only a syncategorematic word. The sentence "Red is a color" would then, in some ways, be like the sentence "It is raining." For what we assert, in assertively uttering this, may be true even though it is not the case that there is something which is raining; nor, in using this sentence, do we use "it" to refer to anything.

Another way of maintaining the view that there are no facts which can be stated by referring to predicables would be to hold that, though there are many propositions which entail that there are predicables, none of these are true. For example, in addition to the possibility of holding that in stating the fact that red is a

color with the sentence "Red is a color" we are not referring to
any predicable, there is the alternative possibility of holding that
it is not a fact that red is a color. Someone who held this view
might agree that 'red is a color' entails that there is such a thing
as the color red, and agree that this is a predicable; but he could
then deny that it is a fact that red is a color—perhaps on the
ground simply that there are no predicables. Someone who held
this view could then either hold that in asserting the (false)
proposition that red is a color with the sentence "Red is a color"
we are not referring to any predicable; or, alternatively, he could
hold that we are referring to the predicable red, though there is
no such predicable.

Just as it can be maintained that there are no facts which can
be stated by referring to predicables, so, along similar lines, it
can be maintained that there are no facts which can be stated by
using terms which must be reckoned as true of predicables. Consider, for example, the sentence "Some virtues are out of fashion."
It is open to someone to maintain that this sentence itself provides us with a way of stating the fact that some virtues are out
of fashion without using a term which must be reckoned as true
of virtues, or of any other predicables. This view would most
naturally—though not of course necessarily—be grounded on the
dual conviction that there are no predicables, and that terms can
be true only of things that there are.

Someone who held these views could hold that it is a fact that
some virtues are out of fashion, but deny that this entails that
there are any virtues, or predicables. And on this ground he
could deny that in using the sentence "Some virtues are out of
fashion" we are using a term which must be reckoned as true of
a virtue, or a predicable. He could insist that "virtue," as it
occurs in this sentence, is not true of anything at all. He could
even go a step farther and deny that it is a term. After all, to
borrow an example from Quine, we use the word "sake" (as in
"He did it for her sake") without there being anything, sakes or
otherwise, of which it is either true or false.

Alternatively, someone could deny that it is a fact that some
virtues are out of fashion. He could allow that the proposition
'Some virtues are out of fashion' does indeed entail that there
are some virtues, and thus, some predicables; but he could insist

that this proposition is false. He could then either hold that, in assertively uttering this sentence, we are not using any term which must be reckoned as true of virtues or any other predicables; or, alternatively, he could hold that we are using such a term, but that a term can be true of some thing without there being that thing.

In these various ways, then, it is open to someone to deny that facts can be stated by referring to, or using terms which must be reckoned as true of, predicables. And if this denial were correct, then of course predicables would be reducible. It will be evident from our previous chapters that, in our view, the denial that facts can be stated by referring to, or using terms true of, predicables, is false. But what this brief discussion shows, I think, is that this denial, though false, is not incoherent. And what it shows is that the nominalist can, if he wishes, hold that all our sentences are quite in order as they are.

3. Let us return to our original line of thought: Every fact which can be stated by referring to predicables and by using terms which must be reckoned as true of predicables, can also be stated without thus referring and without using such terms. Predicables are reducible.

What, then, is the ontological significance—if any—of the fact that predicables are reducible?

Or suppose that, for some reason uncovered by us, they are not reducible. What, if anything, would be the ontological significance of that?

Does it, for example, follow from the fact that predicables are reducible that there are no predicables? Can one *show* that there are no predicables by *showing* that they are reducible?

Or does it follow from the proposition that predicables are not reducible that there *are* predicables? If one could show that predicables are not reducible, would one have shown that there are predicables?

In some passages from Arthur Pap—and he is not at all unusual on this point—one finds something very similar to the claim that if predicables are not reducible, then it follows that there are predicables. Pap is discussing universals rather than predicables; and one thing which he tries to show is that apparent names for universals cannot all be contextually eliminated. What he sees as the significance of this attempt on his part can be gathered from the following passage: "In contemporary discussions of the problem of universals a distinction has been drawn between 'x is red' and 'x has the attribute (quality) Redness.' Predicates, the contemporary nominalists contend, are not names at all, hence it is illegitimate to pass from 'x is red' to 'there is an attribute, redness, which x exemplifies (instantiates).'. . . Yet, while one who is satisfied with the subject-predicate form as irreducible to something more intelligible can say 'this apple is red' without admitting that there is such a thing as redness, can he really justify his ontological abstinence by showing that any apparent name of a universal can be contextually eliminated? The modern nominalists are committed to this daring thesis, but a good empiricist, I contend, ought to reject it on inductive grounds. In the following, I shall discuss a small sample of descriptive statements that refer irreducibly to universals and are intelligible to everybody except philosophers with a nominalistic prejudice."[3]

What Pap says here, as I understand him, is that certain contemporary philosophers (he does not exclude himself) are of the view that if all apparent names of universals cannot be contextually eliminated from intelligible statements then it follows that there are some universals. Hence, if a man is justifiably to hold that there are no universals, he must have some good reason for thinking that all apparent names can be contextually eliminated.

The issue which Pap raises—of whether all apparent names of universals can be contextually eliminated from intelligible statements—is somewhat different from the issue we have raised—of whether every fact which can be stated by referring to some predicable can also be stated without so referring. There is, for one thing, the obvious, but nonproblematic, difference that whereas Pap speaks of universals, we speak of predicables. Secondly, Pap speaks of *apparent names,* and I take it that he would also speak of *apparently referring;* whereas we have formulated our question in such a way as to speak neither of

3. "Nominalism, Empiricism, and Universals—I," pp. 332–33.

apparent names nor of apparently referring. Quite clearly it is Pap's view that if there is no such predicable as so-and-so, so-and-so can at most be *apparently* named and *apparently* referred to. We cannot *really* name or refer to it. Thirdly, there is the difference that whereas Pap speaks of *making intelligible statements* without referring to universals, we have been speaking of *stating facts* without referring to predicables. These last locutions differ significantly, for the purpose at hand, only in that Pap, instead of speaking merely of *true* statements, speaks of *intelligible* (that is, true *and false*) statements.

I think it is clear that these differences are of no great significance for the matter in hand. Pap's claim, adapted to our interests and stated in our terminology, is that if some facts which can be stated cannot be stated without referring to predicables, it follows that there are predicables.

So, would the nonreducibility of predicables have ontological import of such significance? Is this view acceptable? Suppose it were true, for example, that the fact that red is a color cannot be stated without referring to the predicable red. Would it follow that there is such an entity as the predicable red?

The argument which naturally comes to mind here is the following:

(i)   That red is a color, is a fact which can be stated.
(ii) That red is a color is a fact which can be stated only by referring to the predicable red.
(iii) If a fact can be stated, and can be stated only by referring to some predicable, then there is that predicable.
(iv) Hence, there is such an entity as the predicable red.

In evaluating this argument, an important matter to consider at once is the following. What proposition is it that is being asserted in the words of the conclusion: "There is such an entity as the predicable red"?

We saw, in chapter 7, that this sentence may, when used in normal sense, be used to assert various different propositions. The principal possibilities, we saw, were these. It may be used to assert a proposition which is equivalent to the proposition that at some time or other something is red. Or it may be used to assert a proposition which is equivalent to the proposition that at some time or other something *could* be red. Or it may be used to assert a proposition which does not even entail that something could be red. Henceforth, when we wish to assert a proposition of the first sort, let us use the words "there exists"—for example, "There exists such an entity as the predicable red." When we wish to assert a proposition of the second sort, let us use the words "there subsists"—for example, "There subsists such an entity as the predicable red." And when we wish to assert a proposition of the last sort, let us use the words "there is"— "There is such an entity as the predicable red."

Thus we really have before us three different arguments to consider. One runs thus:

(i)   That red is a color, is a fact which can be stated.
(ii) That red is a color is a fact which can be stated only by referring to the predicable red.
(iii) If a fact can be stated, and can be stated only by referring to some predicable, then there exists that predicable.
(iv) Hence, there exists such an entity as the predicable red.

The second argument can be stated by substituting for the word "exists" in the formulation above the word "subsists." And the third can be stated by substituting for the word "exists" the word "is." The question then is whether any of these three parallel arguments is acceptable.

It should be remarked, however, that Pap might very well not accept any of these three interpretations of his argument. For he is arguing against the nominalist, trying to establish something that the nominalist disputes. But neither the nominalist nor anyone else would dispute the conclusion when understood in any of these three ways. He does not dispute that sometimes something is red. But each of the other two propositions is entailed by this one. Thus Pap is presumably operating on the assumption that both he and the nominalist understand 'there is'-claims with respect to predicables as expressing different propositions from any of those we have suggested—propositions which he accepts and which he understands the nominalist to be disputing. But he does not make clear what other force he is giving to the words "there is." He does not make it clear what proposition he thinks it is that these words, when used in conjunction with the name of some predicable, express. So all we can do is adopt our own interpretation.

The crucial premise, apart from the second, in any of the three variant arguments cited, is of course the principle that if a fact can be stated and can be stated only by referring to some predicable, then there exists that predicable. Or the principle that then there subsists that predicable. Or the principle that then there is that predicable.

Now, from the proposition

(1) that some fact can be stated but cannot be stated without referring to a certain predicable,

it of course follows

(2) that that predicable can be referred to.

But the only reason I know of, for supposing that (1) entails

(3a) that there exists that predicable,

is that (1) entails (2), and (2) entails (3a). So also, the only reason I know of for supposing that (1) entails

(3b) that there subsists that predicable,

is that (1) entails (2), and (2) entails (3b). And the only reason I know of, for supposing that (1) entails

(3c) that there is that predicable,

is that (1) entails (2), and (2) entails (3c).

Let us then consider whether (2) does entail (3a) or (3b) or (3c)—whether, if some fact can be stated by referring to some predicable, then there exists that predicable. Or then there subsists that predicable. Or then there is that predicable.

It may be noted first, however, that if someone accepts the principle that (2) entails (3a), then this principle alone, coupled with the first and second premises from the corresponding original argument, yield the same conclusion as that original argument. Thus if one accepts the principle that one cannot refer to some predicable unless that predicable exists, it is then quite irrelevant to argue, concerning such a fact as 'red is a color', that this fact can be asserted *only* by referring to red. All one need argue is that it *can* be asserted by referring to red. Whether it can or cannot be asserted without thus referring is quite irrelevant. And the same thing, mutatis mutandis, is to be said concerning the acceptance of the principle that (2) entails (3b), and the principle that (2) entails (3c). Thus, for the person who accepts one of these three principles—and the acceptance of one of these principles, we said, was the only reason for accepting the third premise in the corresponding original argument—it is quite irrelevant to inquire into the reducibility or nonreducibility of predicables. The real question at issue is not, whether in stating the facts one *must* refer to predicables, but whether in stating anything at all one *can* refer to predicables. Perhaps the various attempts at establishing the nonreducibility of predicables should really be understood as attempts to persuade opponents that predicables *can* indeed be referred to.

Is it then the case that one cannot refer to some predicable unless that predicable exists? Or unless it subsists? Or unless it is?

It seems clear that one can refer to some predicable even though that predicable does not *exist*. And it also seems clear that one can refer to some predicable even though that predicable does not *subsist*. The property of being a round square, for example, can be referred to even though it neither exists nor subsists.[5]

But what about, say, the property mentioned on the first page of this book? We saw earlier that there is no such property, since no property is mentioned on the first page of this book. Can one, in spite of this, refer to the property mentioned on the first page of this book? It seems to me that the answer to this must be, "No, one cannot." For if some predicable is referred to, then it follows that *there is* something such that it is identical with that predicable and it is referred to. So if it is not the case that there is such a predicable as the property mentioned on the first page of this book, then also the property mentioned on the first page of this book cannot be referred to. There just is no such property to be referred to. One cannot refer to some predicable unless there is that predicable to be referred to. Not every word-sequence of the form "The predicable ———" can be regarded as used to refer to some predicable. And a condition of some words being used to refer to a certain predicable is that *there be* that predicable. A predicable need not *exist* in order to

5. On the connection between reference and existence in general, see my "Referring and Existing," *Philosophical Quarterly* (October 1962).

be referred to. It need not *subsist* in order to be referred to. But it must *be* in order to be referred to.

Thus far we have considered whether, if some facts cannot be stated without *referring* to certain predicables, it follows that there exist, or that there subsist, or that there are, those predicables. We must next consider whether, if some facts cannot be stated without *using terms which must be reckoned as true of* certain predicables, it follows that there exist, or that there subsist, or that there are those predicables. Suppose, for example, that the fact that some virtues are out of fashion cannot be stated without using a term which must be reckoned as true of virtues. Would it follow that there exist, or that there subsist, or that there are, some predicables; namely, virtues?

The argument which naturally comes to mind here, with respect to the *existence* of predicables, is the following.

(i)   That some virtues are out of fashion, is a fact which which can be stated.
(ii) That some virtues are out of fashion is a fact which can be stated only by using a term which must be reckoned as true of virtues.
(iii) If a fact can be stated but can be stated only by using a term which must be reckoned as true of certain predicables, then there exist those predicables.
(iv) Hence, there exists certain predicables, namely, virtues.

Parallel arguments for the *subsistence* and the *being* of virtues can easily be derived by substituting for "there exist" in the conclusion and premise (iii), the words "there subsist" or the words "there are."

The crucial premises in these arguments are of course the principles that if a fact can be stated and can be stated only by using a term which must be reckoned as true of certain predicables, then there exist those predicables. And that then there subsist those predicables. And that then there are those predicables. Now, parallel to what was said concerning the argument from reference, the only plausible reason for supposing that if one *must* use a term which must be reckoned as true of certain predicables in order to state some fact which can be stated, then it follows that there exist those predicables, is this:

(4) that one must use a term which must be reckoned as
true of certain predicables in order to state some fact
which can be stated,

entails

(5) that one *can* use a term which must be reckoned as true
of those predicables,

which in turn entails

(6a) that there exist those predicables.

And so also, mutatis mutandis, for subsistence and being.

Now (4) certainly does entail (5). So the question to consider is whether (5) entails (6a); and whether (5) entails (6b):
that there subsist those predicables. And whether (5) entails
(6c): that there are those predicables. We must consider whether
the principle is true, that if one can use a term which must be
reckoned as true of certain predicables, then it follows that
there exist those predicables; and the principle that then it follows
that there subsist those predicables; and the principle that then
it follows that there are those predicables.

It should be noticed, however, that, for reasons also wholly
parallel to those to which we called attention in discussing the
argument from reference, if one accepts some one or another
of these principles, then it becomes quite irrelevant to argue for
the nonreducibility of predicables. For then, *whether or not* a
certain fact can be stated *without* using a term which must be
reckoned as true of some predicables, if it *can* be stated *by* using
such a term, then it follows that there exist, or that there subsist,
or that there are, those predicables. Accordingly, it becomes
irrelevant to inquire whether this fact can also be stated without
using such a term. It becomes irrelevant to argue for the nonreducibility of predicables, unless such argument is interpreted as
an attempt to persuade some opponent that one can indeed use
terms which must be reckoned as true of predicables.

It seems clear that terms can be true of predicables without
those predicables existing or subsisting. Just as we can refer to
predicables that do not exist, and that do not subsist, so too we
can predicate terms of predicables that do not exist, and do not
subsist; and in some cases, the terms which we predicate of non-
existent or nonsubsistent predicables may be true of them. Con-

sider, for example, the sentence "Being a round square is un-exemplified." In assertively uttering this sentence we refer to a predicable which neither exists nor subsists, and we predicate of it "is unexemplified." And the term "is unexemplified" is true of it. In fact, this term is true *only* of predicables which do not exist (as is the term "does not exist"). Similarly, the term "could not be exemplified" is true of the property of being a round square, even though it does not subsist. For it is true of all and only predicables which do not subsist.

Comparable points can be made concerning such things as physical objects, animals, and persons. For example, in assertively uttering "Pegasus is a fictitious creature," we are referring to Pegasus and predicating "is a fictitious creature" of him. And, it being true of him that he is a fictitious creature, the term "is a fictitious creature" is true of him—though, of course, Pegasus does not exist. In fact, "is a fictitious creature" is true only of things that do not exist. And so too, "is dead" and "was destroyed" and "hasn't yet been built" and "was prevented from happening" and "does not exist" are true only of things that do not exist. Or consider the sentence, "Some ghosts are reputed to dwell in cemeteries." This sentence can be used to state the fact that some ghosts are reputed to dwell in cemeteries. In so doing, we use a general term "ghosts"; this term must be true of some of the things reputed to dwell in cemeteries if the sentence is to be used to state the fact. But it does not follow, from the fact that we use such a term, that any of the things reputed to dwell in cemeteries actually exist.

Our conclusion is this: Even if there were no way of asserting the fact that some virtues are out of fashion, other than by using terms which must be reckoned as true of those predicables, it would not follow that there exist or subsist those predicables.

However, the situation with respect to the *being* of predicables again seems different. It does seem that a term cannot be true of some predicable unless *there is* that predicable for the term to be true of. For if a term is true of some predicable, then it follows that *there is* some entity such that it is identical with that predicable and the term in question is true of it. No term at all is true of the property mentioned on the first page of this book, for there is no such property for any term to be true of. Not even the term "is not something of which any term is true" is true of the property mentioned on the first page of this book. Of course, in assertively uttering the sentence "The property mentioned on the first page of this book is not something of which any term is true," one is asserting something true. But in so doing, one is not referring to the property mentioned on the first page of this book and predicating of it a term which is true of it, the term, namely, is not something of which any term is true." A term cannot be true of some predicable unless there is that predicable for it to be true of. A predicable need not exist, nor need it subsist, in order for something to be true of it; but it must *be* in order for some term to be true of it.

From this it follows that the term "has been referred to" cannot be true of some predicable unless there is that predicable.

4. Our contention has been, however, that every fact which can be stated by referring to, and by using terms which are true of, predicables, can also be stated without referring to predicables and without using terms which are true of predicables. We have contended that predicables are reducible. So the question which is immediately relevant is whether it follows from this that no predicables exist, or subsist, or are.

But before we consider this question, it would perhaps be worthwhile briefly to consider a sort of reduction slightly different from that which we have thus far considered. Contemporary logic has served to focus a great deal of the attention of philosophers on quantification sentences (sentences beginning "everything is such that" or "there is at least one thing such that" or with expressions synonymous with these); and many of the discussions concerning 'reducibility' have been conducted by reference to a language consisting exclusively of quantification sentences and sentences which are truth-functions of quantification sentences. So let us introduce the concept of predicables being *quantificationally reducible*. Predicables are quantificationally reducible just in case every fact which can be stated with a quantification sentence (or truth-function thereof) can be stated with one such that no predicables need be reckoned among the entities over which its variables range in order that that sentence be used to state that fact.

Suppose, then, that predicables are *not* quantificationally reducible. Does it follow that some predicables exist, or that some subsist, or that some are? If one could show that predicables are not quantificationally reducible, would one have shown that there exist, or that there subsist, or that there are, some predicables? Could this function as an argument for the existence, or the subsistence, or the being, of predicables?

An example of the sort of argument which comes to mind here is the following:

(i)   That (E*x*) (*x* is a virtue . *x* is admirable) is a fact which can be stated in quantificational language.

(ii) To state that (E*x*) (*x* is a virtue · *x* is admirable) in quantificational language, one must use variables which must be reckoned as ranging over virtues.

(iii) If a fact can be stated in quantificational language, but can be stated only by using sentences whose variables must be reckoned as ranging over certain predicables, then there exist those predicables.

(iv) Hence, there exist certain predicables, namely, virtues.

Variants of this argument can be derived by substituting, in the conclusion and in premise (iii), the words "there subsist" or the words "there are" for the words "there exist."

The crucial premises here are, of course, the claims that if a fact can be stated in quantificational language but can be stated only by using sentences whose variables must be reckoned as ranging over certain predicables, then there exist those predicables. And that then there subsist those predicables. And that then there are those predicables. Now, as our comments on the two parallel sorts of arguments previously considered will immediately suggest, the only plausible reasons for holding these claims are such that the important principles for consideration are the following. If a fact *can* be stated in quantificational language by using sentences whose variables must be reckoned as ranging over certain predicables, does it follow that there exist those predicables? Or that there subsist those predicables? Or that there are those predicables?

As our comments on the two sorts of arguments previously considered also suggest, if one does accept some one or other of these principles, then the issue of the quantificational reducibility or nonreducibility of predicables becomes irrelevant to the conclusion in question. Then it makes no difference whatsoever whether a fact which can be asserted with a quantificational sentence whose variables must be reckoned as ranging over predicables, can or cannot also be asserted with a quantificational sentence whose variables *need not* be reckoned as so ranging. For example, in order that we may assert something true with the quantificational sentence "(Ex) (x = wisdom · Socrates had x)," the predicable wisdom must be reckoned within the range of our variables. But in order that we may assert something true with the quantificational sentence "(Ex) (x = Socrates · x was wise)," it is not necessary that any predicables be reckoned within the range of our variables. Now if the fact that Socrates was wise can be asserted with the quantificational sentence "(Ex) (x = wisdom · Socrates had x)," it matters not whether it can also be asserted with the quantificational sentence "(Ex) (x = Socrates · x was wise)." For if it can be asserted with the former sentence, then, on one of the principles at stake, it follows that there exists such an entity as wisdom.

So are any of these principles acceptable—the principle that if some fact can be stated in quantificational language by using a sentence whose variables must be reckoned as ranging over certain predicables, then there exist those predicables, or the principle that then there subsist those predicables, or the principle that then there are those predicables?

Consider once more the quantificational sentence "(Ex) (x is a virtue · x is admirable)." In order that what is asserted with this sentence may be true, certain predicables must be among the entities over which our variables range. *Or in other words,* in order that what is asserted with this sentence may be true, the two 'functions' in this sentence—"is a virtue" and "is admirable"—must be *true of* certain predicables. And in general, some entities must be reckoned as within the range of our variables just in case these entities must be reckoned as among what our 'functions' are true of.[6]

---

6. Concerning "is true of" and quantification, see Quine, *From a Logical Point of View*, p. 131.

So we can put our question this way. If a certain fact can be stated with a quantificational sentence whose 'functions' must be reckoned as true of certain predicables, does it then follow that there exist, or that there subsist, or that there are, those predicables?

But once the question is put this way, then it becomes clear that we have already answered it in the previous section of this chapter. For 'functions' are terms. And we have already concluded that though a term can be true of some predicable without that predicable existing or subsisting, it cannot be true of some predicable unless there is that predicable. Our conclusion, then, is that, if some fact can be stated in quantificational language by using a sentence whose variables must be reckoned as ranging over certain predicables, then it follows that there are those predicables, though it does not follow that those predicables exist or subsist.

5. To make the point once more, it is academic to inquire whether it would follow from the nonreducibility of predicables that there exist, or that there subsist, or that there are, some predicables. For predicables are in fact reducible. So the relevant question is whether, from the reducibility of predicables, it follows that no predicables exist, or that no predicables subsist, or that there are no predicables.

It would be most implausible indeed to hold that it follows that no predicables exist. For one thing, we have stipulated that the sentence "There exists such a thing as the property of being red" is to be used to assert a proposition equivalent to that normally asserted with "Something is red." And we have claimed that the former is *one* of those normally asserted with "There is such a thing as the property of being red." Now I think that actually there is no reason for not making the stronger claim that 'Something is red' just *is* (rather than, is *equivalent to*) one of the propositions normally asserted with "There is such a thing as the property of being red." Or if this is not true in normal usage, one can stipulate—as we saw earlier—that the words *shall* be used thus. Accordingly, let us take it that in using the words "There *exists* such a thing as the property of being red," as we have agreed to use them, we are asserting that something is red (rather than merely asserting something equivalent to this). Now surely it is a fact that something is red. Hence, we have here a fact which can be asserted by using a singular term standing for a predicable, and thus by referring to a predicable; for in assertively uttering the sentence "There exists such a thing as the property of being red" we refer to the property of being red. But this fact can also be asserted *without* referring to this or any predicable; for we can assert it with the sentence "Something is red." Now it could not possibly follow from the fact that this and other replacement sentences are available, that there does not exist such a thing as the property of being red. For this sentence provides us with nothing less than a way of stating the fact which could also be stated with the sentence "There exists such a thing as the property of being red."

Secondly, not only are predicables reducible to nonpredicables; it is also the case that nonpredicables are reducible to predicables. As a replacement for the sentence "Somebody is wise," we could use the sentence "Wisdom is sometimes exemplified." As a replacement for "Everything is wise," we could use "Wisdom is always exemplified." As a replacement for "Socrates is wise," we could use "Being wise and being Socrates are jointly exemplified." As a replacement for "Some men are wise" we could use "Being a man and being wise are sometimes jointly exemplified." And as a replacement for "All men are wise" we could use "Being a man is, if ever exemplified, always jointly exemplified with being wise." It looks, in fact, as if the reduction of nonpredicables to predicables can be accomplished with far more ease and economy than the reverse reduction. And let us again be reminded that if we find ordinary language too restrictive, we always have available to us the tactic of either introducing words and phrases, or complete locutions, in order to accomplish our replacement project.

But now, given that both predicables and nonpredicables are reducible, if it followed from the reducibility of a certain sort of entity that there exist no entities of that sort, it would be the case that nothing at all exists—a most implausible consequence.

So, from the fact that every fact can be stated without referring to any predicable, and without using a term which must be true of some predicable if that fact is to be stated, it does not follow that no predicables exist. But if it does not follow that no predicables exist, then also it does not follow that there subsist, or that there are, no predicables.

It would be equally implausible to hold that the *quantificational* reducibility of predicables entails that there exist no predicables. The fact that there exists such a predicable as red, can be asserted with the sentence "There is at least one thing such that it is red." And for this sentence, no predicables need be reckoned within the range of its variables. Yet from the fact that this quantificational replacement sentence is available, it can obviously not follow that there does not exist such a predicable as red. There may exist all kinds of things which, for the purpose of stating all the facts, we need not quantify over (though, of course, for other purposes we *may* have to quantify over them). Hence, even if predicables are quantificationally reducible, it does not follow that no predicables exist. In assertively uttering "There is something such that it is identical with Socrates and it is wise," what I assert entails the existence of the property of being wise, and of the property of being identical with Socrates, though neither of these need be reckoned within the range of the variables. But if it does not follow that no predicables exist from the fact that predicables are quantificationally reducible, then also it does not follow that there *subsist,* or that there *are,* no predicables.

6. We have explored, at length, one view as to the ontological significance of the reducibility or nonreducibility of predicables. We can now, very briefly, deal with another. It has sometimes been said that if one sort of entity is reducible to another, then it follows that the latter sort is ontologically more *basic* than the former. The claim is that if predicables are reducible, so that even the claim that there are predicables can be asserted without referring to predicables or using any term which must be reckoned as true of them, then surely predicables are not a *basic* sort of entity. They are, perhaps, logical constructions.

So, is reducibility the linguistic reflection of an ontological hierarchy of more and less basic entities? Not, I think, if the words "more basic than" are used in anywhere near their normal sense. For one thing, it would seem that one could not *make* predicables more basic than nonpredicables; and certainly, that one could not make them more basic just by creating words for the purpose. Yet we have seen that a reduction of predicables to nonpredicables can always be accomplished by fiat, if not by discovery. Secondly, it would seem that if predicables are more basic than nonpredicables, then it cannot also be the case that nonpredicables are more basic than predicables. Yet it is clearly the case that nonpredicables are reducible to predicables as well as predicables to nonpredicables. So the reducibility of predicables to nonpredicables does not show, in any reasonable sense of these words, that nonpredicables are more basic than predicables.

Is there then something else of ontological significance that it shows? So far as I can see, the answer to this must be "No." The fact that all the facts can be stated without referring to predicables, and without using terms which must be reckoned as true of predicables, and without quantifying over predicables, seems to me in itself to have no ontological significance. The fact that one can avoid such linguistic acts and still state all the facts has no ontological significance. On the other hand, the fact that one *can* refer to predicables, and *can* use terms which must be reckoned as true of predicables, and *can* quantify over predicables *does* have ontological significance. For it entails that there are predicables.

Universals

PART THREE

10

Space, Time,
and Universals

1. Thus far in our discussion we have been dealing with what I have called *predicables*. We have distinguished predicables from nonpredicables, or *substances;* and we have drawn this distinction by using the concept of (nonlinguistic) predication. A predicable is what can be predicated, a substance is what cannot be predicated.

It turns out, on these definitions, that the class of substances is a very mixed bag of things. Not only exemplifications, but also cases of predicables are substances; for example, not only Napoleon, but also Napoleon's brashness. And among those substances which are exemplifications of predicables are to be found not only events and physical objects and persons, but also such entities as poems, symphonies, species, classes, groups, organizations, stuffs, and propositions. For though, to give but one example, one can of course predicate *being Bartok's Fifth Quartet* of something, one cannot predicate Bartok's Fifth Quartet itself.

Among predicables, further, we drew a distinction between those which can fittingly be called *universals* and those which cannot be. The distinction was that between those which can be truly predicated of more than one thing, and those which can not be truly predicated of more than one thing. *Being identical with Napoleon* is a predicable nonuniversal, as is *being a round square;* whereas *being identical with someone named "Napoleon"* is a predicable universal, for it is possible that it should be truly predicated of more than one thing.

Just as there can be exemplifications of a single predicable universal, so, analogously, there can be many copies, and many recitations, of a single literary work (for example, "Sailing to Byzantium"). There can be many performances of a single musical work (Bartok's Fifth Quartet). There can be many copies, and many showings, of a single film ("Blowup"). There can be many inscriptions, and many utterances, of a single word or sequence of words. There can be many impressions of a single art-print (Rembrandt's "Hundred Guilder Print"). There can be many performances of a single dance (the Zuni Rain Dance). There can be many castings of a single sculpture (Rodin's "The Thinker"). There can be many productions of a single car-model (the '32 Ford Victoria), of a single house-model (the Tech-Bilt House), of a single chair-model (the Barcelona Chair), of a single flag (the American Flag). There can be many playings of a single game (baseball). There can be many copies, and many productions, and many performances, of a single drama. There can be many issues of a single newspaper (*The Grand Rapids Press*), many numbers of a single journal, many editions of a single book. There can be many executions of a single play or move in a game (the Draw-Play). There can be many doings of a single exercise (the push-up). There can be many uses of a single argument. There can be many printings of a single stamp. There can be many mintings of a single coin (the Buffalo-Head Nickel). There can be many examples of a single genus or species (the Lion). There can be many cases of a single disease.

In all these cases one feels, I think, a strong analogy between the fact cited, and the fact that there can be many exemplifications of a predicable. Now in every such case there is present, of course, a one-many contrast. But the feeling of analogy must have deeper roots than this. For everything whatsoever is such that it bears *some* relation to many things. A painting, for example, can have many reproductions; a father, many children; a house, many doors; but we do not feel any strong analogy between these facts and the fact that a predicable can have many exemplifications. Nor, I think, do we feel any strong analogy between this fact and the facts that a class can have many members, that a group or organization can have many members, and that a stuff can have many quantities of it.

It is well known that more sorts of things than predicables have been called universals. The whole medieval and ancient tradition regarded natural kinds—species and genera—as universals; and contemporary philosophers have frequently cited such things as literary works and musical works as examples of universals. In this and the following chapter I wish to see what, if anything, can be made of this concept of universal, a concept such that both predicables and nonpredicables fall under it. Is there any significant analogy between the relation of a predicable to its exemplifications, on the one hand, and, on the other, the relation of a kind to its many examples, a literary work to its many copies, a musical work to its many performances? Or is our feeling, that there is a significant analogy here, illusory, having no solid basis in fact? Is there any rationale for speaking of substance-universals as well as of predicable-universals?

2. It is common practice, among philosophers of modern and contemporary times, to draw a distinction between those entities which are capable of recurrence, or repetition in space-time, and those which are not. Whitehead, for example, makes the distinction very deliberately. Calling properties and qualities "objects" he says, "We are comparing objects in events whenever we can say, 'There it is again.' Objects are the elements in nature which can be again."[1] In another place he says, "A colour is eternal. It haunts time like a spirit. It comes and it goes. But where it comes, it is the same color."[2] In yet another place he says, "The same object can be found in different parts of space and time, and this cannot hold for events."[3] "Objects have the possibility of recurrence in experience."[4] The very same sort of

1. A.N. Whitehead, *Concept of Nature* (Cambridge, 1920), p. 144.
2. A.N. Whitehead, *Science and the Modern World* (New York, 1931), p. 126.
3. A.N. Whitehead, *Principles of Natural Knowledge* (Cambridge, 1919), p. 66.
4. Ibid., p. 64.

distinction appears, this time almost offhandedly, in Miss Anscombe's book on the *Tractatus*. Criticizing F.P. Ramsey's contention that, since red and something which is red can both enter into several facts, there is no fundamental distinction between them, she says, critically, "It takes a little mental habituation to think that existence in several facts is the only feature that counts, so that since both A and red can exist in several facts, we should not be impressed by A's at least existing in only one place at a time, while red can exist in so many."[5]

Usually the distinction between entities capable of recurrence in space-time and those not capable of such recurrence, has been denominated as the distinction between *universals* and *particulars*. Thus far in our discussion we have ignored this universal-particular distinction. We have concentrated solely on the predicable-substance distinction. Let us now pick up this thus-far neglected distinction and see whether it sheds light on the problem at hand. Is it the case that those predicables which can be truly predicated of many are spatio-temporally repeatable? Is it the case that those which cannot be truly predicated of many are not spatio-temporally repeatable? And is it the case that those things which we feel to be radically different from predicables—events, physical objects, persons—are not spatio-temporally repeatable? And where do such things as musical works, literary works, and natural kinds fall? Are they too repeatable? Is it the case that they, along with those predicables which are truly predicable of many, fit into the framework of space and time in a fundamentally different way from the way of events and physical objects and persons? Is it the case that a single predicable, a single species, a single musical work, a single literary work, a single game, a single word, a single dance, can each be in many different places and/or times; and do they differ in this way from events, physical objects, and persons? If so, this would no doubt ground our feeling of a close analogy between the things in the list given earlier, and justify us in calling them all *universals*.

Whitehead spoke of a thing as being again, whereas Anscombe spoke of one thing as being in different places at the same time. Which of these is to be used to draw the distinction we are con-

5. G. Anscombe, *Introduction to Wittgenstein's Tractatus* (London, 1959), p. 109.

cerned with? Or should we put them together, and say that a thing is repeatable just in case it can be again, or can be in different places at the same time? But then, is being again to be regarded as happening whenever a thing exists at two different times? And is a desk, which has a size of five feet by three feet by two and one-half feet, thereby in many different places at once? Evidently to answer these questions, and so to arrive at a suitable definition of "repeatability," we shall have to look into some of the ways in which things can be in space and time.

3. Let us notice, first, that something may be or take place somewhere, without being or taking place anywhere in space. Suppose, for example, that with my eyes shut there is presented to me a red patch with a black dot superimposed. Then it might be that the black dot is in the middle of the red patch which I am now seeing. Still, I think it is clear that the black dot is not anywhere in space; one thing can bear a spatial relation to another thing, without either of the things being in space. There are, though, other states of consciousness which, so it seems, can be somewhere in space, for example, bodily pains. When I have a pain in my finger, that pain is somewhere in space; and amputees testify that they sometimes have pains in places not occupied by any part of their bodies. There is another class of states of consciousness which seem, in the respects mentioned, a good deal like pains, but which are not, I think, anywhere in space; these are those afterimages which we see somewhere— when we look, for example, from a sheet on which there is a red area surrounded by green, to a white sheet. In such cases, though one sees the gray afterimage *on* the white sheet, and thus sees it somewhere, perhaps even sees it somewhere in space, it would certainly be misleading to say that that is where it is. Thus one can see something somewhere in space, without that thing's *being* anywhere in space.

For the sake of convenience, then, let us henceforth use the phrase "location in space" as follows. A location of a thing in space at a certain time is any place where it is or takes place in space at that time. It is what, if anything, can be given as a true answer to the question, asked of the thing in question, "Where is it, or where does it take place, in space?"

The reason for not saying merely "is in space," but adding "or takes place in space" is this: There are some entities such that though they take place somewhere, still they *are* not anywhere. For example, there is no correct answer to the question, asked of some collision or some performance of a symphony, "Where is it?" though there is a correct answer to the question, "Where did it take place?" And if it is in space that something takes place, as it often is, then we shall say that it has a location in space—its location being, of course, *where* it takes place.

Let us notice, next, that though collisions and symphonic performances do have location in space, they yet do not have a north half and a southern half, a left half and a right half, a top half and a bottom half. On the other hand, my desk, which likewise has location in space, does have a north and south, left and right, top and bottom, half. Thus some of the things which have location in space have spatial parts and some do not. It may be noted that some of the things which lack location in space yet have spatial parts, for example, afterimages.

We are now in a position to distinguish between what I shall call *multiple location in space* and *divided location in space*. A thing which is located in space will be said to have *multiple* location in space at a given time if it has more than one location in space at that time. A thing which is located in space will be said to have *divided* location in space at a given time if at that time it has at least two spatial parts having different spatial locations. The crucial difference, be it noted, is the difference between one thing being at different places in space at a given time, and one thing having spatial parts which are at different places at a given time.

It is evident that physical objects have divided, but not multiple, location. They themselves cannot be in different places at the same time, but they do have parts which are in different locations at the same time. It would seem to be the view of Whitehead and Anscombe that predicables, on the other hand, are capable of multiple location. Whether this view is correct will be considered shortly.

To say that an entity can have multiple location in space at a given time is to say that one of its locations can be to the north of, or above, or to the left of, another of its locations.

Now this is different from saying that the *thing* is to the north of, or above, or to the left of, itself. One can hold that things are capable of multiple location in space, without holding that spatial-ordering relations are reflexive.

Our definition of multiple location allows for both the case in which there is spatial discontinuity among the locations of a thing at a time, and the case in which there is no discontinuity. Predicables are, by reputation, not only capable of multiple location, but capable of spatial discontinuity in their locations at a given time. Perhaps the French Revolution is another example of the same phenomenon. In principle there could, however, also be entities which, though capable of multiple location, are not capable of *discontinuous* multiple locations. Such entities, though they could be in different places at the same time, could only be in adjoining places.

Also our definition of divided location allows for both the case in which there is spatial discontinuity among the locations of a thing's spatial parts, and the case in which there is no such discontinuity. An obvious case of such discontinuity would be the case of a suite of furniture which, as a whole, has a spatial location in a certain room. The part constituting one of the pieces of furniture is spatially disconnected from the part constituting one of the other pieces; there is no place between them which is in turn the location of some spatial part of the thing.

Now before we put these distinctions to use in trying to formulate a satisfactory definition of repeatability, let us make a series of comparable distinctions for the relation of things to time.

We saw, earlier, that a thing could be somewhere, without being somewhere in space. Something similar is to be found in the case of time. In a dream, for example, there are before and after relations among the dreamed events. But these events do not themselves take place in time (though the *dreaming* of them does). So let us define "position in time". A position in time of some thing is whenever it is (was, will be) or takes (took, will take) place in time. It is any time at which or during which it is (was, will be) or takes (took, will take) place. It would seem that everything whatsoever that is (was, will be) or takes (took, will take) place in time has some position in time.

Such a thing as a race, be it noted, can be half over at a certain point. Within the stretch of time from the beginning of the race to that point, the race itself does not take place, only half of the race does. That stretch of time does not constitute the temporal position of the race; rather, it constitutes the temporal position of the first half of the race. But now suppose that my desk endures throughout today—today then being one of its positions in time. It also exists at each component stretch of time—the *desk* does, not half of it, or a quarter of it. And if my green ashtray gradually, over the years of its existence, becomes blackened, it is not the case that part of the ashtray was green, part black, and part somewhere in between. Physical objects, in short, do not have temporal parts, whereas such things as races do. Of course, corresponding to a physical object is what we might call the *life* or *history* of the object. And *that* has temporal parts. During a certain stretch of time not the whole history of my ashtray but only half of it, is to be found. And, for each of us, our life is half over at a certain point, though we ourselves are not; in the stretch of time from our birth to that point is to be found half of our life, but not half of ourself. We are not our histories; we are not our lives.

Corresponding to the distinction between multiple and divided location in space, let us distinguish between *multiple* and *divided* position in time. A thing which is positioned within time will be said to have *multiple position in time* if it is positioned at or during more than one time. And a thing which is positioned in time will be said to have *divided position in time* if it has at least two temporal parts which have different temporal locations. What is to be noted here is just the distinction between the case in which one thing has more than one position in time, and the case in which one temporal part of a thing has one position in time and another temporal part another position in time.

Since physical objects do not have temporal parts, they do not have divided position in time. Obviously, however, they do have multiple position in time; my desk exists now—*it* does, and not some temporal part of it; it also existed a minute ago—*it* did, and not some temporal part of it. Predicables, likewise, have multiple but not divided position in time, and it was this similarity between physical objects and predicables which led Whitehead to assimilate them to each other and call both "objects." A musical performance is a good example of something which has divided position in time, but is incapable of multiple position; for there can be one, and only one, time during which it takes place.

We must distinguish, as we did in the case of space, between the temporal relations of things, and the temporal relations of the temporal positions of things. One of the temporal positions of a thing may be before another; indeed, this will be the case if a thing has more than one temporal position. But it does not follow from this that, in such a case, the thing is before itself. One can allow that some things have multiple positions in time, without allowing that all temporal-ordering relations are reflexive.

Our definition of multiple position in time allows for both the case in which there is temporal discontinuity among the positions of a thing in time, and the case in which there is no such discontinuity—that is, for the case in which a thing is or takes place at or during one time, and another time, and no intervening time; and the case in which, if a thing is or takes place at or during one time, and another time, it also is or takes place at every intervening time. Similarly, our definition of divided position in time allows for both the case in which there is temporal discontinuity among the positions in time of a thing's temporal parts, and the case in which there is no such discontinuity. A symphonic performance, in which there is a pause between the movements, would be an example of the former. At a certain time during the time of the entire performance, no part of the performance is taking place.

4. In one sense, of course, no entity is repeatable; there can be only one of each thing. But quite clearly, when philosophers have spoken of certain entities as repeatable, or capable of recurring, they had in mind the relation of such entities to space and/or time. And no doubt what they were pointing to was the phenomenon of *multiple,* as distinguished from *divided,* location or position. Whether it was the phenomenon of multiple location in space that they had in mind, or multiple position in time, or both, is less clear. To mention just the two cases we have cited, Whitehead seems to have had chiefly multiple po-

sition in time in mind, whereas Anscombe seems to have had multiple location in space in mind. Let us then consider the various possibilities.

Suppose we say that a thing is repeatable just in case it can have multiple position in space at a given time. Can we then single out universals as being those entities which are repeatable? That is to say, do multiply-predicable predicables, and entities which we feel to bear a significant analogy to them, turn out to be distinguished from other entities as being repeatable?

A question to be raised at once is whether predicables, musical works, literary works, natural kinds, and others have spatial locations at all, let alone multiple locations. Are there correct answers to such questions as these:

Where is the property of being six feet tall?
Where is the lion?
Where is Bartok's Fifth Quartet?
Where is Yeats' "Sailing to Byzantium"?

If a copy of "Sailing to Byzantium" is on the mantel, then I think that a perfectly appropriate and true answer to the question "Where is Yeats' 'Sailing to Byzantium'?" is this: "On the mantel." It might be argued that if we regard this as a true answer, then we are really interpreting the question as one which would more strictly be asked with these words: "Where is a *copy* of Yeats' 'Sailing to Byzantium'?" For, the argument would go, a *copy* of Yeats' poem can well be on the mantel, but the poem itself cannot be. And the fact that we can appropriately and correctly answer "On the mantel" to the question "Where is Yeats' 'Sailing to Byzantium'?" just indicates that this is an ambiguous form of words, failing to distinguish between a poem and a copy of a poem.

I see no reason to suppose that this objection is correct. Why should not "On the mantel" be a correct answer to "Where is Yeats' poem 'Sailing to Byzantium'?" as well as to, "Where is a *copy* of Yeats' poem 'Sailing to Byzantium'?" Why should not a poem be wherever some copy of it is? Perhaps, even, we should not regard the question "Where is Yeats' poem 'Sailing to Byzantium'?" and the question "Where is a copy of Yeats' poem 'Sailing to Byzantium'?" as two different questions having the very same answer, but rather as one question asked with two different word-sequences, the same question being also askable with these words: "Where is Yeats' 'Sailing to Byzantium'?"

I think it is much less clear, however, that there is an appropriate and true answer to the question "Where is the property of being six feet tall?" Indeed, it seems to me quite clear that there is no appropriate and true answer to this question. But if not, then, by our definitions, *the property of being six feet tall* turns out to be *non*repeatable. For, being then susceptible of no location in space, it is of course not susceptible of multiple location.

Now quite clearly the basic assumption of those who have tried to distinguish between universals and particulars by reference to the concept of repeatability in space, is that a poem is where its copies are, a musical work where its performances are, a kind where its examples are, a predicable where its exemplifications are. We have seen reason to doubt that this assumption holds for *all* such cases. But suppose it be granted. By granting it, do we achieve the result that universals are those entities which are repeatable in space?

Not at all. Not even all *predicable* universals are repeatable in space. For not all predicables are such that their *exemplifications* have spatial location. *The property of being a thought* is one such, *the property of having no spatial location* is another such. And so the concept of repeatability in space is obviously inadequate for the work we want done. The matter is not improved if we start with the concept of *non*repeatability, define "a particular" as any object which has location in space but is not capable of having multiple location, and define "a universal" simply as a nonparticular. On this definition, *the property of being a thought* and *the property of having no spatial location* would indeed turn out to be universals. But so would God, and angels, and numbers, all of them entities which lack the analogy to predicable universals that we are requiring of universals generally.

What, then, about repeatability in time? Suppose we say that an entity is repeatable just in case it can have multiple position in time. Can we then single out universals as being those entities which are repeatable *in time?*

No. This too is unsatisfactory. For on this definition it turns out that such things as physical objects and persons are universals, since physical objects and persons, as we saw, have multiple position in time. A minute ago was a time at which my desk existed, and half a minute ago was another time at which my desk existed.

At this point it might be suggested that, though predicables and physical objects are alike in that they are both capable of multiple location in time, what differentiates them is that predicables can *be again,* whereas physical objects can only *be yet*— that is, that predicables, unlike physical objects, are capable of *discontinuous* multiple position in time.

Suppose, then, that "a universal" were defined as what is capable of discontinuous multiple position in time. Would *this* be satisfactory for our purposes?

One question to raise, obviously, is whether it is in fact impossible for persons and physical objects to have discontinuous multiple position in time. Is it impossible, *logically* impossible, that a certain sofa should exist for a while, then go out of existence for a time, and then come back into existence? And is it logically impossible that a person should exist for a time, then die and go out of existence, and then be resurrected?

These are difficult questions, involving subtle issues of identity. They must, of course, be answered if the definition at hand proves satisfactory in all other respects. But I think that that is just what it does *not* do.

We saw earlier that the words "there is," when used in connection with predicables, are ambiguous. For example, in assertively uttering, with normal meaning, the words "There is such a thing as the property of being green," I may be asserting a proposition equivalent to the claim that something is green, or one equivalent to the claim that possibly something is green. Now if the condition for there being such a property as being green is understood to be that possibly something is green, then the property of being green cannot go out of and come back into being. But if the condition for there being such a property as being green is understood to be that something is green, then the property of being green can go out of and come back into being. It is, in short, capable of discontinuous multiple position in time. And so far, then, the definition of "universal" as what is capable of discontinuous multiple position in time is satisfactory.

But there are many predicables which are necessarily exemplified at all times; and so, no matter how we understand "being" when used in connection with predicables, these are not capable of discontinuous multiple position in time. One example of such a predicable is this: *Being an animal if a cat.* And another is this: *Being a predicable.*

So neither the concept of repeatability in time, nor the concept of discontinuous repeatability in time, is satisfactory for distinguishing universals from nonuniversals in the manner we desire. And nothing is gained if we use *both* the concept of repeatability in space and the concept of repeatability in time. For if we say that something is a universal just in case it is capable of *both* multiple location in space and multiple position in time, then the predicable *being a thought* turns out not to be a universal, for it cannot have location in space at all. And if we say that something is a universal just in case it is capable of *either* multiple location in space *or* multiple position in time, then physical objects and persons turn out to be universals, for they have multiple position in time.

We have not rung quite all the changes on the concept of repeatability, but enough has been said to show this: Our feeling that there is a fundamental similarity between predicables on the one hand, and such entities as natural kinds, literary works, musical works, and the like, on the other, is not based on the fact that all such entities, as distinguished from those which seem clearly different, are *repeatable.* Even more generally, the various properties of space and time can of course be used to draw various distinctions between sorts of entities. But they will not serve to distinguish universals from nonuniversals in the fashion that we are requiring.

5. It was important to Whitehead, in his ontology, that there be entities which could not be repeated in time and space, as well as entities which *could* be repeated in time and space. It seems to have been his belief, further, that an entity is nonrepeatable if and only if whatever locations in space it has could not have been different, and whatever positions in time it has

could not have been different. The only entities which seemed to him, on this criterion, to be nonrepeatable, were what in his earlier writings he called events, and what later he called actual entities. And by an event, or actual entity, he seems to have meant what has sometimes been called "a four-dimensional chunk" of the spatio-temporal continuum.

Now I think there is a great deal of difficulty in understanding just what such a "chunk" may actually be. But here I wish just to comment on the view that an entity is nonrepeatable just in case whatever location in space it has and whatever position in time it has could not have been different. A physical object cannot, I think, be repeated in space. Yet most, if not all, physical objects might have had different spatial locations from those they do have. My desk might have been one foot to the west of where it now in fact is. Though physical objects are not repeatable in space, their spatial locations are not intrinsic to them. Or again, a given performance of a given symphony is not, I should think, capable of repetition in time. Yet its position in time might have been different from what it is; it might have started ten minutes earlier than it did. Thus this is an example of something which, though not repeatable in time, yet is not such that its position in time is intrinsic to it.

11

Kinds

1. We were unsuccessful, in our previous chapter, in drawing the distinction between universals and nonuniversals by using the concept of repeatability. We were, that is to say, unsuccessful in discovering, in the phenomenon of repeatability, any basis for our feeling that there is a close analogy between, on the one hand, the relation of a single predicable to its exemplifications, and, on the other, the relation of a single literary work to its many copies, a single musical work to its many performances, a single natural kind to its many examples.

In this chapter I should like to make a fresh attempt at discovering a basis for this feeling. I shall conclude that all the entities cited as examples of universals are in fact *kinds* (types). To lay the groundwork for arriving at this conclusion, let us elucidate some features of the concept of a kind (type).

The recognition of kinds is, of course, by no means foreign to the thought of practical life. We are all aware of the fact that there are countless different kinds of things, the things being examples of the kinds. For instance, we recognize that there are various different kinds of cows, the Hereford being one of them; that there are various different kinds of animals, the Lion being one of them; that there are various different kinds of plants, the Lily being one of them. Some, but not all, cows we recognize to be examples of the Hereford; some animals, to be examples of the Lion; some plants, to be examples of the Lily.

Not only do we, in practical life, recognize the existence of kinds, we also, in ordinary speech, name and refer to kinds. I have just referred to three of them: the Hereford, the Lion, the Lily. A linguistic structure was manifested by the names I have used. The name of the kind was composed by prefacing common nouns true of examples of the kinds ("hereford," "lion," "lily") with the word "the." And this is a thoroughly standard way, in English, of forming names of kinds. It is also, though, a standard way, in English, of forming definite descriptions. Suppose, for example, that I begin a story to my children thus: "Once upon a time a boy and a lion were walking in a woods. The boy, as boys will do, was teasing the lion. And the lion, as lions will do, was growling in annoyance." Here the expressions "the boy" and "the lion" are not functioning as names of kinds, but rather as definite descriptions. The expression "the boy" is being used to refer to a particular boy, real or imaginary, the one the speaker had in mind in his first sentence when he spoke of *a* boy; and the expression "the lion" is being used to refer to a particular lion, real or imaginary, the one the speaker had in mind when earlier he spoke of *a* lion. Thus, to tell whether such an expression as "the lion" is being used to refer to the kind, Lion, or is being used to refer to an example of this kind, we must look at how the expression is functioning. Form alone will not tell us.

It must be added that by no means all names of kinds in English are of the form just discussed. "Man," not "the Man," is correct; and the taxonomist does not preface his latinate names of biological kinds with "the." He says simply, for example, *"Quercus imbricaria."*

Just as common nouns prefaced with "the" can be used both to refer to kinds and to refer to examples of the kinds, so, similarly, common nouns themselves are, in standard usage, true both of kinds and of examples of the kinds. The word "plant," or "a plant," for example, is true both of plant-examples and of plant-kinds. This is most clearly seen, perhaps, by noticing the ambiguity in such a question as "How many different plants do you have in your garden?" This may mean either: *How many different plant-examples do you have in your garden?* or *How many different plant-kinds do you have in your garden?* And, depending on what is meant, different answers may be correct. Suppose, for example, that my entire garden consists of one rose bush and two lily corms. Then to the question "How many different plants do you have?" I can answer, truly, either "two" or "three." I can point in the direction of two different plants and say, truly and appropriately, "This is the same plant as that."

Underlying the fact that these two different correct answers can be given, is the fact that there are two different, equally correct, ways of counting what I have in my garden. I can count either plant-kinds, or examples of plant-kinds. Of course, in some situations there may be even more than two ways of counting plants. For example, if it were the case that I had three lily corms and one rose bush in my garden, the lilies being of two different species, then I could correctly say that I had three plants in my garden, as well as two or four. For plant-species can be counted as well as plant-particulars and plant-genera. Kinds are what are counted when, in the situation last indicated, we arrive, after counting correctly, at either the conclusion that there are two, or that there are three, plants in the garden.

Thus far we have cited, by way of example, only natural, as opposed to man-made, kinds: The Hereford, the Lion, the Lily. Further, the kinds we have cited are all ones whose examples are objects capable of repetition in time. But there are also natural kinds of other sorts—for example, the Bee's Honey-Dance and the Wren's Song. Many honey-dances can be performed by bees, all of them examples of the Bee's Honey-Dance; and many songs can be sung by wrens, all of them examples of the Wren's Song. Both of these are kinds whose examples are occurrences, entities incapable of repetition in time. The linguistic form for speaking of such kinds is the same as that available for speaking of the other sort of natural kinds. For example, the name of the Wren's Song is obtained by prefacing the common noun "wren's song" with the word "the"; and the common noun "a wren's song" is ambiguous, true both of wren's song-kinds and wren's song-examples. The question "How many different wren's songs did you hear?" may be an invitation to count wren's song-examples or wren's song-kinds.

The recognition of kinds in practical life is by no means limited, however, to natural kinds. It includes man-made and man-performed kinds. The American Flag and the Barcelona Chair, for instance, are familiar kinds whose examples are temporally repeatable objects; and the Draw-Play and the Zuni Rain Dance are kinds whose examples are occurrences not capable of repetition in time. There can be many American flags, all of them examples of the American Flag; there can be many Barcelona chairs, all of them examples of the Barcelona Chair. Many draw plays can be executed, all of them examples of the Draw-Play; many Zuni rain dances can be performed, all of them examples of the Zuni Rain Dance. Names of these kinds are formed in the now-familiar manner. And just as "plant" is ambiguously true both of examples and kinds, so too "flag" and "chair" and "play" and "dance" are true both of kinds and of examples of those kinds. Suppose, for instance, that someone asks, referring to a football game: 'How many different plays were used in the game?" This is ambiguous in a way which we have found to be typical. It may be that the Draw-Play, if used at all, is to count as one play, or it may be that every *use* of the Draw-Play is to count as one play. Thus different answers will be correct depending on what is actually being asked. So, too, the owner of a furniture store can count the different chairs he has in stock either by counting chair-kinds or by counting chair-examples.

2. So far we have done nothing more than cite, by way of example, various familiar kinds, and point to some features of the language used for talking about kinds. Let us now look briefly at the nature of kinds.

In the first place, is it at all possible to say under what circumstances there *is* such-and-such a kind? We have stuck to familiar, commonly recognized kinds. But of course there are many which go unrecognized. Can we give anything like a criterion for the being of kinds?

If there is *a k,* then it would seem that there is such a kind as *The K.* But is it also a *necessary* condition of there being such a kind as *The K* that there is at least one *k?* Can there not be such a kind as *The K* even though there are no *k's?* Is there not, for example, such a kind as the Square Circle? Or is it at least demanded that there possibly are or were or will be *k's?* Is the criterion this: There is such a kind as *The K* if and only if it is possible that at some time there are one or more *k's?*

There is of course no dodo; though, on the other hand, it is certainly possible that there should be one. Thus one who adopts the criterion just cited is committed to holding that there is such a kind as the Dodo, even though there are no dodoes. But is it true that there is such a kind as the Dodo? Is it not rather perhaps the case that there *was* such a kind as the Dodo? And is not the correct schema perhaps this: There is such a kind as *the K* if and only if there is *a k?* Or is even this satisfactory? Is, perhaps, the correct schema not rather this: There is such a kind as the K if and only if there is at least one and could be more than one *k?*

It is clear that the puzzles and unclarities over the criteria for the being of kinds, which we are here uncovering, are very similar to those which we uncovered in discussing criteria for the being of predicables. And I think the solution must be similar. We must acknowledge that "there is," when used in connection with references to kinds, is highly ambiguous. In using a sentence of the form 'There is such a kind as the K' one may, without departing from normal sense, assert various propositions. One may, for instance, assert a proposition which is equivalent to the corresponding proposition of the form: It is possible that there is *a k.* Or, one which is equivalent to the corresponding proposition of the form: There is at least one *k.* And these two possibilities do not yet begin to exhaust the range of possibilities.

For the sake of clarity in our ensuing discussion, henceforth whenever I use a sentence of the form 'There is such a kind as the *K,*' I shall be using it to assert a proposition such that its truth does not even require that there should possibly be *k's.* There is such a kind of shape as: the Square Circle.

Another issue to consider is whether a kind is not just the same thing as a class. Certainly the two are similar. The relation of a class to its members is much like that of a kind to its examples; in fact, it does not seem incorrect to say that the examples of a kind are *members* of the kind. And there can be kinds of kinds, just as there can be classes of classes.

But in spite of their close similarities, kinds are not the same thing as classes—the decisive differences being the following two. No class can have had different members from those it does have, whereas many kinds can have had different examples from those they do have; and necessarily classes are identical just in case there is nothing which is a member of the one and not of the other, whereas there may well be nonidentical kinds such that there is nothing which is an example of the one and not of the other.

Let us consider the latter point first. The standard criterion for the identity of classes is the one cited. That this is not the criterion for the identity of kinds, however, is perhaps most clearly seen from the case of a kind which has no examples. Consider, for instance, the Dodo and the Passenger Pigeon. Both of these kinds are extinct—that is, no examples of either exist. Yet the Dodo is surely not the same kind of bird as the Passenger Pigeon. However, the class of all currently existing dodoes is identical with the class of all currently existing passenger pigeons—it is the null class. So also, even if it were the case that all and only pro soccer players were stonecutters, still the Pro Soccer Player would not be the same kind as the Stonecutter.

We have seen before in chapter 8 that a class cannot have had different members from those it does have. The phrase "the class of the apostles of Christ" might have stood for a different class from that for which it does in fact stand (if, for instance, fewer or more or other men had followed Christ than did). And the class of men which the phrase "the class of the apostles of Christ" does in fact stand for might have existed even though none of the men who did in fact follow Christ had followed him, or if no one had followed him (though in either of these cases we could not, of course, *refer to* the class of the apostles of Christ with the phrase "the class of the apostles of Christ"). But the class which this phrase does in fact stand for could not have had different or more or fewer members than it does have.

Kinds are not so. The null class could not have had members.[1] But the Dodo, though it is extinct, might not have been extinct; there might have been some examples of the Dodo now existing. And there might have been more examples of the Pure-Blooded Indian than in fact there are. Kinds—many of them— are constantly changing with respect to their examples; examples of Man come and go, while the kind perdures. But the class of men cannot change with respect to its membership. The class of all men now existing is a different class from the class of all men who exist at some time or other; but the kind of which all men now existing are examples by virtue of being men, is the same kind as that of which all men who exist at any time are members by virtue of being men.

The feature of kinds which has engendered the most philosophical discussion and perplexity is that of the relationship between predications true of kinds and predications true of examples of the kinds. So let us turn to this issue.

The Grizzly is a kind. And the Grizzly is hairy. Does it follow that a certain kind is hairy? Can kinds be hairy?

It is true, is it not, that the Lion has four feet, that it roars, and that it is found largely in tropical countries? But how are we to understand such a proposition? Is it equivalent to this: There is something such that it is identical with the kind, Lion, and it has four feet and it roars and it is found largely in tropical countries? And if it is equivalent to this, does it follow that if we were making a list of all the things capable of roaring, we would have to include the kind, Lion, on the list; that if we were making a list of all the four-footed entities, we would have to include the kind, Lion; and that if we but searched long enough in tropical countries we would find the kind, Lion? Can kinds roar? Can kinds have four legs? Can kinds dwell in tropical countries? Or is it that the kind, Lion, can indeed roar, but not roar in the usual sense of the word "roar"; have four legs, but not have four legs in the usual sense of the words "have four legs"; live in tropical countries, but not in the usual sense of the words "live in tropical countries"? Do our dictionary-

---

1. Professor Peter deVos has pointed out to me that the null class must not be confused with the kind, the Null Class. This *kind* has an example, namely, the null class.

makers manifest a serious blind spot in not systematically distinguishing these nonusual senses of predicates for us? But suppose they tried to correct the blind spot, how would they define the nonusual sense of, say, "roar"? Evidently something in all this needs clarification.

What seems clear is that one can indeed assertively utter, and thereby speak truly, the sentence "The Lion roars." What also seems clear is that either it is not true of the kind, Lion, that it roars; or if it is true of it, what one asserts about the kind, Lion, in truly asserting of it that it roars, is different from what one asserts of some example of the kind, Lion, in truly asserting of *it* that it roars. And so it seems that in assertively uttering "The Lion roars," either one is not referring to the kind, Lion, in using the words "the Lion," or one is not using the word "roars" in its more usual sense. How are we to choose between these two possibilities?

One feels, intuitively, that there is some connection between the truth or falsehood of 'The Lion roars' and the roaring or not roaring of examples of the kind, Lion. Schematically, one feels some connection between The K being f, and at least some k's being f. Perhaps if we can discover what this connection is, the situation will clarify itself.

It seems that the Lion has four legs just in case lions have four legs, and that the Grizzly roars just in case grizzlies roar. In fact, I see no reason to doubt that the proposition 'The Lion has four legs' is not only equivalent to but identical with the proposition 'Lions have four legs'; and that 'The Grizzly roars' is identical with 'Grizzlies roar.'

Time, of October 28, 1966, contained an essay entitled "What the Negro has—and has not—gained." Sprinkled throughout the essay is the phrase "the Negro," often with adjectival modifiers.[2] So far as I can see, one could, throughout, change "the Negro" to "negroes," and the very same proposition would be asserted. The only other change necessary would be a change in the gram-

---

2. I can appreciate, I think, something of the offensive connotations that this word now has for many blacks. I use the example—so apt for my purposes—with apologies to them. It may be added that I *mention* rather than *use* the word.

matical number of the verbs for the sake of grammatical propriety. Here are just a few examples from the article:

1. The attitude of many white Americans is influenced by the belief that the Negro has made great gains in a relatively short time. . . .
2. . . . these two opposing views pose a root question about the state of the Negro in the U.S. today.
3. The Negro has enthusiastically participated in the U.S.'s steadily increasing material prosperity.
4. The middle-class Negro, on the other hand, is troubled by the riots and the chants of black power. . . .

Thus in many cases it seems to be no more than a matter of diction as to whether one shall use "the Negro" or "negroes," "the Lion" or "lions," "the Grizzly" or "grizzlies." Whichever one uses, the same proposition is asserted.

If this sort of choice were never anything more than a matter of diction, then one could conclude that the concept of the Negro was the same as the concept of negroes, that the concept of the Lion was the same as the concept of lions; schematically, that the concept of the K was the same as the concept of k's. But I think that this quite clearly is not the case. Following is a list of examples in which it is far from clear that we can replace ⌜the K⌝ with ⌜k's⌝ and save the proposition. For in each case, though the proposition of the form *The K is-f* is true, still it may well be that the corresponding one of the form *No k is-f* is also true.

1. The Lion is a symbol of strength.
2. The Lion is king of the beasts.
3. The Apple-Blossom is the state flower of Michigan.
4. The Sheep-Liver Fluke will be our subject of investigation in this course.
5. The Lion is a species of animal.
6. In the Cleveland Zoo is an example of the Dodo.
7. Audubon painted a picture of the Robin.
8. The Grizzly is widely distributed across North America.
9. The Wren's Song is to be heard in all the settled areas of Michigan.

So I think that the admittedly inviting temptation to regard the concept of the K as the same concept as the concept of k's, will have to be resisted; there seems no reason to doubt that in each of the above nine cases one is referring to a distinct entity, a kind, and saying something about it. Yet, on the other hand, we have seen that in many other cases it is no more than a matter of diction as to whether one shall use ⌜the K⌝ or ⌜k's⌝.

We were inquiring into the connection between the truth of 'The Lion has four feet' and the four-footedness of lions; between the truth of 'The Grizzly roars' and the roaring of grizzlies. What we have seen is that 'The Lion has four feet' is the same proposition as 'Lions have four feet,' that 'The Grizzly roars' is the same proposition as 'Grizzlies roar'. But we have still not really discovered the connection we wanted to discover. For just what is it that one is saying, in assertively uttering "Lions have four feet"? Is one saying that *all* lions have four feet? Is one saying that *some* lions have four feet? Is one saying that *most* lions have four feet? Upon reflection, it is clear that unquantified plurals— "lions," "grizzlies," "negroes"—are themselves puzzling.

In an essay of his, Wilfrid Sellars suggests that the following equivalence schema is the acceptable one:

The K is f $\equiv$ All K's are f (necessarily).[3]

This suggestion, however, does not seem correct—neither in the case in which ⌜the K⌝ is replaceable by ⌜k's⌝, nor in the case in which it is *not* so replaceable. What is immediately to the point here is the former sort of case. It may be true that negroes have (the Negro has) made great gains, even though it is not true, and certainly not *necessarily* true, that *every* negro has made great gains. Some negroes may have made no gains whatsoever, and it could still be true that negroes have (the Negro has) made great gains. So also, it is true that lions have (the Lion has) four feet, but it is probably not true that every lion has four feet. Here or there, in all likelihood, there is a maimed or defective lion which has only three feet. And certainly it is not *necessarily* true that all lions have four feet.

The situation is rather, I think, that locutions of the form 'The K' and 'k's,' when interchangeable *salva propositione,* are ambig-

3. "Abstract Entities," *Review of Metaphysics* (June 1963), p. 632.

uous, depending a great deal for their sense on the particular sentence and the particular context in which they occur.

In assertively uttering "The Negro has made great gains," or "Negroes have made great gains," one is simply claiming, I should think, that *most* (if not all) negroes have made great gains. And so also, in assertively uttering "Negroes have enthusiastically participated in the U.S.'s steadily increasing material prosperity," one is simply claiming, I should think, that *most* negroes have enthusiastically participated in the U.S.'s steadily increasing material prosperity. Often, then ⌜k's⌝, when interchangeable with ⌜The K⌝, has the force of ⌜most k's⌝.

In other cases, however, a sentence of the form *k's are f,* when interchangeable with one of the form *The K is f,* seems not to bear a reference to what is true of the majority of k's, but, rather, to what is true of *normal, properly formed k*'s. The whole sentence has a normative rather than a statistical force. In assertively uttering, for example, "Lions have four feet" (or, "The Lion has four feet") one is simply claiming, I should think, that every properly formed lion has four feet. It might be the case that most lions did not have four feet, that most of them were maimed, and still be true that lions have four feet. So also, in assertively uttering "Grizzlies roar" (or, "The Grizzly roars") one is claiming that every normal, properly formed grizzly roars. And this may be true even though some are mute; indeed, it may be true even though most are, for some reason or other, muted.

Similarly, suppose it is true that "The Wren's Song has an interval of a sixth between the first and second notes"—that is, that wren's songs have an interval of a sixth between the first and second notes. It certainly does not follow from this that it is true of *every* wren's song that there is an interval of a sixth between the first and second notes. For it may happen, in a given case, that something prevents the normal progress of the song; the wren "chokes up." But it does follow that it is true of *every properly executed* wren's song that there is an interval of a sixth between the first and second notes.

If we turn from the objects and occurrences of nature to the products and performances of men, the same phenomena confront us. For example, in assertively uttering "In draw-plays (in the Draw-Play) the quarterback hands off the ball to his fullback

and then . . . ," one is not asserting that in *every* draw-play the
quarterback hands off the ball to his fullback and then. . . . For
it may be that, in certain executions of the Draw-Play, the
quarterback does not succeed in handing off, but instead rather
luckily *fumbles off,* the ball to his fullback. That would then be
a defective draw-play, but a draw-play nonetheless. But in assertively uttering such a sentence, one is also not merely claiming
that in *most* draw-plays, the quarterback hands off the ball to
his fullback and then. . . . Rather, what we are claiming is that
in *every properly executed* draw-play the quarterback hands off
the ball to his fullback and then. . . . Similarly, in assertively
uttering "Barcelona chairs are some (the Barcelona Chair is one)
of the strongest ever constructed," we are not claiming that *every*
Barcelona chair is one of the strongest ever constructed. For it
may be that one of them has a flaw, and is defective, so that the
first time anyone ever sits on it, it collapses. Rather, we are claiming that *every properly formed* Barcelona chair is one of the
strongest ever constructed.

We have seen, then, that 'The Lion has four feet' is the same
proposition as 'Every well-formed lion has four feet'; and that
'The Negro has made great gains' is the same proposition as
'Most Negroes have made great gains'. So then, in assertively
uttering "The Lion has four feet," are we referring to the kind,
Lion, with "The Lion"; and are we predicating something of
the kind, Lion, namely, that it has four feet; and is it true of the
kind, Lion, that it has four feet just in case every normal lion
has four feet; and are we asserting something which entails that
there is something such that it is identical with the kind, Lion, and
it has four feet? Or does "The Lion" stand for nothing at all in
"The Lion has four feet"? Is this really not a subject-predicate
sentence at all? Is "The Lion" here just an alternative locution for
"every normal lion"; and does what we assert not entail that
there is something such that it is identical with the kind, Lion,
and it has four feet? Shall we say that the predicate in "The Lion
has four feet" has a somewhat unusual sense, a sense which can
be explained, nonetheless, by pointing out that it holds of the
kind just in case it holds in the more usual sense of every normal
example of the kind? Or shall we say that "The Lion" here has
a peculiar function, not the function of a definite description, not

the function of the name of a kind, but the same · function as "every normal lion"?

So far as I can see, there is no good reason for preferring either of these alternative analyses to the other. There are, we have seen, important differences between the sentence "The Lion has four feet" and "Leo has four feet."[4] But so far as I can see, there is no good reason for preferring the view that "The Lion" in "The Lion has four feet" is standing for the kind, Lion, on which analysis the predicate "has four feet" does not have the same sense as that which it has in "Leo has four feet"; nor for preferring the alternative view that "The Lion" is just a dummy for "lions" or "every normal lion," in which case the sentence is not a subject-predicate sentence, though "has four feet" has the same sense as that which it has in the subject-predicate sentence "Leo has four feet." That is, there is no good reason for holding the view that the analogy to "Leo has four feet" breaks down because of the different function of "The Lion," instead of holding the view that the analogy breaks down because of the different sense of "has four feet."

Further, whether 'The Lion has four feet' entails 'There is something such that it is identical with the kind, Lion, and it has four feet' depends on what this second proposition is understood to be. If it is understood as the claim that the kind, Lion, has four feet in the same sense of "has four feet" as that in which it is true of some individual lions that they have four feet, then I think that 'The Lion has four feet' does not entail this proposition. But if 'There is something such that it is identical with the kind, Lion, and it has four feet' is understood as identical with the proposition 'Lions have four feet' and with 'Every normal lion has four feet', then I think that 'The Lion has four feet' does entail this. And thus it also entails 'There is something such that it has four feet'. It is also, though, the case that 'Leo has four feet' entails 'There is something such that it has four feet'. But these, then, are two different propositions which are entailed.

I think that we can see in Aristotle a failure to clarify some of the points we have canvassed in this section. Aristotle, it will be remembered, distinguishes between *things present in,* and

4. "Leo" here being used to name some *particular* lion.

things predicable of, something. The things predicable of something, or secondary substances, as he also calls them, are kinds, of which the thing in question is an example. "These, then, are called secondary substances, things such as the Man and the Animal" (*de Categoriae* 2a 18). But not every kind of which the thing is an example is something predicable of it; rather, only those of which the thing is necessarily an example. Socrates is necessarily an example of the kind, Man; but he is not necessarily an example of the kind, Stonecutter.

Now as to the relation between a thing and what is predicable of it, this is what Aristotle says: "When you predicate this or that of another thing as of a subject, whatever is said of the predicate can also be said of the subject. We predicate Man of a certain man; so also of The Man do we predicate The Animal. Therefore, of a certain man we can predicate The Animal too. For a man is both animal and man" (1b 10–15). And "But of secondary substances, the species is predicated of the individual, the genus both of the species and of the individual" (3a 37–38).

On Aristotle's view, it is impossible that Bucephalus should not have been a horse—that is, that he should not have been an example of the kind, Horse. On his view it is also impossible that the Horse should not have been an animal. And so on his view it is impossible that Bucephalus should not have been an animal, that is, that he should not have been an example of the Animal. But now, if the kind, Animal, is what is predicated (in Aristotle's sense) of Bucephalus in assertively uttering "Bucephalus is an animal," then in assertively uttering "The Horse is an animal," we are not predicating the kind, Animal, of the kind, Horse. For if Bucephalus is the sort of thing which the kind, Animal, has as examples, then the kind, Horse, is not an example of the kind, Animal. Individual horses are, but the kind, Horse, is not. In assertively uttering "The horse is an animal," and speaking truly, we are either not with "the horse" referring to the kind, Horse; or, if we are, we are predicating something quite different of it from what we are predicating of Bucephalus in assertively uttering, and speaking truly, "Bucephalus is an animal." What we are claiming is that most—indeed all—*horses* are animals; that is, all *horses* are examples of the kind, Animal.

It is perhaps worth noting that not even the following schema is universally valid. If the K is a kind of L, then examples of the K are L's. It is, of course, the case that if the Lion is a kind of animal, then examples of the Lion are animals; and if the Lily is a kind of plant then examples of the Lily are plants. But though it is the case that the Grizzly is a kind of animal which is widely distributed across western North America, it is not the case that examples of the Grizzly are animals which are widely distributed across western North America.

3. What I now wish to suggest is that the things cited at the beginning of the preceding chapter as examples of nonpredicable universals—literary works, musical works, films, words, prints, dances, sculptures, car-models, house-models, furniture-models, flags, games, newspapers, journals, books, plays, exercises, arguments, stamps, coins, diseases, biological species and genera— are, all of them, kinds. Perhaps this seems as dubious in the case of literary works and musical works as any, so let us make out the case for them.

There is, presumably, such a kind as: Copy of *Tom Jones*. This is a certain kind of copy. Copies, like other things, come in kinds, and the kind, Copy of *Tom Jones,* is one of them. For comparable reasons, there is the kind, Performance of Bartok's Fifth Quartet. This is a certain kind of performance. Performances, too, come in kinds, and this is one of them.

The question I wish to raise now is this: Is there any reason for not identifying the kind, Copy of "Sailing to Byzantium," with the poem "Sailing to Byzantium"? And is there any reason for not identifying the kind, Performance of Bartok's Fifth Quartet, with Bartok's Fifth Quartet?

It must be admitted that we do not *say* that a copy of the poem "Sailing to Byzantium" is an example of it, nor do we *say* that it belongs to or is a member of it. And we do not *say* that a performance of Bartok's Fifth Quartet is an example of the Quartet, nor do we *say* that it belongs to or is a member of it. But, as we have seen repeatedly, such linguistic facts are not ontologically decisive.

It is also the case that we do not customarily form names of literary works and musical works in the fashion usual for familiarly recognized kinds. We do not, that is, take some common noun true of examples of the kind and preface it with "the." The name is simply "Sailing to Byzantium" and "Bartok's Fifth Quartet." But not only is *this* linguistic fact also not ontologically decisive; the linguistic pattern itself breaks down in some cases in which we are dealing with familiarly recognized kinds. As we have seen before, "Man" is the common English name for the kind, Man. Further, it is worth noting that we do in fact have "The Bible" and "The Koran" corresponding to "a Bible" and "a Koran."

In short, I think it must be admitted that some features of the language standardly used in our speech about familiarly recognized kinds find almost no echo in the language standardly used in our speech about literary and musical works. But this phenomenon does not constitute a good reason for not regarding a literary work as a kind whose examples are its copies, and a musical work as a kind whose examples are its performances. Nor do I see any other phenomenon which constitutes such a good reason.

But is there anything *in favor* of making the identification? Or must the case rest on the fact—if it is one—that there is nothing against it? Two sorts of considerations, I think, can be given in favor of the identification. These considerations are not decisive; they do not quite deserve the title of "arguments." Yet they do show that the view fits in with certain other relevant phenomena.

One consideration is the following. The relation between what is true of a literary work and what is true of its copies, and what is true of a musical work and what is true of its performances, follows the pattern which we have discovered for the relation between what is true of a kind and what is true of its examples.

Sometimes, what is true of a musical work is true of it without being true of any performance of it; and sometimes what is true of a literary work is true of it without being true of any copy of it. For example, it is true of the *Missa Solemnis* that it was composed by Beethoven; but it is not true of any performance of it that it was composed by Beethoven. And if A.E. Housman's own testimony can be believed, some of his poems were composed while he was shaving; but it is in all likelihood not true that any copy was composed while he was shaving.

In other cases, what is true of a musical work seems to be true of it just in case the same thing is true of most if not all performances of it; and what is true of a literary work is true of it just in case the same thing is true of most if not all copies of it. For example, it would seem to be true of Bartok's Fifth Quartet that it sets people's nerves on edge just in case it is true of most if not all *performances* of Bartok's Fifth Quartet that they set people's nerves on edge. And it would seem to be true of "Sailing to Byzantium" that it is about a page long just in case it is true of most if not all *copies* of "Sailing to Byzantium" that they are about a page long.

But in yet other cases—and these are certainly the most interesting ones—something is true of a literary work just in case it is true of every *correct* copy of the work; and something is true of a musical work just in case it is true of every *correct* performance of the work. Suppose, for example, that someone claims that the third word of "Sailing to Byzantium" is "no." That could certainly be true even though not every copy of "Sailing to Byzantium" has "no" as its third word; for there could very well be some defective copy somewhere which has, say, "on" as its third word but which is a copy of "Sailing to Byzantium" nonetheless. In fact, "Sailing to Byzantium" could have "no" as its third word even though, because of some early printer's error, *most* copies do not have "no" as their third word. The situation would then be that most copies were defective, incorrect, copies. What does seem to be the case is this: It is true of "Sailing to Byzantium" that it has "no" as its third word just in case every *correct* copy of "Sailing to Byzantium" has "no" as its third word.

Similarly, suppose someone claims that a G flat occurs at the end of the fourth measure of Bartok's Fifth Quartet. That could certainly be true even though not every performance has a G flat at the end of the fourth measure; there might be a faulty performance of it—though a performance of it nonetheless—in which a G natural rather than a G flat gets played. Indeed, it may be that the difficulty of performance is such that *in most* performances it is a G natural rather than a G flat that gets played, even though the *work* has a G flat. Again, the situation seems to be this: It is true of Bartok's Fifth Quartet that it has a G flat at the end of the fourth measure just in case it is true of every *correct* performance of Bartok's Fifth Quartet that it has a G flat at the end of the fourth measure.

So there we have one consideration in favor of the view that a musical work is a kind of performance, and that a literary work is a kind of copy: The relation between what is true of a musical work and what is true of its performances, and the relation between what is true of a literary work and what is true of its copies, follow the same threefold pattern that we uncovered when we discussed, for familiarly recognized kinds, the relation between what is true of the kind and what is true of its examples.

A second consideration in support of the view we are propounding, is the fact that a literary work is a word-sequence which can be repeatedly copied out or uttered, along with the fact that such word-sequences, in general, are kinds; and the fact that a musical work is a sound-sequence which can be repeatedly sounded out, along with the fact that such sound-sequences, in general, are kinds.

That a literary work is a word-sequence, definite words in a definite sequence, the whole sequence capable of being repeatedly uttered and repeatedly copied out, seems clear enough. But the claim that all such words and word-sequences as can be repeatedly uttered or inscribed are kinds, needs perhaps a bit of explanation.

It has often been noted by philosophers that such a question as "How many different words are there on this page?" is ambiguous. For example, if "the" occurs three times, it may be that each distinct occurrence is to be counted as a distinct word, or it may be that each occurrence is to be counted as nothing more than another occurrence of the *same* word. Or, to take another example, suppose it is asked how many different words are contained in this box:

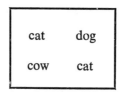

This too is an ambiguous question. The correct answer could be either "four" or "three," depending on what is to be counted as *a* word.

It will be evident, at a glance, that such questions as "How many different phrases are there on this page?" and "How many different sentences are there in this book?" are ambiguous in exactly the same way.

Now, though I know of no decisive argument in favor of the view, it seems plausible to regard words qua repeatable and word-sequences qua repeatable as *kinds*—kinds of word-occurrences, and kinds of word-sequence-occurrences, respectively. Word-occurrences, and word-sequence-occurrences, do after all come in kinds; and there seems to be nothing against identifying certain of such kinds with words qua repeatable and with word-sequences qua repeatable. Further, that words qua repeatable are not to be identified with the *class* of their occurrences, nor word-sequences qua repeatable with the *class* of their occurrences, seems clear enough. For these classes cannot have had different members from those they do have, whereas words qua repeatable and word-sequences qua repeatable can very well have had different occurrences from those they do have.

Of course, we do not customarily form the name of a specific word qua repeatable by prefacing a common noun true of word-occurrences with "the." One can, perhaps, without gravely offending usage, speak of each of the occurrences of the word "the" as *a* "the." And one can ask how many "the's" there are on a page. But the name of the word qua repeatable is not "the 'the'," but rather just "the." So names of words qua repeatable are not formed in the fashion which we have found to be typical of familiarly recognized kinds. But this—as we have already learned from several similar cases we have considered—is no good reason for doubting that words qua repeatable and word-sequences qua repeatable are kinds. So if it is indeed true that literary works are word-sequences capable of repeated utterances and repeated inscriptions, and if it is indeed true that such word-sequences are kinds, then of course we have our conclusion. A literary work is a kind—a kind whose examples are certain word-sequence-occurrences, those, namely, which are copies and utterances of the work.

That a musical work is a sound-sequence, definite sounds in a definite sequence, the whole sequence capable of being repeatedly sounded, is also clear enough. But again, what perhaps needs a bit of explanation is the claim that sound sequences, understood as entities capable of being repeatedly sounded, are kinds. The point can be made in the same way that we used to make the parallel point for words, namely, by first pointing out the ambiguity in such a question as "How many different sounds did you hear?" This may be either a request to count the different *kinds* of sounds heard or a request to count the different soundings. It may be, for example, that middle C as played by the oboe is to count as one sound, no matter how often it occurs; or it may be that each occurrence of middle C as played by the oboe is to count as one sound. Now sound-occurrences certainly come in various kinds, and there seems no reason whatsoever not to identify certain of these with sounds qua repeatable. And, if it is indeed the case that musical works are repeatable sound-sequences, then we have our conclusion. Musical works are kinds—kinds whose examples are certain sound-occurrences, those, namely, which are performances of the work.

The thesis we are maintaining here—that literary works and musical works, and their components, words and sounds, are kinds—is not, of course, wholly novel. C.S. Peirce is famous for having distinguished between a word understood as what he called a *type* and a word understood as what he called a *token*. Perhaps it is worth quoting what he says: "There will ordinarily be about twenty *the's* on a page, and of course they count as twenty words. In another sense of the word 'word', however, there is but one word 'the' in the English language; and it is impossible that this word should lie visibly on a page or be heard in any voice, for the reason that it is not a Single thing or Single event. It does not exist; it only determines things that do exist. Such a definitely significant Form, I propose to term a Type." "A Single event which happens once and whose identity is limited to that one happening or a Single object or thing which is in some single place at any one instant of time, such event or thing being significant only as occurring just when and where it does, such as this or that word on a single line of a single page or a single copy of a book, I will venture to call a *Token*." "In order that a Type may be used, it has to be embodied in a Token which shall be a sign of the Type, and thereby of the object the Type signifies. I propose to call such a Token of a Type an *Instance* of the Type. Thus there may be 20 Instances of the Type 'the' on a page."[5]

Peirce in these passages is pointing to a distinction to which we also have been pointing—that between a word which is capable of many occurrences, and a word which is a word-occurrence. And though, so far as I know, he does not, he might well have pointed to the parallel distinction in the case of word-sequences. What is not clear, though, from the words we have quoted from Peirce, nor, so far as I know, from any other words of Peirce, is how he understands the ontological nature of what he calls a type. Is a type a kind? Or is it a class? Or is it yet some third sort of thing?

C.L. Stevenson, in a discussion of the nature of the poem, applies Peirce's distinction and terminology to poems. He says: "A poem is a sequence of words, understanding this either as a token sequence or a type sequence, the latter being a *class*. Copies, then, are *of* the kind (class)."[6] Here Stevenson explicitly says that types are kinds, but he also explicitly indicates that he regards a kind as the same sort of thing as a class. Our contention is that kinds and classes are not the same sort of thing; and that literary works are kinds, not classes. That they are not classes can be seen by noting that they are not identical just in case they have exactly the same copies. For consider a literary work without copies; its copies have all vanished, or it never had any, being one of those poems which occurred to Housman as he was shaving, but which he neglected ever to inscribe. Such a literary work, if it were a class, would be identical with the null class; and since there are no prime numbers between five and seven, it would be identical with the class of prime numbers between five and seven. But this conclusion is absurd.

Another point, raised by both Peirce and Stevenson, should be considered. We heard Peirce saying that a type-word cannot be seen or heard. And in his essay Stevenson says that a type-poem, as contrasted with a token-poem, cannot be written down, cannot be recited, cannot be on the top shelf of my bookcase, and so on. However, neither Peirce nor Stevenson gives any reason for hold-

5. Collected works of C.S. Peirce (Cambridge, 1933), 4:537.
6. *Philosophical Review* (July 1957), p. 330.

ing these paradoxical views. And is it not much more plausible to
hold that *in* seeing or hearing the token-word, one sees or hears
the type-word? *In* writing or reciting or laying down a token-
poem, one writes or recites or lays down a type-poem? *In* hearing
a performance of Bartok's Fifth Quartet, one hears Bartok's
Fifth Quartet? In general, we often do one thing *by* or *in* doing
another. Why should that not also be the case here?

4. The question which remains to be considered is our principal question in this and the preceding chapter. Is there any significant analogy between kinds and predicables? Is there any basis
for our vague feeling that those predicables which can be truly
predicated of many, and those kinds which can have many
examples, have some significant analogy to each other, an analogy
which justifies us in calling entities of both sorts, *universals?*

We have seen, in earlier chapters, that predicates can be regarded as standing for predicables; and that a person, in assertively uttering a subject-predicate sentence, can be regarded as
claiming a predicative relation to hold between whatever the
subject stands for and the predicable for which the predicate
stands. For example, in assertively uttering "Socrates is wise," a
speaker claims that Socrates has or possesses the property of
being wise; and the predicate, "is wise," stands for this property
of being wise.

Now, in their role in the activity of predication a significant
similarity can be seen between predicables and kinds. For at
least some predicates can also be regarded as standing for kinds;
and in assertively uttering a subject-predicate sentence whose
predicate stands for a kind, a speaker can be regarded as claiming that what the subject stands for is an example of that kind
for which the predicate stands. Suppose, for example, that someone assertively utters, "Bucephalus is a horse." The predicate
can be regarded as standing for the kind, Horse, and the speaker
can be regarded as claiming that Bucephalus is an example of the
kind, Horse. Similarly, in assertively uttering "Socrates was a
stonecutter," a speaker is claiming that Socrates was an example
of the kind, Stonecutter; and the predicate can be regarded as
standing for the Stonecutter.

So there is a significant similarity between kinds and predicables. But still, it can seriously be questioned whether we have found what we were looking for. For it must be noted that classes can function in exactly the same way as kinds in the activity of predication; whereas what we were looking for was an analogy which held between predicables and kinds, but did not also hold between predicables and classes. Suppose, once more, that someone assertively utters "Socrates was a stonecutter." It would seem, in such a case, that "was a stonecutter" can be regarded as standing for the class of all things who were stonecutters, and that the speaker can be regarded as claiming that Socrates is a member of this class.

So let us pursue, yet farther, the answer to our question.

Corresponding to the predicable, wisdom, there is the kind, Case of wisdom. Corresponding to the predicable, being green, there is the kind, Case of being green. And in general, corresponding to every predicable there is a kind whose examples are cases of that predicable.

Is there any good reason for supposing that the kind, Case of wisdom, is a distinct entity from wisdom? Is there any good reason for supposing that the kind, Case of being green, is a distinct entity from being green? And, in general, is there any good reason for not identifying a predicable with the kind whose examples are the cases of that predicable?

I myself see no good reason whatsover for not making these identifications. In addition, I think some positive reasons can be given for making them.

For one thing, it looks as if the identity criteria for predicables, and the identity criteria for those kinds whose examples are cases of a certain predicable, are the same.

From our discussion in an earlier chapter we can conclude that the predicable *being a brother* is identical with the predicable of *being a male sibling* if and only if the assertible *that it is a brother* is identical with the assertible *that it is a male sibling;* that is, if and only if in saying of something that it is a brother one says the same thing of it that one says of something in saying of it that it is a male sibling. But now, it would seem that the very same criterion holds for the correlative kind. The kind, Case of being a brother, would seem to be identical with the kind, Case of being a male sibling, if and only if the assertible *that it is a brother* is identical with the assertible *that it is a male sibling.*

Though distinct predicables can have all the same exemplifications in common, they cannot have the same cases; and so, in an earlier chapter, we considered whether predicables can, in general, be identified with the *classes* of their cases. We concluded that this general identification could not be made because, while some predicables might have had different or more or fewer cases from those they do have, no class can have had different or more or fewer members from those it does have. In this respect, kinds are like predicables rather than like classes; for, as we have already seen in this chapter, many kinds can well have had different or more or fewer examples than those they do have. Thus the sort of argument which we marshalled against the identification of a predicable with the class of its cases, cannot be marshalled against the identification of a predicable with the *kind* whose examples are cases of that predicable.

Further, if our discussions concerning the existence criteria for predicables and the existence criteria for kinds are correct, it will not be possible to show any divergence on this point between predicables and those kinds whose examples are all cases of some predicable. As we use "there is" in conjunction with names of predicables, it is true that there is such a predicable as *being a round square.* And as we use "there is" in conjunction with names of kinds, it is true that there is such a kind as Case of Being a Round Square. In general, every view which we canvassed concerning the identity criteria for predicables has its obvious parallel for identity criteria for kinds. I, at least, see no hope of showing that some one of these views is correct for predicables, whereas the corresponding one for those kinds whose examples are cases of predicables is incorrect.

It is apropos here to consider, for a moment, the alternative view that a predicable is identical with the kind of its *exemplifications,* rather than the kind of its cases. For example, should not the property of being a horse be identified with the kind, Horse (that is, exemplification of being a horse), rather than with the kind, Case of Being a Horse? And should not the property of being white be identified with the kind, White Thing (exemplification of being a white thing), rather than with the kind, Case of Being White?

It might seem that this alternative view, on its face, is absurd. After all, is it not true that the Horse has four legs? But can it with any plausibility whatsoever be held that the *property* of being a horse has four legs? And the White Thing is colored. But can it with any plausibility whatsoever be held that the property of being white is colored?

We saw earlier, however, that when someone assertively utters "The Horse has four legs," we need not view him as referring to a kind, The Horse, and saying something of it; we can instead view him as saying what could also be said with the sentence "Every properly formed horse has four legs." So it is not at all clear that having four legs is a property which the kind, Horse, has, but which the property of being a horse lacks. And comparable remarks are to be made concerning the suggestion that the kind, White Thing, is colored, whereas the property of being white is not colored.

Further, though the force of "there is" when used in connection with *cases* of predicables, is not especially clear, it is certainly possible to hold that there is a case of a certain predicable if and only if there is an exemplification of it; and there *can be* a case of a certain predicable if and only if there *can be* an exemplification of that predicable. There seems no hope then of showing that the criteria for the being of a certain predicable is the same as those for the being of its case-kind, but diverges from those for the being of its exemplification-kind.

Yet there are good reasons for rejecting the view that predicables are, in general, identical with their excmplification-kinds. Perhaps the most decisive one is that nonidentical predicables can have identical exemplification-kinds. Consider, for example, the property of being a member of the genus *Metasequoia,* the property of being a member of the redwood family and growing natively only in an isolated valley of western China, and the property of being a member of a genus unknown to Western botanists before it was brought out of China in 1948. These seem clearly to be distinct properties. Yet the kind, *Metasequoia,* is identical with the kind, Member of the redwood family and growing natively only in an isolated valley of western China. And it is also identical with the kind, Member of a genus unknown to Western botanists before it was brought out of China in 1948. But of course it cannot be that three nonidentical properties are, each of them, identical with one and the same exemplification-kind.

Such considerations of identity and nonidentity are not the only reasons for resisting the view that predicables are identical with their exemplification-kinds. There are such considerations as these: The Apple Blossom is the state flower of Michigan, but certainly it is not the case that the property of being an apple blossom is the state flower of Michigan. And the Lion is a symbol of strength, whereas it is not the case that the property of being a lion is a symbol of strength.

I conclude that predicables are just kinds, of a certain sort. They are certain kinds of cases. And, if this is correct, then of course we have found a basis for our feeling that there is a close analogy between predicable universals on the one hand, and nonpredicable or substance universals on the other. For these latter, we have seen, are also kinds. Predicable universals—indeed, predicables generally—are one kind of kind; substance universals are another kind of kind.

Predicables in
Divine and Human Life

PART FOUR

12

Paradigms, Exemplars and God

What we have thus far said about universals provides almost no clue to the great importance which has sometimes been ascribed to them. We have said that universals—some of them anyway—enter into human life through being predicated, being perceived, being thought about. But this pales into insignificance when we listen to what has on occasion been said concerning their actual and proper role in human life and, indeed, in divine life as well. For it has been said of universals that they ought to function as *paradigms* for all human and divine thought and action. And it has been said of universals that they do function as *exemplars* for God's creative activity.

I wish, in this concluding chapter, to consider the view that universals ought to function as human and divine paradigms, and also to consider the view that they do in fact function as divine exemplars. Plato will be used to illustrate the former view, and Augustine and Aquinas, the latter. Further, we shall find ourselves naturally led into a consideration of Aquinas' claim that universals are all either identical with, or brought about by, God. Finding all these views unsatisfactory, we shall close with some brief remarks on how, then, the relation between God and predicables should be thought of.

1. From our discussion thus far it must seem, to someone fresh to philosophy, inexplicable that Plato or anyone else should have regarded universals as paradigms. But what we have so far not at all discussed is that long tradition, initiated by Plato, in which universals are thought of as ideal examples of themselves. It is because they are thus conceived that some of them, at least, are regarded as fit paradigms for human and divine thought and action.

It is, however, by no means an uncontroversial interpretation of Plato's thought to hold that he regarded universals as perfect examples of themselves. So it is with a defense of this interpretation that we must begin our discussion.

Let us begin by noticing that Plato refers to and speaks of what he calls *Forms,* or *Ideas,* both as one would refer to and speak of universals, and also as one might refer to and speak of perfect examples of universals.

Over and over Plato uses abstract nouns to refer to one and another of his Forms. For example, in *Phaedo* 65 he uses the terms "greatness" (μέγεθος), "health" (ὑγιεία), and "strength" (ἰσχύς). And, to cite just one more passage from a multitude of possible ones, in *Parmenides* 128e–131a he uses the terms "similarity" (ὁμοιότης), "plurality" (πλῆθος), "beauty" (κάλλος), and "justice" (δικαιοσύνη). He also frequently uses common nouns functioning like kind-names to refer to certain of his Forms. For example, in *Parmenides* 130c he uses "Man" (ἄνθρωπος); and in *Republic* 596b he uses "Bed" (κλίνη) and "Table" (τράπεζα). Thus, to refer to Forms, Plato uses just the sorts of expressions which we ourselves would use to refer to predicables and kinds.

In addition, Plato speaks of Forms as we would speak of predicables. For repeatedly he says that things other than the Forms have, or possess, or share in (μετέχω, μεταλαμβάνω), the Forms; and we ourselves have often spoken of things as having, or possessing, or sharing, predicables.

But this is just one side of the matter. Plato also refers to and speaks of Forms as one might refer to and speak of, not universals, but rather examples of universals which are perfect in a certain way.

In addition to using abstract singular terms to refer to his Forms, Plato has a standard alternative way of referring to them.

He uses expressions composed of an adjective prefaced with the neuter definite article, frequently with the addition of "itself" (αὐτό): "The just" or "The just itself," "The beautiful" or "The beautiful itself," and the like. In the *Republic,* for example, he rather consistently says, not that the aim of the philosopher is to contemplate goodness, but rather that his aim is to contemplate The good, or The good itself. Plato also sometimes supplements a *common noun* with "itself"—"The bed itself" or simply "Bed itself." In short, Plato often uses the schema αὐτὸ τὸ ——— to compose names of Forms, allowing adjectives and common nouns, and occasionally even mass-terms, to fill in the blank.

It is not at once evident, however, that such expressions are the sort of expressions that one might use to refer to perfect examples of universals. To see this, we must look into the significance which Plato in all likelihood attached to such expressions.

In referring to something as *The* just (thing) *itself,* Plato clearly meant to pick it out from among all the just things. The just thing itself is of course just, but it is not merely one just thing among others. There is something special about it, on account of which it can appropriately be referred to as *The* just (thing) *itself.* This is confirmed by the following passage from *Phaedo* (74a), where the example happens to be The equal itself: "Do we not say that there is something equal? I do not mean one piece of wood to another, nor one stone to another, nor anything else of that sort, but something else beyond all these things—The equal itself [αὐτὸ τὸ ἴσον]."

But what is it that is special about that one just thing, so that it can appropriately be referred to as *The* just (thing) *itself?* What is it that is special about that one equal thing, so that it can appropriately be referred to as *The* equal (thing) *itself?*

Plato regarded The just itself as *just in a special way,* The equal itself as *equal in a special way.* Some of what he regarded as special about the way in which The equal itself is equal is made clear in the same section of *Phaedo* (74–75) from which we have just quoted. In this passage, Plato says that equal stones and equal pieces of wood fall short of being equal in the way in which that which is equal itself (αὐτὸ ὅ ἔστιν ἴσον) is equal (74d). All the equal things, he says, are aiming to be like the equal itself (αὐτὸ τὸ ἴσον), but fail of their aim. They are deficiently equal (75).

What is deficient about them is made clear slightly earlier (74b). It is that they do not seem to us to be simply, *unalloyedly,* equal. Plato does not deny that ordinary sticks and stones may well be equal to each other. What he insists on, however, is that ordinary equal things seem equal in certain respects and unequal in others, whereas this variation in appearance does not characterize The equal itself. The same sort of point is made in *Republic* 479. There Plato says that all the ordinary beautiful things appear ugly as well as beautiful, whereas this is not true of The beautiful itself.

Quite clearly, though, this does not exhaust what Plato thought to be special about the way in which The just (thing) itself is just in contrast to the ordinary just things, the way in which The equal (thing) itself is equal in contrast to the ordinary equal things. He quite clearly thought that the ordinary just things did not merely *seem* both just and unjust, but that they *were in fact* just in some respects and not in others, whereas this is not true of The just itself. Ordinary just things both seem to be, and are, alloyedly just, whereas The just itself both seems, and is, un-alloyedly just. This point is clear from *Parmenides* 129 where Plato says, by way of example, that while The one itself is unalloyedly one, ordinary single things are not one in every respect. It is also clear from *Republic* 479 where, after saying that ordinary beautiful things seem also to be ugly, ordinary just actions seem also to be unjust, and so on, Plato says that ordinary things "always have a claim to both opposite designations." He asks rhetorically, "Whatever any one of these many things may be said to be, can you say that it absolutely *is* that, any more than that it *is not* that?"

Even this, however, does not exhaust what Plato thought to be special about the way in which The just (thing) itself is just in contrast to other things, The equal (thing) itself is equal in contrast to other equal things, and the like. For it was also Plato's view that a Form is *unchangeably* whatever it is and seems to be, whereas non-Forms are only *changeably* whatever they are and seem to be. In *Phaedo* 78d, for example, Plato insists that The just itself is unchangeably just, The equal itself is unchangeably equal, whereas ordinary just things, though they may indeed be just, are just only for a while and then they are no longer just, and ordinary equal things, though they may indeed be equal, are equal only for a while and then they are no longer equal. The same sort of contrast, between things that are changeably so-and-so and things that are unchangeably so-and-so, is hovering in the air in *Republic* 479, without ever being quite explicitly drawn.

It is often suggested by commentators on Plato that, in his view, ordinary just things differ from The just (thing) itself in that they are only approximately just, not genuinely just; or that they are just in a different sense of "just."[1] So far as I know, Plato nowhere says that this is the difference between a Form and its participators. Rather, his thought seems consistently to be that The just itself stands out from the ordinary just things in that it is and seems unalloyedly and unchangeably just; the ordinary just things are and seem just only in certain respects and only at certain times. So, provided that we take a *perfectly* just thing to be a thing which is and seems unalloyedly and unchangeably just, we may say that The just itself is a *perfect* example of justice, and that ordinary just things are *imperfect* examples of justice. In *Symposium* 211a, Plato says that The beautiful itself "is not beautiful in part and in part ugly, nor is it such at such a time and other at another, nor in one respect beautiful and in another ugly, nor so affected by position as to seem beautiful to some and ugly to others."

I think we can conclude that when Plato used such phrases as "The equal itself" and "The beautiful itself," he meant them to suggest or connote that The equal itself is an equal thing which is and seems unalloyedly and unchangeably equal, that The beautiful itself is a beautiful thing which is and seems unalloyedly and unchangeably beautiful. The equal itself, like some other things, is equal; but it is *the* equal thing *itself*—that is, the *perfectly* equal thing. And The beautiful itself is, like some other things, beautiful. But is it not merely one among other beautiful

---

1. *Cf.* R.E. Allen, "Participation and Predication in Plato's Middle Dialogues," in R.E. Allen, ed., *Studies in Plato's Metaphysics* (London, 1965). Perhaps also, G. Vlastos, "The Third Man Argument in the *Parmenides*" in Allen, ibid., p. 252.

things. Rather, it is *the* beautiful thing *itself*—that is, the *perfectly* Beautiful thing.

If Plato's expressions of the form "the ———— itself" do in fact bear the connotations which we have suggested they do, then these referring expressions have close affinities with a standard way Plato has of alluding to, or reminding his hearers of, his theory of Forms, and with yet another, though somewhat less frequently used, form of expression used to refer to specific Forms.

We have already quoted Plato's comment, in *Republic* 479, about things other than Forms: "Any such thing will always have a claim to both opposite designations." And we have also quoted his rhetorical question from the same passage: "Whatever any one of these things may be said to be, can you say that it absolutely *is* that, any more than that it is *not* that?" Plato is suggesting that of a Form we can say that it *is* so-and-so, whereas of other things we cannot speak thus; we must, speaking strictly, say that they are *and are not* so-and-so. Whatever they are, they are only alloyedly and changeably so. Now frequently Plato alludes to the Forms as each being a thing which he is accustomed to call "that-which-is"; and I think we are justified in hearing in this locution an echo of the doctrine that Forms are unalloyedly and unchangeably whatever they are, whereas other things are not so. In *Phaedo* 78, for example, Socrates speaks thus:

"Let us then," said he, "turn to what we were discussing before. Is the entity itself [αὐτὴ ἡ οὐσία], which we in our dialectic speak of as being [τὸ εἶναι], always the same or is it susceptible to change? The equal itself, the beautiful itself, each that-which-is [ὃ ἔστιν] itself, being [τὸ ὄν]—do they ever admit of any change whatsoever?"

In *Republic* 507 he says:

We say that many beautiful things and many good things each are, and we define them in our dialectic. And we assume the beautiful itself, and the good itself, and so for all which we formerly assumed as many, considering them again according to one idea [ἰδέαν], of each thing, existing as one; and we call each thing that-which-is [ὃ ἔστιν]. . . .

And in *Phaedo* 65 he says:

I am speaking of all such things as greatness, health, strength, and in

short of the being [τῆς οὐσίας] of everything, of that which each is
[ὃ τυγχάνει ἕκαστον ὄν].

Not only does Plato allude to Forms, generally, as each being
a that-which-is; he also, on occasion, refers to a specific Form
with a locution of the form "that which is ————." In *Republic*
597c he speaks of That-which-is-bed (ὃ ἔστιν κλίνη), in *Symposium* 211d he speaks of That-which-is-beautiful-itself (αὐτὸ . . .
ὃ ἔστιν καλόν), and in *Phaedo* 74d he speaks of that-which-is-
equal-itself (αὐτὸ ὃ ἔστιν ἴσον). I think it likely that when Plato
used such expressions as "that which is bed" and "that which is
beautiful," he meant them to connote that that-which-is-bed is
not also, in some respect or at some time, not a bed, that that-
which-is-beautiful is not also, in some respect or at some time,
not beautiful, etc. He meant them to connote, in short, that the
thing referred to was the perfect bed, the perfectly beautiful thing,
and the like.[2]

In short, the connotations of Plato's referring expressions of
the form "that which is ————" would seem to be the same as
those of his referring expressions of the form "the ———— itself."
Both sorts of expressions connote that Forms, as distinguished
from what participate in the Forms, are and seem to be unchangeably and unalloyedly whatever they are. They connote
that Forms are perfect examples.

This interpretation of the significance of these two modes of
referring to Forms fits in with a well-known feature of Plato's
speech *about* the Forms, namely, with his frequent suggestion that
ordinary things *resemble,* or *are like,* or *are similar to,* the Forms,
this similarity deriving from the fact that ordinary things are
copies of the Forms. It is clear that Plato meant this resemblance
in a quite literal sense; equal things are like The equal itself (that-
which-is-equal), in that they along with it are equal; they are
unlike in that they are and seem to be only alloyedly and
changeably equal.

2. H. Cherniss ("The Relation of the *Timaeus* to Plato's Later Dialogues,"
in Allen, *Studies in Plato,* pp. 370–72) understands the force of the ὃ ἔστι
x locutions, not as "that which is unalloyedly and unchangeably *x*," but as
"that which is identical with *x*." And he thinks the contrast is with "that
which possesses *x*." But this interpretation is even grammatically unlikely
in the case of, for example, ὃ ἔστι καλόν; since "what is identical with the
beautiful" is grammatically ill-formed.

So we are brought to the conclusion that Plato does indeed refer to and speak of Forms both as one would refer to and speak of universals, and also as one might refer to and speak of perfect examples of universals. Further, Plato clearly refers to and speaks of *the very same Form* in these two divergent ways. He does not refer to and speak of some of the Forms in one way, and others of the Forms in the other way. He refers to and speaks of them as *each* a perfect example of *itself*.

One might suspect that this was the case, upon noticing that Plato himself nowhere points out that the Forms he is referring to and speaking of when he uses the universals mode of speech are distinct from those he is referring to and speaking of when he uses the perfect-examples mode of speech. One's suspicions would be confirmed, I think, by the fact that Plato clearly uses these two modes of speech—which to us seem so different—interchangeably.

For instance, in *Phaedo* 100e, immediately after saying that beautiful things (τὰ κάλα) are beautiful on account of The beautiful (ὅτι τῷ καλῷ), he says that great things are great on account of greatness (μέγεθει). In *Parmenides* 129a he suggests that there is such a Form as similarity (ὁμοιότης), and, as opposite to it, that-which-is-unlike (ὅ ἐστιν ἀνόμοιον). In 129b he says that all things are one by sharing The one (μετέχειν τοῦ ἑνος), and that things are plural by sharing plurality (πλήθους); and then immediately he reverts to speaking of That-which-is-one (ὅ ἐστιν ἕν). In 129e he gives a list of Forms which runs thus: similarity, dissimilarity, plurality, the one, rest, motion. In 130b he gives a list which runs thus: The just, The beautiful, The good; and then in 131a, with no indication that he is now referring to different things, he speaks of beauty and justice. From Plato's constant unsystematic shifting back and forth in his mode of reference to Forms, I think one can only conclude that he was referring to the same thing when he used the expressions "beauty," "the beautiful itself," and "that which is beautiful"; to the same thing when he used the expressions "justice," "the just itself," and "that which is just"; and so on.

Nowhere does Plato remark that if the relation between beautiful things and the beautiful itself is that of possession, then it cannot also be that of copy-resemblance; or if it is that of copy-resemblance, then it cannot also be that of possession. In addition, there is nothing in his usage to indicate that, in his judgment, the relation could not be both of these at once. Indeed, he may even have thought that possession and copy-resemblance were the very same relation. In *Phaedo* 74 he repeatedly speaks of things as resembling the Forms, whereas in *Phaedo* 100 he speaks of them as possessing the Forms. In *Phaedo* 102 and *Parmenides* 131 he says that things other than the Forms are 'named' as they are because they partake of the Forms, whereas in *Timaeus* 52 he says that they are 'named' as they are because they resemble the Forms.

The only passage in which Plato himself considers the relation between participation and copy-resemblance is *Parmenides* 132d–133a. The speakers, Parmenides and Socrates, are trying to clarify the concept of participation, and, late in their attempt, Socrates says this: "But, Parmenides, the best I can make of the matter is this: that these Forms are as it were paradigms fixed in the nature of things; the other things are made in their image and are likenesses; and this participation they come to have in the Forms is nothing but their being made in their image." Parmenides then argues—and Socrates meekly assents—that the view that things and Forms resemble each other leads to an infinite regress. And he states the conclusion to his argument thus: "It follows that the other things do not partake of Forms by being like them; we must look for some other means by which they partake." Now if we had clear evidence that Plato himself regarded this argument as decisive, while still holding that there are Forms and that things participate in them, then we would have to allow that at some time he came to the conclusion that things do not both participate in and resemble the Forms. But the significance for Plato's *own* thought of the *Parmenides* arguments is just the most moot of all points in Platonic scholarship; so nothing can, I think, be concluded from this passage. There is, on the contrary, considerable evidence, cited by Cherniss, that Plato continued to speak of things as both participating in and resembling the Forms.[3]

So our conclusion thus far is this: Surely at some points in

---

3. Cherniss, in Allen, *Studies in Plato*, pp. 361, n. 5; 363–64.

his career, and probably to the end of his career, Plato used both the universals mode of speech and the perfect-examples mode of speech to speak of a given Form. Plato spoke of at least many of his Forms as if they were universals which were perfect examples of themselves.

What has so far been said would not be seriously contested by most of Plato's commentators, for so far we have spoken only of Plato's mode of speech. But obviously Plato needs interpreting, and there has been a persistent tendency, in the attempts of recent commentators to *interpret* Plato's views, to stress one of these ways of referring to and speaking of Forms at the expense of the other. There has been a persistent tendency either to insist that Plato is giving us a theory of universals, while admitting that he lapses into the language of perfect-examples now and then; or to insist that Plato is giving us a theory of perfect examples, while admitting that he lapses into the language of universals now and then. To maintain our thesis that Plato *thinks* of universals as perfect examples of themselves, we must combat both of these "levelling off" tendencies.

The view that Plato actually *thought* of at least some of the Forms as universals which are perfect examples of themselves has been opposed in various ways. Given the pervasive reverence by European intellectuals for Plato's genius, there is, of course, always the temptation to conclude, simply on the ground that the view is absurd, that Plato did not hold it. One may suspect many commentators of having fallen prey to this temptation; rarely though, if ever, will someone explicitly offer the absurdity of the view as ground for concluding that Plato did not hold it. One will, however, find those—for example, R.E. Allen—who say that the absurdity of the view is ground for trying at all costs to avoid interpreting Plato as holding it.

A somewhat more substantial reason for concluding that Plato did not think of Forms as each an example of the universal that it is, is to be found in the writings of Harold Cherniss. He argues that Plato himself was quite aware of the distinction between *being* a certain property or characteristic, and *having* that property or characteristic. On this ground he rejects the view that Forms are conceived as having the characters that they are. He points to two passages in Plato—*Republic* 597c and *Parmenides*

158a—as places where Plato himself draws the distinction in question. The former of these runs thus: "If [the god] made even as many as two [of that-which-is-bed-itself], then again one would appear whose Form [*eidos*] those two would have, and that one, not those two, would be that-which-is-bed." Concerning this passage, Cherniss says that the distinction between being and having a character is here "expressly applied to prove that the idea of *x*, since it is identical with *x*, cannot have *x* as a character or property, as it necessarily would if it were one of a plurality of entities alike in 'being *x*', and that such entities, however 'perfect' they might otherwise be, would still be 'particulars' and not ideas of *x*, because they would 'have *x* as a character' and therefore would not be 'what *x* is'."[4]

Now this passage from the *Republic* is a peculiar one. In it, Plato does not, as Cherniss suggests, draw a distinction between *being* that-which-is-bed and *having* that-which-is-bed; but rather, between being that-which-is-bed and having the *form* (*eidos*) of that-which-is-bed, this form of that-which-is-bed (not that-which-is-bed itself) being what the two god-made things would have if there were two. It would have been quite possible for Plato here to say that the two god-made those-which-are-beds would have the Form That-which-is-bed. In fact, he does not say this. I suspect that Plato is speaking loosely here in distinguishing between that-which-is-bed and its *eidos;* normally that-which-is-bed would itself be called an *eidos* which things possess.[5] But if Plato is speaking loosely here, no conclusions should be drawn from the passage; whereas if he is speaking strictly, he is not making the distinction that Cherniss says he is.

The *Parmenides* passage to which Cherniss points runs thus: "But its participation in The one clearly implies that it is other than one; for if not, it would not partake of, but would be One itself. But really it is impossible for anything except The one itself to be one." Here, I think, Plato is quite clearly distinguishing between possessing a Form, and being identical with a Form. Still, from his awareness of this distinction it cannot be concluded that Plato did not think that Forms are what we should describe

4. Cherniss, *ibid.,* p. 372.
5. Cf. R.S. Bluck, "Logos and Forms in Plato," in Allen, *Studies in Plato,* pp. 34–35.

as perfect exemplifications of the characters that they are. Of course, he would then have been confused; for though some properties—for example, being a property—are examples of themselves, certainly not all are. Yet, to show that Plato did not think of Forms as universals which are perfect examples of themselves, it will not be sufficient to show that he had in hand the distinction between being an example of a universal and being identical with a universal. In addition, it must be shown that he consistently used it. And it may be noted that the passage just cited from *Parmenides* may itself be read as saying that The one itself is something which is one.

The view of many commentators that Plato did not think of Forms as universals which are perfect examples of themselves still leaves open, of course, the question as to whether he thought of them as universals but not as perfect examples, or whether he thought of them as perfect examples but not as universals. In the literature one finds both positions argued.

We have defended the view that Plato thought of Forms as perfect examples by, among other things, pointing to the fact that he speaks of ordinary things as resembling the Forms. Now there have been various attempts to argue that, though perhaps Plato did indeed speak of things as resembling Forms, he did not in fact *think of,* say, an ordinary beautiful thing and beauty as resembling each other in that both are beautiful. Before we look at one or two of these arguments, though, it should be noticed that even if Plato did not hold that an ordinary beautiful thing and beauty resemble each other in that both are beautiful, he might still, without incoherence, have held that beauty is a perfect example of beauty. For he might, without incoherence, have held that there is only one example of beauty, namely, the perfect example, beauty itself, The beautiful itself. The view that The beautiful itself does not share a common character, beauty, with any ordinary things, is not incompatible with the view that it is in fact a beautiful thing, indeed, the only beautiful thing.[6] But this, I think, is not in fact Plato's view.

Edith Schipper is one who holds that Plato's talk of resemblance is not to be taken literally. She says that ". . . the re-

6. For a statement of the view here being opposed, see ibid., p. 44.

semblance to or imitation of the Forms by things cannot be literal. For a sensed thing cannot literally be like an unsensed Form."[7] To this it must again be said that the fact that *we* cannot see how there could literally be a resemblance between a sensed thing and an unsensed Form is not sound evidence for concluding that *Plato* did not hold that there was this resemblance. But further, Plato does not, of course, hold that sensed things are like unsensed things in every way. Rather, his point is that, for example, beautiful things are like The beautiful itself in that they too are beautiful, though not unchangeably and unalloyedly so. Beauty is not in all ways similar to what participates in it; Plato does say, though, that it along with what participates in it is beautiful.

Harold Cherniss also holds that Plato does not, in spite of his speech, actually *think of* Forms and ordinary things as sharing common characters. But his opposition is somewhat different and more subtle. For he holds that Plato thought of non-Forms as likenesses or images or imitations of the Forms, but not as like the Forms, not as sharing some character with the Forms. "So, for example, a human image is not itself *human;* but it is a human *image* precisely because it does not have as its own the 'humanity' that it signifies."[8] And, ". . . even before Plato wrote the *Parmenides* he must have believed that the 'likeness' of particular to idea does not imply that the idea and the particular are 'alike'."[9] Cherniss supports his interpretation by pointing to passages in various dialogues in which Plato makes it clear that, on his view, if *a* is an image of *b,* then it is not the case that *b* is an image of *a.*[10] But it scarcely follows from this that we must discount all the passages in which Plato speaks of things as similar to the Forms of which they are likenesses. Cherniss is surely correct in suggesting that the relation of one thing being like another is a relation distinct from that of one thing being a likeness of another. The former is symmetrical, the latter is not.

7. Edith Schipper, *Forms in Plato's Later Dialogues* (The Hague, 1965), p. 7. See also W.D. Ross, *Plato's Theory of Ideas* (Oxford, 1961), pp. 87–88.
8. Cherniss, in Allen, *Studies in Plato,* p. 377.
9. Cherniss, *Aristotle's Criticism of Plato and the Academy* (Baltimore, 1944), p. 298. Cf. Allen, *Studies in Plato,* pp. 48–52.
10. Cherniss, in Allen, *Studies in Plato,* pp. 297–98.

But the view that *being a likeness of* is not a symmetrical relation is quite compatible with the view that two things, of which one is a likeness of another, are like each other (in at least some respects). And further, Cherniss cites no evidence to the effect that Plato thought these views incompatible.

One can also find, in the literature, arguments to the effect that Plato's universals mode of speech is to be played down in the interpretation of his thought. One example of this approach is the view of P.T. Geach.[11] He points out that our way of referring to and speaking of *standards* has many analogies to Plato's way of referring to and speaking of Forms. And this is certainly a true and illuminating comment. But it scarcely justifies Geach's view that we should interpret Plato's other ways of referring to and speaking of Forms as, for us, misleading ways of expressing his conception of them as standards. For it is equally the case that our way of referring to and speaking of *universals* has many similarities to Plato's way of referring to and speaking of Forms.

The approach of R.E. Allen is somewhat different, but no more successful. He first argues that Plato thought of Forms as perfect examples. And then he argues that if Plato had held the absurd view that they are also attributes, the result for his philosophy as a whole would have been shipwreck. "Now commutative universals or attributes clearly cannot be identified with standards and paradigms; for the latter are things characterized, not characters; and if there is confusion on this point, self-predication follows immediately. But Forms clearly function in Plato's ontology as standards and paradigms; therefore, if he also thought of them as common characters or attributes, the result is shipwreck."[12] What then follows this passage in Allen's discussion is a page or two in which he tries to show just what would be the consequences, for Plato's view generally, if he thought of the Forms as both universals and perfect examples. But to this line of argument it must be said that we need more evidence for supposing that Plato did not think of Forms as perfect examples of themselves, than just that *we* see various calamitous consequences for his views as a whole if he did so think of them.

So I think that all the attempts to show that one but not the

11. Geach, "The Third Man Again," in ibid., pp. 265–277.
12. Ibid., p. 53.

other of Plato's two ways of referring to and speaking about Forms must be taken seriously, fall very short indeed of establishing their case. Nowhere is there any hint from Plato that one must think of Forms as universals but not as perfect examples, nor that one must think of them as perfect examples but not as universals. Nowhere is there any hint from Plato that he wants us to take one, but not the other, of his two modes of speech seriously. All indications are that he means both modes of speech to be taken with equal seriousness.

There is, perhaps, one other interpretation which merits consideration, though it too, I think, proves unsuccessful. In *Phaedo* 102 Plato very clearly distinguishes between the greatness in Simmias and greatness as such, between the smallness in Socrates and smallness as such; and in *Parmenides* 130, between the likeness in us and likeness as such. In short, he distinguishes between Forms and what we have, in earlier chapters, called *cases* of predicables.[13] In commenting on the *Phaedo* passage, W.D. Ross suggests that it was Plato's view that cases are *present* in the ordinary things, whereas they *resemble* or *are copies of* the Forms.[14] Possibly this was Plato's view. But it seems clear that Plato did not hold this view to the exclusion of the view that ordinary things themselves *both* participate in and resemble the Forms. Probably it was Plato's view that whenever some ordinary thing resembles and participates in some Form, there is present in it a case which resembles the Form as well. Of course, it is attractive to suppose, further, that whenever Plato says that some ordinary thing resembles and participates in a Form, he means this to be taken as a loose way of saying that present in that thing is a case which resembles the Form in question. Then most of the difficulties in Platonic ontology which we have been canvassing would be dissolved. But if Plato did in fact hold this view, one would expect him to put it forth clearly somewhere, especially in *Parmenides*. Nowhere is it in fact put forth at all.

The conclusion is inescapable. Plato conceived of universals as perfect examples of themselves.

13. Perhaps the same ontology is expressed in *Tamaeus* 49–52. Cf. the comments on this passage by F.M. Cornford, *Plato's Cosmology* (New York, 1952).
14. Ross, *Plato's Theory of Ideas*, p. 30.

What motivates the attempts of many of Plato's twentieth-century commentators to flatten out his thought in the ways indicated, is their own conviction that most universals are not examples of themselves at all, let alone being perfect examples of themselves. On this point they are, of course, correct. It was a confusion on Plato's part to think of beauty as beautiful, to think of justice as just, to think of The Bed as a bed. The confusion is perhaps understandable; if one has ever tried to teach students some of these matters, one knows how endemic it is in human beings to think that justice is just, that greenness is green, and the like. But, understandable or not, it is confusion nonetheless.

That Plato regarded Forms—and thus universals—as fit *paradigms* for divine and human thought and action is so well-known a feature of his thought as to need little comment here. It will suffice to cite just a few passages in which he himself *calls* them paradigms. Many other such passages might be cited instead; in addition, many might be cited in which, though he does not use the word "paradigm," his thought is yet that the Forms should be paradigms for one and another action.

In *Euthyphro* 6d, where we find the rudimentary beginnings of Plato's theory of Forms, Socrates says: "Tell me then what this idea (ἰδέα) is, that I may keep my eye fixed upon it and employ it as a paradigm and, if anything you or anyone else does is similar to it, may say that the act is holy, and if not, that it is unholy." In *Republic* 500e Socrates says: ". . . Happiness can only come to a state when its lineaments are traced by an artist working after a divine paradigm." And somewhat later (592b) he says: "But perhaps there is a paradigm set up in the heavens for one who desires to see it and, seeing it, to found one in himself." In short, it was Plato's view that the Forms ought to serve as models or paradigms for all our thoughts and actions, from the most trivial to the most fundamental. Thus the Forms acquire a religious status for Plato. In the Hebrew and Christian religions it is God's will that ought to guide our thoughts and actions. In Platonic religion it is, instead, universals that ought to guide our thoughts and actions. In Christianity it is the historical figure of Jesus of Nazareth that is the paradigm for human life. In Platonic religion it is the universal, Man itself, that is the paradigm for human life.

In Platonic thought, universals function as paradigms for the gods as well. In no fundamental way is God's making different from ours. In *Timaeus* 38b Socrates says: "Time, then, came into existence along with the heaven, to the end that having been generated together they might also be dissolved together, if ever a dissolution of them should take place; and it was made after the paradigm of the eternal nature, to the end that it might be as like thereto as possible. . . ." And later (39e–40a): "Now, in all other respects this World has already, with the birth of Time, been wrought in the similitude of what whereunto it was being likened, but inasmuch as it did not as yet contain generated within it the whole range of living creatures, therein it was still dissimilar. So this part of the work which was still undone He completed by moulding it after the nature of the paradigm." And in *Parmenides* 132d Socrates says: "But Parmenides, I think the most likely view is, that these forms (εἴδη) exist in nature as paradigms, and the other things resemble them and are imitations of them. . . ." In short, universals are bound up not only in Platonic religion, but also in Platonic theology and cosmology.

But it should be clear that, unless one regards universals as perfect or ideal examples of themselves, it just makes no sense to say that they should be treated as paradigms or models. The presupposition of the Platonic religion and the Platonic theology is that universals are perfect examples of themselves. But the religion and the theology are not even viable options, for the presupposition is untenable. One could indeed try to govern one's state on the model of The perfectly just thing—if there were one. One could indeed try to live one's own life on the model of The perfectly good thing—if there were one. But one cannot try to govern one's state on the model of the property of justice; one cannot try to live one's own life on the model of the property of goodness; one cannot try to make a bed on the model of the property of being a bed, nor on the model of the kind, Bed.

2. Such thinkers as Augustine and Aquinas seem not to have noticed the confusion in Plato's notion that exemplifications of

predicables and examples of kinds are in the likeness of those predicables and kinds. They did, however, notice Plato's view that
predicables and kinds are independently existing entities which
God, if he is to create well, must imitate as closely as possible.
And they, rightly, saw in this view quite a different understanding
of the nature of creation from that of the Christian faith. Augustine remarks that "God was not fixing his gaze upon anything
located outside Himself to serve as a model when he made the
things he created, for such a view is blasphemous."[15] And
Aquinas, following in the footsteps of Augustine, says: "But it
seems contrary to faith that the forms of things should subsist of
themselves without matter outside the things themselves, as the
platonists held, asserting that *life-in-itself* and *wisdom-in-itself* are
certain creative substances. . . . Therefore, in the place of the
Ideas defended by Plato, Augustine said that the exemplars of
all creatures existed in the divine mind. It is according to these
that all things are formed. . . ."[16]

As can perhaps be gathered from these passages, both Augustine and Aquinas hold that God's creative activity must not be
understood on the analogy of someone who executes a painting
by copying some other, independently existing, painting. Rather,
they both insist that it must be understood on the analogy of an
artist who has an idea for a painting and then, in accord with
his own idea, executes his painting. Thus, it is God's *ideas* which
are the exemplars for his creative activity. In fact, both Augustine
and Aquinas use "Idea" as a technical term for those divine
ideas which function as exemplars; and whenever I capitalize
"Idea," I shall be using it in this way. Let us quote Augustine on
his conception of God's Ideas: "The Ideas are Original Forms or
fixed and changeless patterns of things which have not been
fashioned from the Forms themselves and consequently, being
eternal and always the same, are contained in the Divine Mind.
And while these themselves neither come to be nor cease to
exist, it is maintained that, in accordance with them, everything
is fashioned capable of having a beginning and end, as well as

---

15. "De Ideis," Migne, *PL* 40, pp. 30–31; tr. J.A. Mourant, *Introduction
to the Philosophy of St. Augustine* (University Park, Pa., 1964), p. 205.
16. *Summa Theologica*, I, Q. 84, a. 5.

whatever actually comes into or goes out of existence."[17] Aquinas would call anything at all in accord with which something is made—be it a divine Idea or not—an exemplar. But it was his conviction—as it was Augustine's—that the only things which function as exemplars for God are his ideas.

Now both Augustine and Aquinas identify (at least some) predicables and kinds with the divine Ideas. But their understanding of the nature of divine Ideas, though similar, is not the same. Thus their understanding of the nature of (at least some) predicables and kinds, and of the relation of these to God, turns out to be somewhat—even considerably—different.

Augustine says that ". . . all things have been fashioned according to an intelligible principle [*ratione*]. Neither has man been made by the same intelligible principle as the horse, since this is an absurd supposition. Each thing . . . has been created according to its own intellectual principle. . . . It is by participating in these Ideas that a thing comes to exist, whatever its mode of being."[18] Now Augustine never, so far as I know, makes the general claim that predicables are all identical with the divine Ideas. Nor does he ever, with full explicitness, say of some particular predicable that it is identical with a divine Idea. But that he did in fact hold, concerning at least some predicables, that they are divine Ideas, is reasonably concluded from, among other passages, the following one from *De vere religione:*

But who can find absolute equality or similarity in bodily objects? Who would venture to say, after due consideration, that any body is truly and simply one? All are changed by passing from form to form or from place to place, and consist of parts each occupying its own place and extended in space. Thus equality and similitude, true and primal unity, are not perceived by the eye of flesh or by any bodily sense, but are known by the mind. How is equality of any kind demanded in bodies, and how are we convinced that any equality that may be seen there is far different from perfect equality, unless the mind sees that which is perfect? If indeed that which is not made [*facta*] can be called perfect [*perfecta*]?

All things which are beautiful to the senses, whether they are produced by nature or are worked out by the arts, have a spatial or temporal beauty, as for example the body and its movements. But the

17. "De Ideis," p. 204.
18. Ibid.

equality and unity which are known only by the mind, and according
to which the mind judges of corporeal beauty by the intermediary of
the senses, are not extended in space or unstable in time. . . . This
law [lex] of all the arts is absolutely unchangeable, but the human
mind, which is given the power to see the law, can suffer the muta-
bility of error. Clearly, then, the law which is called truth is higher
than our minds.

We must not have any doubt that the unchangeable substance which
is above the rational mind is God. The primal life and primal essence
is where the primal wisdom is. This is unchangeable truth, which is
the law of all the arts and the art of the omnipotent artificer.[19]

Though Augustine does not actually say so, I think the only
reasonable interpretation of his thought in this passage is that
what he here calls *laws,* and shortly afterwards *intelligible principles,* are in fact Divine Ideas. And if so, then it is clear that
at least some predicables are to be counted among the Divine
Exemplars. For in 55–57 he cites equality, similarity, unity, and
squareness as examples of what he calls laws.

But with *which* Ideas would Augustine identify equality, similarity, unity, and the like? I think it is clear that he regarded
squareness as identical with God's idea of a square thing, perhaps, of a perfectly square thing; unity, with God's idea of a unified thing, perhaps, of a perfectly unified thing; and so on. This,
of course, is what one would expect, given his Platonic back-
ground. But he also constantly says such things as these: "Things
seen with the eyes are better the nearer they are in their own
kind to the things I know with my mind."[20] "No material thing
can possibly achieve the unity it aims at. . . . Material things
imitate but cannot completely achieve unity."[21] ". . . we must
rather ask whether [corporeal things] deceive by resembling unity
or in failing to achieve unity."[22] In short, he constantly speaks of
ordinary, somewhat unified, things as similar to, though not fully
similar to, unity; and as more similar to it the more unified they
are. And this scarcely makes sense unless he is thinking of the
idea of unity as the idea of a unified, or perfectly unified, thing.

19. *De vere religione,* secs. 55–57. The translation given is mainly that in
St. Augustine: Of True Religion, tr. J.H.S. Burleigh (Philadelphia, 1953).
20. Ibid., sec. 57.
21. Ibid., sec. 60.
22. Ibid., sec. 61.

Indeed, if Augustine did *not* identify God's idea of unity with God's idea of a (perfectly) unified thing, it is hard to see how he could think of God as creating things in accord with his ideas. Presumably, if God creates something in accord with his idea of *x,* he creates something which is or approximates *x.* When God creates something in accord with his idea of Augustine, He creates Augustine. When he creates something in accord with his idea of a man, he creates a man. But Augustine does not hold that God creates *unity* in accord with his idea of unity. Rather, unity is an idea in accord with which he creates unfied things. Presumably then unity, the idea in accord with which he creates unified things, is the idea of a (perfectly) unified thing.

Augustine's theory of Divine Ideas is undoubtedly similar to Plato's theory of Forms, and he himself indicates that this is the provenance of his theory.[23] But it must also be noted how radically he has transformed the Platonic theory. Men, on the Platonic conception, were created by God on the model of The Ideal Man. The Ideas were all *perfect examples.* But men, on the Augustinian conception, were created by God in accord with his own idea or concept of a man. And the idea or concept of a man is not itself a man, let alone the Ideal Man. Augustine has transformed the Platonic theory of divine *paradigms* (that is, of perfect examples functioning as models for making, or functioning as exemplars), into a theory of divine ideas functioning as divine exemplars.

Of course, an idea in accord with which one creates or produces something may be an idea of something which in fact exists. This perhaps explains Augustine's apparent identification of certain predicables with God himself. He seems, for example, to have made such an identification in the case of unity.[24] His thought is, apparently, that God is the perfectly unified thing; accordingly, for God to create something more or less in accord with (satisfying) his idea of a perfectly unified thing, is at the same time to create something more or less in accord with (resembling) himself. So God himself, being the perfect example of unity, can be regarded as that in accord with which he creates all unified things (in which case God himself functions as paradigm for

23. In "De Ideis."
24. *Of True Religion,* secs. 58, 66.

his making). This raises the question as to whether Augustine would wish to identify the predicable, *unity,* with God's idea of a perfectly unified thing, or with the perfect example of unity, that is, God. I think it is unclear which of these alternatives he would have preferred, for he does not seem clearly to have distinguished them. That is, he does not seem clearly to have distinguished between God's idea of the perfectly unified thing, and the perfectly unified thing (himself). Accordingly, he does not seem always clearly to have distinguished between God's ideas functioning as exemplars, and God as a perfect example functioning as exemplar (that is, as paradigm). He does now and then speak as if God himself *is* unity. It seems unlikely, though, that he would have identified, say, squareness with God himself. This, and many other predicables, would, by Augustine, surely be identified with a divine idea but not with God himself. They would not be regarded as paradigmatic exemplars.

It should be evident that Augustine's identification of certain predicables with divine Ideas cannot satisfactorily be broadened into a *general* theory on the matter; that is, predicables cannot in general be identified with divine Ideas. For one thing, predicables which are never exemplified can obviously not be identified with ideas in accord with which God does create, and predicables which can never be exemplified cannot even be identified with ideas in accord with which God *could* create. Further, it is not even satisfactory to identify those predicables which *are* exemplified with ideas of God in accord with which he *does* create; or predicables which *can* be exemplified with ideas of God in accord with which he *can* create. For though square things can be produced by making them in accord with the concept of a (perfectly) square thing, they cannot be produced by making them in accord with squareness. Squareness is simply not this sort of thing. And though things are more or less square insofar as they are more or less closely in accord with (that is, more or less closely satisfy) the concept of a (perfectly) square thing, they are not more or less square insofar as they are more or less closely in accord with squareness. Similar remarks, of course, hold for other predicables. It is simply a confusion to identify a predicable with an idea or concept in accord with which exemplifications of the predicable are produced.

Aquinas followed Augustine in holding that when someone makes something intelligently but does not copy a paradigm, there is in the mind of the maker an idea in accord with which, or in the likeness of which, he makes the thing in question. This exemplary idea, Aquinas says, is the *form* of the thing made. So also, since God creates intelligently but does not copy paradigms (unless they be identical with himself), there are in God's mind ideas in the likeness of which he creates things; and these are the forms of the things created. "[B]y ideas are understood the forms of things, existing apart from the things themselves. Now the form of anything, existing apart from the thing itself, can be for one of two ends; either to be the exemplar of that of which it is called the form, or to be the principle of the knowledge of the thing, according as the forms of knowable things are said to be in him who knows them. . . . [T]he likeness of a house preexists in the mind of the builder. And this may be called the idea of the house, since the builder intends to build his house like the form conceived in his mind. Since, then, the world was not made by chance, but by God acting by His intellect . . . there must exist in the divine mind a form to the likeness of which the world was made. And in this the notion of an idea consists."[25]

Actually, Aquinas chooses to apply the term "Idea" not just to those divine ideas in the likeness of which God *does* create things, but also to those in the likeness of which he *could* create something. "[A] thing can be called an exemplar merely if something else can be made in imitation of it—even though this other thing is never made. The same is true of ideas."[26]

To clarify further what he has in mind by an idea, Aquinas points out that it is not to be thought of as that *by which* something is understood, but as *that which is* understood. It is not a concept, or intelligible species (likeness) as he would call it, by the having of which we understand something. It is, rather, something understood, and in the likeness of which something can be made. "[T]he idea of the thing to be produced is in the mind of the producer as that which is understood, and not as the likeness

25. *S.T.*, I, Q. 15, a. 1, resp. See also *De Veritate*, Q. 2, a. 5, resp; and Q. 3, arts. 1, 7, and resp.
26. *De Veritate*, Q. 3, a. ad. 3; see also a. 3, art. 7, resp. Tr. R.W. Mulligan in *Truth: St. Thomas Aquinas* (Chicago, 1952).

whereby he understands, which is a form that makes the intellect in act. For the form of the house in the mind of the builder is something understood by him, to the likeness of which he forms the house in matter."[27]

Now Aquinas held that in God's case all his Ideas are identical with himself. Thus it was his view that God makes everything in the likeness of himself. Yet he thought it not inappropriate to speak of there being *many* Ideas. His thought on this point was, apparently, something like the following. Suppose that a painter produces several paintings in accord with a certain painting-idea which he has. Suppose, further, that none of these paintings is a perfect execution of his idea, but that each is designed as a different, albeit imperfect, imitation of the one idea. Then one can say that his one painting-idea is the exemplar for all these different paintings. But equally one can say that his painting-idea treated as imitable in a certain fashion, is the exemplar for one of his paintings; that his painting-idea treated as imitable in a certain different fashion, is the exemplar for another one of his paintings; and so on. In one sense, then, there is but one exemplar; in another sense, there are several exemplars. So also in the case of God. Nothing but God is *perfectly* like God. Everything is but an imperfect imitation of God, each thing resembling God in a different fashion. Thus, in one sense all created things are made in accord with the same thing. One thing is made in the likeness of God considered as imitable in one fashion; another is made in the likeness of God considered as imitable in another fashion; and so on. Every divine Idea is God considered as imitable in a certain fashion. "God, who makes all things by means of His intellect, produces them all in the likeness of His own essence. Hence, His essence is the idea of things. . . . Created things, however, do not perfectly imitate the divine essence. . . . Now, different things imitate the divine essence in different ways, each one according to its own proper manner since each has its own act of existence, distinct from that of another. We can say, therefore, that the divine essence is the idea of each and every thing, understanding, of course, the different proportions that things have to it. Hence, since there are in things different pro-

27. *S.T.*, I, Q. 15, a. 2, resp. See also *De Veritate*, Q. 3, a. 2, resp.

portions to the divine essence, there must necessarily be many ideas. If we consider the essence alone, however, there is but one idea for all things; but if we consider the different proportions of creatures to the divine essence, then there can be said to be a plurality of ideas."[28]

Now it was Aquinas' view that when a universal—a form or nature—is known by someone, then there indeed *is* something that is known, namely, that universal. It exists *in intellectu*. But a universal can exist *in intellectu*—can *be* something that is known —without existing in reality, *in re*. There is, according to him, such and such a universal *in re* just in case it is instantiated, just in case it is the form or nature *of* something.[29] Accordingly, since the Divine Ideas all exist eternally, universal natures or forms all, in one sense, exist eternally, for they just are God considered as imitable in a certain fashion. But this is only existence *in intellectu,* existence *as* a divine idea. It is only by virtue of God's bringing men into existence that there exists *in re* such a thing as human nature. There will exist *in re* such a thing as human nature just in case something bears what one might call man-resemblance to God. Before men were brought into existence, there was indeed God considered as imitable in this certain way; that is, human nature existed *in intellectu.* But human nature did not exist *in re;* there was *in fact* nothing bearing man-resemblance to God.[30]

It was Aquinas' view that with the exception of God's nature —which, he thought, was identical with God—all natures which exist *in re* have been brought into existence by God. In short, it was his view that all universals which exist *in re* are either identical with God or brought into *in re existence* by God.

It will have been noticed that here too, as in the case of Plato and Augustine, the idea of things being made in accord with or

28. *De Veritate,* Q. 3, a. 2, resp. See also ibid., ad 2 and ad 6, in which we find this: "The one first form to which all things are reduced is the divine essence, considered in itself. Reflecting upon this essence, the divine intellect devises—if I may use such an expression—different ways in which it can be imitated. The plurality of ideas comes from these different ways." See also *S.T.,* I, Q. 15, a. 2, resp.; and Q. 44, a. 3, resp.
29. *S.T.,* I, Q. 85, a. 2, ad. obj. 2.
30. See *S.T.,* I, Q. 14, a. 12, resp.; and *summa contra Gentiles,* I, 50 (9), and 54 (5).

in the likeness of universals plays a dominant role. But Aquinas' elaboration of this idea is quite different from that of either of his predecessors. In Plato, squareness was conceived as identical with the ideally square thing, and square things were thought of as resembling squareness in respect of being square. In Augustine, squareness was conceived as identical with God's idea or concept of a (perfectly) square thing, and square things were thought of as made in the likeness of this idea. When Aquinas first explains what he means by "Idea," it sounds as if his thought is the same as Augustine's. In fact, however, it turns out to be quite different; he has as radically transformed Augustine as Augustine transformed Plato. For Aquinas holds that all things are made in the likeness of God. But he does not hold that God is the perfectly square thing, so his thought does not follow the pattern of Plato—he does not identify squareness with the perfectly square thing. But also he does not think that God is the concept of a square thing, so his thought does not follow the pattern of Augustine—he does not identify squareness with God's *concept* of a square thing. Square things are not likenesses of God in the way in which deficiently square things are likenesses of the perfectly square thing; nor are they likenesses of God in the way in which square things are in accord with or in the likeness of the concept of a square thing. Rather, they are likenesses of God in the way in which something which is made as an imperfect likeness of something else is yet a likeness of it.

Suppose, for example, that I make something which is an imperfect likeness of a cube. What I make may, in fact, be a sphere. But it still is something having a shape. It is like—and also unlike—the cube *in a specific way*. Anything like—and unlike—a cube in this specific way will also be a sphere.

But Aquinas' view seems quite clearly to have the astounding consequence that such entities as squareness and man are identical with God. "By ideas are understood," he says, "the forms of things," the force of saying of some form that it is an idea or exemplar being simply that God can create things in its likeness. But in fact it is God himself who is the sole exemplar for all his creative activity; he makes things in the likeness of solely himself. Now squareness, Aquinas holds, is a form, an accidental form; man is also a form, a substantial form. The conclusion must be that Aquinas identifies squareness and man with God. And this is grossly untenable.

Of course, Aquinas would want to say something more. He would want to say that it is God considered as imitable in the fashion peculiar to square things that is the exemplar for square things; and so, he would want to say that it is God considered as imitable in the fashion peculiar to square things that is to be identified with the form of square things, that is, with square-ness. Now if *God* were something distinct from *God considered as imitable in the fashion peculiar to square things,* then we would have to choose between two possibilities as to what Aquinas wishes to identify squareness with. The crucial question is how Aquinas understands such a phrase as "considered as imitable in the fashion peculiar to square things." Unfortunately, he never makes his thought explicit on this point, and we can only specu-late. It does seem clear that he holds that God is the sole exem-plar for all things. Hence, whatever the force of "considered as imitable in the fashion peculiar to square things," it seems that God is identical with God considered as imitable in the fashion peculiar to square things. However, considering God as God seems different from considering God as imitable in the fashion peculiar to square things, and this, in turn, seems different from considering God as imitable in the fashion peculiar to men. (Simi-larly, to say of something *that it is God* is to say something differ-ent of it from saying of it *that it is imitable in the fashion peculiar to square things;* and this, in turn, is to say something different of it from saying of it *that it is imitable in the fashion peculiar to men.*) So perhaps Aquinas' full point is the following: Squareness is identical with God. But to consider God as (identical with) squareness, is not to consider him as God, but is rather to con-sider him as imitable in the fashion peculiar to square things. (And correspondingly, to say of God *that he is squareness* is not to say of him *that he is God* but is rather to say of him *that he is imitable in the fashion peculiar to square things.*)[31]

---

31. There is perhaps some slight reason for thinking that, on Aquinas' view, squareness is a certain *resemblance* to God rather than God considered as imitable in a certain way. For he says in *S.T.*, I, Q. 14, a. 6, resp.: "[T]he nature proper to each thing consists in some particular participation of the divine perfection."

But God is not a universal, and certainly he is not all universals. Predicables and kinds are not, as Plato held they were, perfect examples of themselves of which God is obligated to create likenesses. Nor are they as Augustine held they were, concepts in the likeness of which God creates things. Nor are they as Aquinas held they were, God himself considered as imitable in certain ways. Predicables and kinds are simply not entities whose examples are made by God in the likeness of, or in accord with, themselves.

3. But, as we have already suggested, there is more which motivates the identification of universals with divine Ideas, on the part of Augustine and Aquinas, than just their confused notion that instances of a universal are somehow in the likeness of that universal. Both were concerned to develop a theory of universals which was in harmony with the biblical conception of a creating God. This led them both to repudiate the Platonic notion that God, in creating, creates in the likeness of entities separate from himself. But it also led Aquinas to the view that any theory of universals which is to be in accord with the biblical doctrine of creation must yield the consequence that all universals are either identical with or brought into being by God. For it was his view that the biblical teaching on creation includes the belief that *all* things are either identical with or brought into being by God. In *Summa Theologica*, I, Q. 44, art. 1, resp., in answer to the question "is God the efficient cause of all things?" he says firmly: "I answer that, It must be said that everything, that in any way is, is from God." So part of the intent of Aquinas, in constructing his theory of universals, was to construct a theory which conformed to this understanding of the doctrine of creation. So also Augustine says that "Existence as such is good, and supreme existence is the chief good. . . . Every good thing is either God or derived from God. . . . All that exists receives its potential existence from God."[32] And apparently he understands the divine ideas as, if not identical with God, in some way derived from him.

Indeed, the great Christian theologians seem remarkably

32. *De vere religione*, secs. 35–36.

unanimous in holding that the biblical teaching is that all entities, other than God himself, owe their existence in some way to God. Ockham says, "Everything that is not from God as its efficient cause, is uncaused; and everything of this nature is God; therefore everything different from God is from God as its efficient cause."[33] Calvin says, ". . . God, by the power of his Word and Spirit, created out of nothing the heaven and the earth . . . from them he produced all things animate and inanimate."[34] Karl Barth says, "[M]an owes his existence and form together with all the reality distinct from God, to God's creation. . . ."[35] And Emil Brunner says, "He who is 'above' all and 'before' all is the One who originates all things and is Himself originated by none; He is the One who determined all things and is determined by none."[36] In short, these theologians are all of the view that the Creator-Creature distinction is exhaustive of all reality. And they all suggest that in holding this view they are conforming to the view of the biblical writers. Aquinas, for example, cites this biblical passage: "For from him and through him and to him are all things" (Rom. 11:36).

What I wish to discuss briefly is whether Aquinas and the other theologians cited were correct in supposing that it is an implication of the biblical teaching on creation that all predicables are either identical with or brought into being by God. If one holds that there are some predicables which fall into neither of these classifications, *must* he then repudiate or revise the biblical-Christian belief in a creating God?

To begin, it seems clearly to be a consequence of the biblical-Christian teaching on creation as well as on other matters, that *not* all predicables and kinds are either identical with or brought into being by God. The teaching of the biblical writers surely presupposes that God has many properties—the properties of having created, of being faithful, and others. Further, it clearly presupposes that God is not identical with these properties, for it presupposes that God is not a property. Now no doubt some of God's properties have been brought into *existence* by God

33. Boehner, *Ockham,* p. 228.
34. *Institutes,* I, xiv, 20.
35. *Church Dogmatics,* III, I, p. 3.
36. *Christian Doctrine of Creation and Redemption,* p. 8.

himself, for example, his property of having created. But if he has the property of having created, then he also has the property of having been able to create. And *this,* it seems clear, he did not bring into existence. Nor, of course, did he bring the property of being identical with God into existence, nor the property of being identical with something that exists.[37] God himself has properties (attributes) which are neither identical with himself nor brought about by himself.

Further, supposing it not to be the case that God exists necessarily—and it seems to me that this is indeed not the case—then we cannot even say that whatever might not have existed but does exist, depends on God's creative activity for its existence. For if God might not have existed, then the property of being able to create might also not have existed; but this property was not brought into existence by God's creative activity.

It might be replied that such properties as being able to create, though they were not brought into existence by God's creative activity, still are dependent on God in that they are properties of him, and exist because he does. And so someone might claim that though the classical theologians whom we have cited were mistaken in thinking that everything is either God or created by God, at least it can be held that everything is either God or dependent on God. But then consider the fact that propositions have the property of *being either true or false.* This property is not a property of God. But it is presupposed by the biblical writers that not all exemplifications of this property were brought into existence by God, and thus that it was not brought into existence by God. For the propositions 'God exists' and 'God is able to create' exemplify *being true or false* wholly apart from any creative activity on God's part; in fact, creative ability on his part presupposes that these propositions are true, and thus presupposes that there exists such a property as *being either true or false.*

Further, if God did not exist, then the proposition 'God exists' would be false. And then the property of being either true

37. The reader should be reminded that, throughout, we are distinguishing between the claim that a certain predicable *exists,* and the claim that it *is.* Cf. chap. 9. A predicable *exists* if and only if it is exemplified. It may *be,* even though it neither is exemplified nor could be exemplified.

or false would still be exemplified; it would still exist. The existence of this property seems not to depend on God even in the sense that if God did not exist *it* would not exist.

So the biblical teaching on creation and on other matters clearly presupposes that there are various predicables which are neither identical with God nor brought into existence by God. Is the proper conclusion, then, that Christian belief is contradictory? Is it part of the teaching on creation that all things are either identical with or brought into existence by God? But is it at the same time an implication of this teaching that *not* all things are either identical with or brought into existence by God?

There are certainly prima facie grounds for suspecting that the biblical teaching on creation is being mis-interpreted when it is interpreted as entailing that everything is either identical with or brought into existence by God. For can it plausibly be supposed that the biblical writers, when they confessed their belief in God the Creator, had *universals* in view in speaking of "all things"? If so, why are they never mentioned? Would anyone now, unless he were engaging in some theoretical inquiry, have universals in mind when he spoke of "all things"? When the biblical writers drew the contrast between things in heaven and things on earth and things in the sea, and spoke of God as creator of heaven and earth and sea and all that is in them, did they mean to include universals? Where would universals fit into this classification?

I shall not explore what the biblical writers may have meant to include when they spoke of heaven and earth and sea and all that is in them—though such a linguistic or philological investigation might very well prove to be a profitable line of investigation.[38] Rather, I wish to get at the scope of their claim by looking at the function of the belief in creation in the *religion* of the biblical writers. Surely this approach is apropos; for the biblical writers were not propounding some abstract, theoretical, more or less indifferent, ontology. Rather, their belief in creation was always a matter of religious confession on their part. It functioned in their religion. And to see the import of it, we must look at how it functioned in their religion. The question to ask

38. See von Rad, *Old Testament Theology,* tr. D.M.G. Stalker (New York, 1962), 1: 152, 426.

is whether the religious significance of this creator-creature distinction demands that it be exhaustive of all reality.

Let us, for the moment, focus our attention on the Old Testament writers. In them, the belief in God as Creator seems to have had a dual religious function. For one thing, it was used to help ground their conviction that God has a claim on man's praise and obedience, that he is rightfully the Lord of man's life. And secondly, it was used to ground their claim that man can rely on God without fearing that he will prove to be lacking in power over what happens.

The Old Testament writers saw God's act of creation as one among others of his mighty acts.[39] And it was on account of his mighty acts, acts incomparably greater than those of anything else, that they said that God rightfully calls forth praise and worship and religious awe. God does not, in their thought, merit praise and worship and awe just on account of what he is, wholly apart from what he does. It is not his mere ontological status which grounds their claim that to him and him alone must be given religious praise and worship. Rather, it is his incomparably mighty acts that rightfully call for praise and worship and awe. And among these, creation, of course, occupies a signal place. The writer of Psalm 33 puts it thus:

> Praise the Lord with the lyre,
>   make melody to him with the harp of ten strings!
> . . . .
> By the word of the Lord the heavens were made,
>   and all their host by the breath of his mouth.
> . . . .
> Let all the earth fear the Lord,
>   let all the inhabitants of the world stand in awe of him!
> For he spoke, and it came to be;
>   he commanded, and it stood forth.

Not only does God have a claim on man's worship and praise and awe, on account of his incomparable greatness manifested in his mighty acts, including that of creation. He also, because of his mighty acts, including that of creation, has an incontestable claim

---

39. See ibid., pp. 136–39, 449–53. See also T.C. Vriezen, *Hoofdlijnen der Theologie van het Oude Testament* (Wageningen, Netherlands, 1966), pp. 359–70, 468–70.

on man's obedience. This strain of thought comes out clearly in Isaiah 45:

"Woe to him who strives with his Maker
  an earthen vessel with the potter!
Does the clay say to him who fashions it, 'What are you making'?
  or 'Your work has no handles'?
Woe to him who says to a father, 'What are you begetting?'
  or to a woman, 'With what are you in travail' "
Thus says the Lord, the Holy One of Israel, and his Maker:
"Will you question me about my children,
  or command me concerning the work of my hands?
I made the earth, and created man upon it;
  it was my hands that stretched out the heavens, and I commanded
  all their host.
I have aroused him in righteousness, and I will make straight all his
  ways;
  he shall build my city and set my exiles free not for price or
  reward."

God's act of creation, along with his other mighty acts, is not only used by the Old Testament writers to ground their conviction that God is worthy of praise and of obedience.[40] It is also used to ground their conviction that man can, without fear, trust and rely on God. Man can, without fear, lay his destiny in God's hands. For he has the might—as evidenced by his act of creation and his other mighty acts—to accomplish his gracious purposes. There is nothing capable of frustrating his purposes. The prophet puts it thus in Isaiah 51:

"I, I am he that comforts you;
  who are you that you are afraid of man who dies,
  of the son of man who is made like grass,
and have forgotten the Lord, your Maker,
  who stretched out the heavens
  and laid the foundations of the earth,
and fear continually all the day
  because of the fury of the oppressor
when he sets himself to destroy.

The New Testament writers take up and repeat these Old Testament themes, adding to them the note that God's Word, by which and for which he creates, was embodied in Jesus of Nazareth.

40. See also Isaiah 44 and 48; Jeremiah 10; Psalm 8, 89, 104; Job 38–40.

Now if what we have said does indeed capture the religious import which the biblical writers attached to their belief in God the Creator, then it is clear that the existence of predicables and kinds which are neither identical with God nor brought into existence by God, is no threat whatsoever to their religion. The fact that certain predicables are neither creator nor created is absolutely irrelevant to the religious import of the creator-creature distinction. The biblical writers proclaim that God alone is entitled to religious praise and worship and awe, this on account of the incomparable greatness of his acts, including his act of creation. The fact that certain predicables and kinds have not been brought into being or existence is certainly no slur on the incomparable greatness of God's acts. Nothing else brought them into being or existence either. They proclaim that God has an incontestable claim on our obedience because of his mighty acts, including his act of creation. But the fact that certain predicables and kinds have not been created certainly does not introduce a contest for our obedience. They proclaim that God can without fear be relied on, on the ground of his act of creation along with his other acts. But again, the fact that certain predicables and kinds have not been created does not introduce some question as to whether he can be relied on. When the biblical doctrine of creation is seen in its religious context, it becomes clear that it speaks neither one way nor the other to the issue of whether all predicables and kinds have been brought into being or existence by God.

So Aquinas, in taking the biblical doctrine of creation as a guide for his thought on the matter of universals, misinterpreted that doctrine. This doctrine does not entail that all universals are either creator or created. On the contrary, as we have already seen, it presupposes that some are neither. Predicables ·are not all brought into being or existence by God. Nor is it even the case that all those not brought into being or existence by God are ones of which God is an exemplification.

4. We have seen that predicables and kinds are not perfect examples of themselves, and so they cannot be paradigms for God's creative activity. We have also seen that they are not exemplars for God's creative activity, whether exemplars be con-

ceived in Augustinian fashion as ideas in God's mind, or in Thomistic fashion as God himself qua imitable in various ways. And we have just seen that they are not all either brought into being by God or instantiated by God.

But, it may be asked, how then, if one believes in the existence of God as conceived in the Christian or Jewish religion, can one understand the relation of predicables to God?

A word is said on this matter in the Epilogue.

Epilogue

The predicable/case/exemplification structure holds for all reality whatsoever—necessarily so. Everything whatsoever is either a predicable, a case of a predicable, or an exemplification of a predicable. Nothing does or can fall outside this structure; everything falls within it. Nothing is unique in that it falls outside this fundamental structure of reality. God too has properties; he too acts. So he too exemplifies predicables. The predicable/case/exemplification structure is not just the structure of created things. Nor is it just the structure of 'appearance'. Nor is it just a structure of our thought about things. Nor is it just a structure of our language about things. It is a structure of reality, of what there is.

If reality is to be a *structure* of predicables, cases, and exemplifications, then entities of one of these sorts must be related to entities of another of these sorts—cases to predicables, predicables to exemplifications, exemplifications to cases. And for this, it is in turn necessary that there be relations in which they stand to each other, the relations of being a case of, of being an exemplification of, of being an aspect of. And this is accounted for, since relations are themselves predicables. It is further required that there should be such an entity as *standing in some relation to*.

And this demand too is satisfied. For this in turn is a relation, and thus a predicable.

If reality is to be a structure of predicables, cases, and exemplifications, there must also be relationships—not just relations and things, but things related, things standing in relation, relationships. This too is accounted for; relationships are themselves just cases of relations.

But predicables—so we have seen—are kinds, kinds of cases. Hence another structure holding for all reality is the kind/example structure. Everything whatsoever is one or the other, kind or example, and that necessarily. For all predicables are kinds; all cases are examples of those special kinds which are predicables; and every instance will at least be an example of the kind, Instance of a Property. The kind/example structure is a structure which nothing does or can fall outside of, which everything falls within.

That reality should be a *structure* of kinds and examples, it is necessary that these be related, examples to kinds, kinds to examples. And for this, it is in turn necessary that there be a relation in which they can stand to each other, the relation of being an example of. But this demand is compatible with everything's being an example or a kind; since relations, being predicables, are themselves kinds.

What is also necessary, if reality is to be a structure of kinds and examples, is that there should be relationships between examples and kinds—things actually standing to kinds in the relation of being examples of them. And this demand is also compatible with the claim that everything is a kind or an example. For relationships, being cases, are themselves examples of those kinds which are predicables.

Index

Abelard, 50, 142, 173–74, 186, 187–88
Abstractive attention, 128–41, 149; Aquinas's view of, 143–48
Abstractive descriptions, 130, 134–41
Actions, 75–76; identity of, and assertibles, 151; identity of, and predicates, 155–57; relation of, to assertibles, 79–80; relation of, to properties, 79
Action-names, 75–76
"Affirm of," 41
Allen, R.E., 267, 272, 276
Anscombe, Elizabeth, 224, 226
Aquinas, Thomas, 63, 142–48, 263, 279–81, 290–91, 296; and abstraction, 143–48; and individualized forms, 143–48; and universals, 142–48, 285–90
Arguments from multiple affirmability, 116–23; evaluation of, 117–23; general form of, 118; relation to arguments from resemblance, 116, 120–21
Arguments from resemblance, 108–15; evaluation of, 111–15; general form of, 110–11; relation to arguments from multiple affirmability, 116, 120–21
Aristotle, 138, 184, 247–48
"Aspects," 133–34
Assert about: distinguished from say about, 26–27
Assertibles, 76–77, 107; identity of, and predicates, 155–57; identity of, and properties and actions, 151; identity of, and propositions, 152; relation to properties and actions, 79–80
Assertion, 18–21, 24–25
Assertive clue, 30–35
Assertively utter, 19 n
Augustine, 8, 263, 288, 290; and universals, 279–85

Interchangeability *salvo sensu,* 70–71, 73–74, 76

John of St. Thomas, 63–64, 66, 142
Johnson, W.E., 37–38
Joseph, H.W.B., 16, 29, 32, 49

Kant, I., xii
Keynes, J.N., 39, 42, 50
Kinds, 235–49; difference between, and classes, 240–41; examples of, 235–38; existence criteria for, 238–39; modes of referring to, 236; and predicable universals, 256–60; predications true of, and predications true of examples of, 241–49; and substance universals, 249–56

Links, 95, 101
Location in space, 225–26; divided, 226; multiple, 226, 230–31
Locke, John, 142, 186, 188
Logical predicates: concept of, not applicable to every sentence, 28–29; defined, 28, 35; distinction between, and logical subjects, 11, 12, 13–16, 21–28; and general and singular terms, 47–49, 57–60; and identity of assertibles, properties, and actions, 154–57; incompleteness of, 30–31
Logical subjects: completeness of, 30–31; concept of, not applicable to every sentence, 28–29; defined, 28, 35; distinction between, and logical predicates, 11, 12, 13–16, 21–28; and general and singular terms, 47–49, 57–60

Martin, G., 66
Mill, J.S., 49–50
Moody, E., 184 n
Moore, G.E., 137
Multiple affirmability, 117–19; objective justification for, 121–23. *See also* Arguments from multiple affirmability

Negatives, definition of, 164
Nominalism, 106, 168–70, 204–6

Ockham. *See* William of Ockham;
Pap, Arthur, 198, 203–6
Paradigms, 263, 283, 296–97; Augustine's rejection of universals as, 283–84; Plato's view of universals as, 278–79
Particulars, 224, 231
Peirce, C.S., 17, 254–55
Philosophy of language, 2
Plantinga, A., xiv, 124
Plato, 4, 7, 87–89, 108, 137–38, 263, 283, 288; and universals, 264–79
Position in time, 227–28; divided, 228; multiple, 228, 231–32; and position in time, 227–29
Predicability: and arguments from resemblance, 115; concept of, and concept of universals, 65–66
Predicable entities, 65; Aquinas's view of, 142–48, 285–90; Augustine's view of, 280–84; concept of, and concept of cases, 181–93; distinctions between, 67–86; empirical investigations and identity of, 157–58; existence criteria for, 158–67; identity criteria for, 151–58; identity of kinds with, 256–60; and negative predicates, 80–83; nonreducibility of, 203–12; Ockham's view of, 181–93; Plato's view of, 264–79; relation of God to, 290–97; and relational sentences, 83–84
Predicable expressions, 13
Predicable universals, 65; identity with kinds, 256–60
Predicables. *See* Predicable entities
Predicate entailment principles, 114–15, 123–27, 168–69; evaluation of, 123–26. *See also* General predicate entailment principle
Predicate function, 47–49
Predicate, logical. *See* Logical predicate
Predicate position, 47–48
Predication, 27–28; nonlinguistic, 64–66; theories of, 64
Predicative relations, 67–84; objections to, 87–104